January 1987

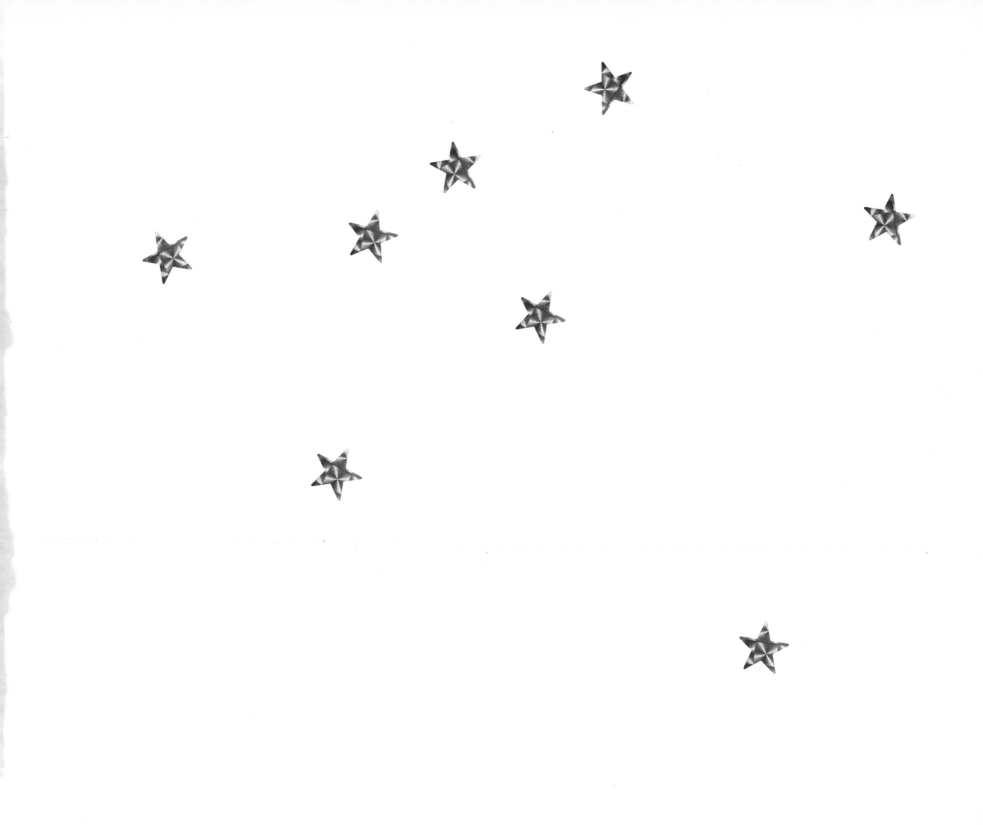

HOLLYWOOD:

Legend and Reality

HOLLYWOOD

Legend and Reality

Edited by Michael Webb

A New York Graphic Society Book

Little, Brown and Company · Boston

in association with

Smithsonian Institution

Traveling Exhibition Service

This book was published on the occasion of the exhibition "Hollywood: Legend and Reality," organized by the Smithsonian Institution Traveling Exhibition Service and shown from April 1986 to February 1988 at the following museums:

National Museum of American History, Smithsonian Institution, Washington, D.C.

Cooper-Hewitt Museum, The Smithsonian Institution's National Museum of Design, New York City

Center for the Fine Arts, Miami

Cincinnati Art Museum

The Denver Art Museum

Los Angeles County Museum of Natural History

This exhibition was made possible by the generous support of Time Inc.

Library of Congress Cataloging-in-Publication Data

Main entry under title:

Hollywood, legend and reality.

  "A New York Graphic Society book."
  Bibliography: p.
  Includes index.
  1. Moving-picture industry — United States — History. 2. Moving-pictures — United States — History. I. Webb, Michael, 1937–
PN1993.5.U6H5914 1986   791.43′0973   85-23141
ISBN 0-8212-1588-4
ISBN 0-8212-1589-2 (pbk.)

Acknowledgments of permission to reprint copyrighted material appear on page 227.

New York Graphic Society Books are published by Little, Brown and Company (Inc.). *Published simultaneously in Canada by Little, Brown & Company (Canada) Limited*

Printed in Great Britain

Designed by Carl Zahn
assisted by Mary Reilly

Production coordination by Nancy Robins
assisted by Christina M. Holz

Composition in Gill Sans Light by DEKR Corporation

Printed and bound by Balding + Mansell

Jacket/cover designed by Carl Zahn

Front: Based on a photograph by David Strick

Back: Filming David O. Selznick's *The Garden of Allah* (1936). Cinematographer W. Howard Greene lines up a shot of Charles Boyer and Marlene Dietrich. Courtesy Ron Haver.

Frontispieces:
Way Down East (1979), construction in painted aluminum by Red Grooms, inspired by a classic scene in the 1920 movie in which director D. W. Griffith and cinematographer Billy Bitzer filmed Lillian Gish cast adrift on ice floes in the Connecticut River. Collection of the University of Northern Kentucky.

Outdoor Lot, MGM Studios, 1939: photo by Edward Weston. Standing sets and sternwheelers were routinely recycled, art directors dressing up whatever was closest to hand. Courtesy Arizona Board of Regents, Center for Creative Photography.

Opposite page:
Neon-lit sign, ca. 1932, that ornamented New York's Radio City Music Hall when it was the flagship of the RKO theater chain.

CONTENTS

Lent by the Kenneth Anger Collection

John Huston mugging for the benefit of
Bernadette Peters and other members of the
cast of *Annie* (1983). Photo by Garry Winogrand.

# PREFACE

A major museum exhibition, "Hollywood: Legend and Reality" pays homage to film entertainment as a central motif of the twentieth century. It celebrates the collective imagination and resourcefulness of a place that has been transformed into a symbol of glitter and glamor.

Time Inc. has had a long and fruitful relationship with Hollywood, ranging from the classic "March of Time" news films to our HBO and Cinemax pay-TV networks. In addition, *Time, Life, People,* and *Fortune* have over the years provided extensive coverage of Hollywood. We have been and are today a significant part of Hollywood's history.

It is therefore with considerable pride and a close feeling of kinship that we are sponsoring this noteworthy project in collaboration with the Smithsonian Institution Traveling Exhibition Service (SITES). It is especially gratifying that our archives and the resources of our many corporate groups have helped make this a comprehensive and memorable exhibition.

Our thanks to SITES and the participating museums in the United States, Japan, and Europe for their enthusiasm for and appreciation of Hollywood's contribution to society. We are pleased to have this opportunity to work with them as part of our continuing program in support of the arts.

RALPH P. DAVIDSON
Chairman of the Board
Time Inc.

New York Movie, 1939, painting by
Edward Hopper.

FOREWORD

Years from now when historians look back and try to understand life in the twentieth century, they will consider our art as much as our actions. They will read our literature, view our paintings and sculptures, listen to our music, and perhaps more than anything, they will watch our movies. For it is there that we have dramatized all aspects of our lives — our humor, fears, heartbreaks, and dreams.

The story of how Hollywood came to be the film capital of the world is as rooted in chance and conflicting motive as the plot of any movie ever made. In the early days of the cinema, the American film industry was based in the theatrical and financial center of the United States, New York City, and cowboy films were shot out West . . . in the wilderness of New Jersey. Southern California, a long train ride away, was occasionally used by enterprising filmmakers, but few producers could imagine making films so far from Broadway and its steady source of actors. At that time, however, the cinema resembled today's "venture industries," and it naturally attracted ambitious, imaginative entrepreneurs.

One such entrepreneur was Chicago glove salesman Samuel Goldfish, who formed a business partnership with Jesse Lasky, a vaudeville musician, and with New York actor-manager Cecil B. De Mille. Goldfish — who later changed his name to Goldwyn — purchased the rights to a Western novel and in 1913 began production on their first motion picture. Initially, they planned to film the movie near Flagstaff, Arizona, but — according to one account — snow-capped mountains in the background interfered with their concept of the "Old West." Even then, they realized a Hollywood axiom: when real life doesn't fit a preconceived image, create another reality. De Mille loaded his equipment back on the train, headed west again, and filmed *The Squaw Man* in a rented barn in Hollywood. It was the first full-length motion picture made there, and a decisive step in the growth of the Hollywood movie industry.

Hollywood has always been a concept as much as a place. Today, only one major studio is located in Hollywood proper, and many back lots have been replaced by busy offices that coordinate activities for filming elsewhere. Yet when you say "Hollywood," everyone conjures a mental image of movie cameras, bright lights, exotic stage sets, and glamorous stars. Somehow, that was the case almost from the beginning.

When Hollywood was still a small town far removed from eastern urban centers, it attracted artists from around the globe. After World War One brought to a halt cinematic activity in Europe, Hollywood became the world's dominant force in film production, bolstered by the talents of immigrants who flocked to America. Foreign-born directors such as Ernst Lubitsch, Erich von Stroheim, and F. W. Murnau, assisted by the finest European designers and craftsmen, brought art to a growth industry.

With the advent of "talkies," in 1929, films were able to treat themes with greater perception and poignancy than ever before . . . and legend and reality were further entwined. The industry produced films on subjects related to audience experience, even if the portrayal was exaggerated to extremes. In films about the Depression, bankers were villains and the heroes, self-made men; the rich were satirized and the humble, praised.

Hollywood has always offered us an escape from our everyday lives. Through films, we can identify with a courageous hero, grateful that we are not in danger. We allow ourselves to be thrilled by a tragic romance or a horror film, safe in the thought that it is only a vicarious experience. And motion pictures endure across generations. We are still uplifted by Jimmy Stewart's discovery of life's pleasures in *It's a Wonderful Life* and understand Henry Fonda's frustration with social injustice in *The Grapes of Wrath*. As it always has, Hollywood continues to give us the chance to know ourselves better.

Here, in a museum setting, we have brought together the history and the artistry of this great medium. This is a serious exhibition about a serious form of art and a remarkable collection of creative people, drawn to a place where fantasy is honored, dreams valued, initiative rewarded, and, significantly, there is daily evidence that the American dream can come true.

This exhibition would not have been possible without the enthusiastic cooperation of many public and private lenders and numerous project participants, who are listed elsewhere in this catalogue. Most of all, the Smithsonian Institution would like to acknowledge with gratitude the generous support and creative contributions of Time Inc., which have made possible the presentation of "Hollywood: Legend and Reality."

ROBERT McC. ADAMS
Secretary, Smithsonian Institution

H O L L Y W O O D:

Legend and Reality

Early fan magazines, which helped create and
sustain the popularity of stars in the years
after 1910.

INTRODUCTION

For seventy years, Hollywood has been the symbolic capital of the American film industry. Run by businessmen in pursuit of profit, Hollywood has marshaled ideas and talent to create a popular art form that has expressed and shaped the dreams of audiences everywhere. Its movies have transformed the mundane into the stuff of legend; sharpened our appreciation of the world around us; transported us to distant or imaginary places. For good and bad, they have defined America to the world. The best of these movies endure, allowing us to experience anew the tastes and values of past decades, to savor the achievements of outstanding artists, performers, and technicians.

Hollywood is a bundle of contradictions: a speculative business that strives for certainties; a mass entertainment medium that is sometimes an art. It is vulnerable and resilient; superficial yet revealing. What appears on the screen is a stylized version of real life (or a plausible vision of imaginary worlds) that is made possible by the prolonged collaborative effort of hundreds, working in support of a celebrated few. Thus a legend — of colorful personalities and extravagant exploits — has obscured the reality of moviemaking much as real-life issues, characters, and events have been enlarged and absorbed into Hollywood's reel world.

The exhibition "Hollywood: Legend and Reality" celebrates the creative process by which ideas are transformed into movies and explores Hollywood's influence on artists and audiences. Like a movie, it seeks to entertain and inform, telling its story in images, with light and sound. And, as in a movie, much depends upon the imagination and emotional response of the audience. This catalogue has a similar goal, drawing upon the vast literature and oral history of film to suggest how professionals do their jobs and how the movies have helped shape or been shaped by society.

Change and Continuity

Seventy-five years ago, Hollywood was a boom town — five days by train from New York, which was still the hub of moviemaking. In New York, the movies were overshadowed by Broadway: serious actors disdained to perform in ten-minute "flickers" that were shown to a working-class audience in storefront theaters. The movies were profitable and disreputable — a marvel-ous opportunity for a new breed of showman-entrepreneur. The established producers and distributors, led by Thomas Edison, formed the Motion Picture Patents' Trust in 1908. Their attempt to monopolize this new invention was challenged by a feisty band of independents, headed by such Jewish immigrants as Adolph Zukor, Carl Laemmle, Marcus Loew, and William Fox. They defied the Trust's strong-arm tactics, then defeated it in the courts. They went on to found four of the companies that still dominate the industry: Paramount, Universal, Loew's–MGM, and Fox (later merged with Twentieth Century Pictures).

These first moguls grasped — more quickly than the Trust — that well-publicized stars, more ambitious, feature-length movies, and palatial theaters would enlarge the audience. Zukor spoke of killing "the slum tradition in movies." By 1919, they had won — decisively. The Trust was dead; its member companies were fading from the scene. War had crippled the once-vibrant European studios. Hollywood had become the world capital, producing four out of every five movies, dominating 80 percent of foreign screens and almost 100 percent of domestic theaters. The movie industry was America's fifth largest, grossing over $700 million a year.

Why Hollywood? The pioneers were drawn to Southern California by the promise of cheap land and labor, spectacular locations, and a benign climate. Contrary to myth, it was not a refuge for independents seeking to escape the Trust by running over the border to Mexico. The first company to arrive was Selig — a Chicago-based Trust member. Both sides shared the territory, occasionally shooting it out in frontier tradition. The pioneers were a tough breed, unfazed by physical hardship, rattlesnakes, and gun-toting rivals.

Crude studios and outdoor sets were thrown up over a 300-square-mile area from 1908 on. Hollywood — then a bucolic settlement of 5,000 — became the principal focus. It was conveniently close to the hills and to downtown L.A., but its first settlers — staid Midwesterners who had outlawed saloons and theaters — were unfriendly. Recalled pioneer director Allan Dwan: "We were beneath them. If we walked in the streets with our cameras, they hid their girls under the beds, closed doors and windows, and shied away." "No dogs, no actors," read a sign at the Hollywood Hotel.

"Movies," as the pioneers were called, sometimes earned this hostility. The town was treated like a standing set. Cowboys would ride over front lawns; Mack Sennett covered intersections with oil and filmed the skids. Henry "Suicide" Lehrman — a former streetcar conductor — once released a lion among a crowd of volunteer extras to film their reactions.

In the next ten years, Hollywood transformed itself from a mining camp into a factory town. Power was consolidated: by the mid-1920s, MGM, Paramount, and Fox dominated the industry, much like the big three auto companies. Hollywood appropriated the Detroit assembly line. Early movies were largely improvised, without a script, and actors shared production chores. A handful of top stars and directors enjoyed almost unlimited authority. Then, spurred by their bosses in New York and by a financial crisis in the early 1920s, the studio heads tightened up. Supervisors were put in charge of every picture — from budget and script, through assigning the actors and crew, to the final editing — reporting, or deferring, only to the studio's head of production.

Top studios produced a major feature almost every week, on average, and distributed them to their own theaters through their own exchanges, across America and abroad. Paramount had studios in Hollywood and New York, in London, Paris, and Berlin. Far behind in wealth and prestige were such majors-to-be as Universal, Warner Bros., and Columbia. Then, as now, there was a host of independent producers. Some, like United Artists, enjoyed respect; most ground out low-budget comedies and Westerns for small town/small theater audiences.

Hollywood's instinct for survival was soon put to the test. It beat back a succession of challenges. Its productions balanced the puritan tradition and "the new morality" with consummate, if cynical, skill. The forces of censorship were rallied by the Arbuckle scandal of 1921 and other well-publicized allegations of depravity behind the cameras. The studio heads counterattacked by firing a few offenders and hiring Will Hays, an upstanding Presbyterian and a member of President Harding's cabinet, to refurbish their image. European films again offered stiff competition; Hollywood devastated the German and Swedish industries by recruiting their best talent.

Filming at the Flying "A" studio in Santa Barbara, ca. 1912. The painted flats, rough stage, and retractable cotton awning to diffuse sunlight were employed by all the pioneers.

Shooting a Western on an outdoor stage at Universal Studios, which Carl Laemmle established in 1915. He charged visitors a nickel to watch from the gallery and sold them eggs from his hatchery as they left.

The Babylon set for *Intolerance* (1916), D. W. Griffith's most ambitious epic, towering over the bungalows of East Hollywood.

Hiring extras at Paramount Studios, 1928. The establishment of the Central Casting Office in the mid-1920s reduced but did not eliminate "cattle calls" at the studio gates.

Sound was a challenge the industry resisted for as long as it could. Thomas Edison had tried to combine sound with moving pictures in the 1890s; Lee De Forest and others had demonstrated the feasibility of sound films by the early 1920s. Hollywood shied from the disruption and the huge expense of changing its methods of production and exhibition. By the middle of the 1920s, the industry was enjoying a commercial and artistic peak; silent movies could be shown in any country, simply by translating a few title cards. The growing threat of radio was as little regarded as that of television twenty-five years later. Americans were staying home to listen to their favorite entertainers, but the dip in movie attendance was not of critical size.

Warner Bros., an outsider struggling to break into the big league, gambled on sound as a means of reproducing music without the expense of live performers. Early failures to synchronize the human voice with film had discredited the idea of talkies. In 1926, Warners released *Don Juan* and a batch of shorts with surprisingly sophisticated music accompaniment that was played on discs synchronized with each reel. Fox brought out sound-on-film newsreels.

These novelties were popular, but silent films were already accompanied by live orchestras and sound effects. What radio had, and the movies needed, was dialogue. Al Jolson's improvised line "You ain't heard nothing yet" was an obituary for the silents, and the public sensation sparked by *The Jazz Singer* in October 1927 vindicated Warners' daring. By summer 1928, 300 theaters were wired to show the first crude talkies. Other studios scrambled to secure equipment, build soundproof stages, and sign Broadway stars and directors. By late 1929, everyone but Garbo and Chaplin had been compelled to talk — or to quit the business.

It was a technical and economic revolution. Sound intensified the appeal of movies — attendance jumped to record levels — and enabled Hollywood to ward off the competition from radio and probably to delay the introduction of television. Without the visceral quality of sound films, the industry might not have weathered the Depression. But the price of survival was high. Many actors and musicians became unemployable. To make the changeover, studios borrowed heavily from New York banks. Hollywood was insulated from the initial impact of the Depression, but by 1932 half the major studios were teetering and a third of the nation's theaters were shuttered. Studios slashed sala-

ries and production costs; the authority of executives over contract artists, and of New York financial interests over studio heads, was more strictly enforced.

Crisis presented a creative opportunity: Warners and Columbia were more agile than the majors in turning headlines into movies and exploiting the realities of everyday life. But every studio brought a new candor and sophistication to its product. The best movies of the early 1930s have a raw vitality that well expressed America's crisis of confidence and the desperation of 25 percent unemployment.

The inauguration of President Roosevelt in March 1933 and the formation in 1934 of the Legion of Decency as an influential guardian of movie morality set Hollywood on a new course. Spurred by the optimism of the New Deal, and constrained by a tough production code that was, for the first time, rigorously enforced, Hollywood shifted its emphasis: from gangsters to G-men, from the

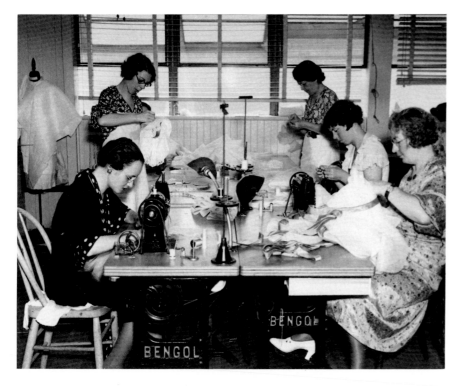

Seamstresses in the MGM Wardrobe Department in the mid-1930s. They earned $16 a week, a fair wage for the time; studio head Louis B. Mayer received $1.6 million a year in salary and benefits.

exotic to the wholesome, from exposés to boosterism. Hollywood's resilience and self-confidence were a model to the rest of America. Its moguls had climbed from rags to riches (Louis B. Mayer's remuneration for 1936 was $1.6 million) and lived their dreams; they invited moviegoers to participate vicariously in their good fortune.

Pearl Harbor found Hollywood better prepared for war than other industries. It had rehearsed its mission — to inspire, to entertain, and (more recently) to expose the Nazi menace. No retooling was required; the studios responded eagerly to the challenge. Leading directors donned uniform and made documentaries to explain to Americans why and how to fight. Top stars enlisted or went on tour to entertain the troops. Movies strengthened resolve, promoted recruiting and bond sales, forged a link between battlefield, factory, and home. They codified and dramatized national myths, celebrated ethnic diversity, and held out the promise of integration to blacks — while attacking the Japanese in

viciously racist terms. Theater attendance soared to near-record levels, boosted by the lack of other leisure activities and by the appeal of newsreels in a pretelevision era.

For Hollywood, more than the nation, the peace was bitter and troubled. Labor unrest, contained by earlier curbs on unions and by wartime regulations, broke out in prolonged and sometimes violent strikes, which were conveniently blamed on left-wing agitators. Britain — Hollywood's chief foreign market — imposed a 75 percent tax on American film earnings, and the industry retaliated with an unsuccessful boycott. Other European countries followed Britain's lead in limiting the repatriation of foreign earnings.

The Justice Department pressed its antitrust suit, initiated in 1938. A Supreme Court decision of 1948 compelled the major studios to give up restrictive booking practices and to sell their theater chains — the guaranteed outlet for their product. Young people — then, as now, the core audience — moved to the burgeoning suburbs. Mortgages and babies, cars and appliances consumed their time and disposable income.

Chastened by these losses, the industry proved vulnerable to the paranoia and intolerance that succeeded this war as they had the previous one. In 1941, studio heads brushed aside the attacks of isolationist senators, who sought to investigate Hollywood's propaganda for intervention in the European war. They took pride in their mildly antifascist movies. During the war they made a handful of pro-Soviet movies — spontaneously, and in response to the White House. (Jack Warner claimed that Roosevelt confided, early in the war: "We can't afford to lose Russia at this stage.")

But in 1947, when the House Un-American Activities Committee began its hearings into subversion in the movie industry, industry leaders panicked. They denounced and fired employees who had faithfully executed their orders and, to extirpate an ineffectual handful of Communists and radicals, instituted a secret blacklist against the thousands of innocents who were denounced by vigilantes.

Monsters lurked beneath the surface calm of America in the 1950s, stirred to life by war in Korea and witch-hunts at home — dark, irrational fears of subversion and conformity, of alienation and unleashed technology. Even the lib-

Song of Russia (1944), one of a handful of movies made in support of the new ally. Critic Nora Sayre later remarked that MGM stereotyped Russians as it had blacks: "a jubilant race, addicted to music and laughter, blessed with an inborn rhythm."

Violence on the picket line at Warner Bros.' Burbank Studios during the prolonged labor dispute of 1945.

eral voice of Adlai Stevenson warned that America's enemies "planned a total conquest of the human mind."

In 1949, Samuel Goldwyn showed himself to be a remarkable prophet when he wrote:

"Even the most backward-looking of the topmost tycoons of our industry cannot now help seeing just around the corner a titanic struggle to retain audiences. The competition we feared in the past — the automobile in early movie days, the radio in the 1920s and 1930s, and the developing of night sports quite recently — will fade into insignificance by comparison with the fight we are going to have to keep people patronizing our theaters in preference to sitting at home and watching a program of entertainment. It is a certainty that people will be unwilling to pay to see poor pictures when they can stay home and see something which is, at least, no worse." [1]

Few heeded his warning. Hollywood first ignored, then tried to fight, television with such short-lived novelties as 3-D and Cinerama. Other technical breakthroughs were ballyhooed, and Cole Porter captured the frenzy in lyrics he wrote for a song in *Silk Stockings* (1955):

> *Today to get the public to attend a picture show*
> *It's not enough to advertise a famous star they know.*
> *If you want to get the crowd to come around*
> *You've got to have*
> *Glorious Technicolor, Breathtaking CinemaScope, and Stereophonic sound.* [2]

Nothing stemmed the growth of the television audience nor the decline of moviegoing. In the 1950s, the studio system crumbled, as production declined and contracts were allowed to lapse. Agents bid up the price of top talent; stars regained the clout their predecessors had lost to the studios thirty years before. Moguls who had ruled for decades — Louis B. Mayer, Harry Cohn, Darryl Zanuck, Samuel Goldwyn — retired or were fired. Ownership of the studios passed to conglomerates, whose managers had no loyalty to — or experience of — moviemaking. Back lots were sold off; human and material resources dispersed.

Rising costs drove moviemakers to Europe, where armies could be hired to don armor and charge across the enlarged screen, and American stars could

find relief from taxes. Hollywood camped beside the Thames and the Tiber and on the plains of Spain. Cheap extras and convincing locations came in useful for the spate of biblical epics that were prompted by a religious revival and a need to justify the gimmicks that Cole Porter sang of.

At home and abroad, independents filled the vacuum left by the decline of the studios. As symbolic as the demise of RKO Pictures was the revival of United Artists. Established in 1919 as an artists' cooperative by Mary Pickford and Douglas Fairbanks, Charlie Chaplin and D. W. Griffith, it had never fulfilled expectations and by 1951 was moribund. A syndicate, headed by entertainment lawyers Arthur Krim and Robert Benjamin, bought the company and made it the most adventurous in Hollywood. The revived United Artists had no studio and was unencumbered by overhead; its role was to finance and distribute the work of independent producers. Increasingly, independents — including graduates of Broadway and live television drama — made similar agreements with the established studios.

By the late 1960s, obituaries for Hollywood were disturbingly frequent. The industry seemed to have lost touch with its audience: the profits on such hits as *The Sound of Music* were squandered on a score of uninspired and overblown sequels. Production was down; only television kept the lots busy. MGM, proudest of the majors, auctioned its props and (for a few years) withdrew from moviemaking to run hotel-casinos in Nevada. In 1968, the industry's Production Code — once impregnable armor, now a withered fig leaf, was abandoned and replaced by the present Ratings System.

A few low-budget pictures — *Bonnie and Clyde, The Graduate, Butch Cassidy and the Sundance Kid,* and *Easy Rider* among them — heralded a renaissance and mirrored the iconoclasm of American youth in the late 1960s. The commercial success of such movies opened the gates to young talent: graduates of film schools and of Roger Corman's low-budget exploitation pictures. The new freedom given to young directors resulted in some stunning grosses and staggering losses; in innovation and self-indulgence. Ned Tanen, one of the studio executives who most encouraged young talent, observed: "The film business is cyclical and it has always had a crisis mentality . . . it lurches between crazed optimism and total gloom. A great deal of success is accidental."[3]

Drive-ins proved increasingly popular with
teenagers and families in the 1950s. Charlton
Heston playing Moses in Cecil B. De Mille's
The Ten Commandments (1956). Photo by
J. R. Eyerman for *Life*.

Hollywood's greatest myth is that of a Golden Age, an elusive El Dorado conjured up by every moviegoer over thirty. It is easy to romanticize the past when only the better work has survived, and the best of today's is obscured by a mountain of dross. David McClintick, a former reporter for the *Wall Street Journal*, offers a more balanced assessment:

"**Myth:** *The Hollywood of today is totally different from the Hollywood of a half century ago.* **Truth:** *Even with a more diverse group of power seekers, even with all the changes wrought by television in the fifties when it became a mass medium competing for audiences with movies, even with all of the impending changes posed by new forms of home entertainment, the institution of Hollywood has changed far less than is conventionally believed. More than a place, Hollywood is a state of mind. And the same elemental forces that drove it in the twenties and thirties still drive it today. In addition to the pleasures of power, there are money, fame, sex, a stake in creating American popular culture, and an opportunity to have a great deal of fun in the pursuit of these pleasures.*

"**Myth:** *By the 1970s, movies had become a rational business, with much of the risk eliminated.* **Truth:** *Despite attempts to rationalize it — and even a modicum of success — the fundamental process of conceiving, producing, and distributing a motion picture is more arcane now than it was fifty years ago. There has never been any mystery about how a refrigerator is made. There has always been a mystery about how a movie is made. 'Not half a dozen men have ever been able to keep the whole equation of pictures in their heads,' wrote F. Scott Fitzgerald in* The Last Tycoon *(1940). Fitzgerald's comment was still apt four decades later. And the presence of television only thickened the plot.*

"**Myth:** *The spirit of the old moguls, with their consummate showmanship and their insistence on quality, even at the expense of profit, is gone forever. Hollywood today is run by accountants concerned about nothing but profit.* **Truth:** *The old moguls were far from homogeneous. Some were skilled showmen with good taste. Some were inept fools with bad taste. All of them, however, were in business for the money more than for the art. Pictures of high quality were the exception rather than the rule, just as they are today. And despite many obvious differences from their predecessors, the men who vie for power in Hollywood today are the direct cultural and psychological descendants of the men who founded and ran* Hollywood from the early 1900s until the fifties, men whom Irving Howe has called 'the dozen or so Yiddish-speaking Tammarlanes [sic] who built enormous movie studios [and] satisfied the world's hunger for fantasy, [men who were] bored with sitting in classrooms, too lively for routine jobs, and clever in the ways of the world.'

"**Myth:** *The studio system is dead. Independent producers and agents now hold the power in Hollywood.* **Truth:** *Despite many structural changes, the power wielded by the major studios in the production of motion pictures and television programs remains formidable. The studios no longer directly employ large numbers of actors, directors, and writers. Instead, they normally contract with 'independent' producers who in turn hire the talent. But the change is hardly revolutionary. The studios still put up most of the money for movies and retain the considerable power that resides with the money. With few exceptions, the studios still have a major voice — frequently veto power — in the producer's assembly of a film project and in the production of the film itself. Most 'independent' producers in fact are dependent producers.*

"**Myth:** *Studio bosses used to have absolute power but are impotent today.* **Truth:** *The heads of the film studios have — and always have had — less power to function independently of their corporate parents than has been commonly portrayed. Louis B. Mayer was one of the most famous figures in America from the twenties until the fifties, and was thought to have absolute power over his Hollywood domain, the Metro-Goldwyn-Mayer studio. Fewer people had heard of Nicholas M. Schenck (pronounced Skenk), the president and chief executive officer of Loew's Incorporated. Loew's Incorporated, however, owned MGM, and L. B. Mayer did not function in a vacuum. He reported to Nick Schenck. They talked by telephone two or three times a day in an age when coast-to-coast telephone calls were not made so casually as they are today. Nick Schenck was the 'undisputed boss of the whole shebang,' reported* Fortune *in 1939, and had an 'uncanny eye for profitable pictures.' It was Nick Schenck, not L. B. Mayer, who spoke perhaps the most prescient sentence ever uttered about the movie business: 'There's nothing wrong with this business that good pictures can't cure.'*"[4]

The failings of today's Hollywood seem large because we are standing close to the subject. Escalating costs are an obvious example. The two most extravagant productions of all time are *Intolerance* (1916) and *Cleopatra* (1963). Both are well ahead — in real dollars — of *Heaven's Gate* (1980). But even a modestly conceived picture costs substantially more today than ever before to produce and promote. And the result is that moviemaking has become a high-stakes gamble, in which the failures outnumber the successes, and only a megahit can carry the rest. This puts a curb on originality and innovation, and encourages the production of sequels and an obsession with teenagers — the one group that goes to movies with any regularity.

None of this is new in kind, only in degree. Hollywood's extravagance has always shocked outsiders; the studios have always cloned their successes; and the young have, from the earliest years, been a mainstay of the audience. The rapid rise in costs is largely explained — and covered — by new sources of investment. The right package can attract huge advances from foreign and private investors; network and cable television are beginning to coproduce theatrical movies — following the example of European television, which has rescued native film industries from near-certain extinction.

Theater attendance is about 22 million a week, way down from the 1946 peak of 90 million. But movies have never been more profitable. Domestic theatrical grosses for 1984 were a record $4 billion, which yielded distributors about $1.4 billion in gross rental income. It has been estimated that television and videocassettes yielded a similar amount, and that rentals from abroad totaled $700 million in 1984.

Another example of the industry's vitality is, ironically, the decline of Hollywood as the production center. There's a new kind of runaway production that is as likely to be shooting in Paris, Texas, or Rome, Georgia, as in Europe. "See America first" has become the motto of a new wave of foreign and independent directors, lured by Hollywood gold and by the freedom to shoot in their own way and in a place of their own choosing.

The fragmentation of production activity is made possible by the introduction of lighter equipment, by smaller crews and better communications. New York has recovered much of the importance it lost to Hollywood, but other cities and states are competing successfully, often by advertising lower costs, cheaper and more flexible labor, fresh locations, and an absence of restrictions — the same factors that drew the industry to Southern California in the 1910s. Such competition can only help to strengthen the movies by offering diversified opportunities and perspectives that have been lacking in the hothouse of Hollywood. Already there are signs that a viable regional cinema is emerging, drawing on the enthusiasm and expertise developed in film schools and workshops, and in federal and state support programs for independent filmmakers.

Quotations

1. Samuel Goldwyn, "Hollywood in the Television Age," *Hollywood Quarterly*, Winter 1949–50; reprinted in *The Movies in Our Midst*, edited by Gerald Mast (Chicago: University of Chicago Press, 1982), page 635.

2. Cole Porter, "Stereophonic Sound," from *Silk Stockings*, © 1955 and 1958 by Chappell & Co., Inc.

3. Ned Tanen, *Sight and Sound*, British Film Institute, London, Winter 1983.

4. David McClintick, *Indecent Exposure* (New York: Dell, 1983), pages 49–51.

Other sources

Tino Balio, *The American Film Industry* (Madison, Wis.: University of Wisconsin Press, 1976).

Rudy Behlmer, *America's Favorite Movies* (New York: Frederick Ungar, 1982).

Kevin Brownlow, *The Parade's Gone By* (New York: Alfred Knopf, 1968; University of California Press, 1976).

———, *Hollywood: The Pioneers* (New York: Alfred Knopf, 1980).

Christopher Finch and Linda Rosenkrantz, *Gone Hollywood* (Garden City, N.Y.: Doubleday, 1979).

Aljean Harmetz, *The Making of "The Wizard of Oz"* (New York: Alfred Knopf, 1977).

Garth Jowett, *Film: The Democratic Art* (Boston: Little, Brown, 1976).

Ephraim Katz, *The Film Encyclopedia* (New York: Perigee, 1982).

Donald Knox, *The Magic Factory* (New York: Praeger, 1973).

Budd Schulberg, *Moving Pictures: Memories of a Hollywood Prince* (Briarcliff Manor, N.Y.: Stein & Day, 1981).

Alexander Walker, *The Shattered Silents* (New York: William Morrow, 1979).

Moviegoing in the Depression. Photo of a theater in Cincinnati by John Vachon for the Farm Security Administration, 1938.

A *Paramount Picture*, 1934, painting by
Reginald Marsh.

1 SPELLBOUND IN DARKNESS

"As an adolescent, I went to the movies as often as I could, and for the same reasons as young people do today: I needed images I could emulate in forming my personality. And I was eager to learn about those aspects of life and adulthood which were still hidden from me. Moving pictures, more than any other art, give the illusion that it is permitted to spy upon the life of others, which is exactly what children and adolescents love to do, in order to find out how these adults manage their lives and, even more important, how they manage to satisfy their desires.

"Also, I wished to escape from reality to daydreams, and the movies provided content for these. Waiting for the next installment of The Perils of Pauline *gave us all something exciting to look forward to and fantasize about in class instead of listening to our teachers. The moviehouses to which I went as a youth were true pleasure domes, very different from those of today, which are characterized by their spareness and cold functionality. As soon as one entered these old dream palaces, one felt transposed to another world. Inside, there were nooks and crannies and boxes with heavy curtains which suggested privacy and intimacy. Here one could escape the watchful scrutiny of one's parents and all other adults, and do nothing constructive whatsoever — but daydream.*

"The moviehouses also provided unique opportunities for letting down one's defenses and experimenting with being in love. The unreality of the setting, and its attractiveness, encouraged both sexual experimentation and uninhibited reaction to what was seen on the screen. I do not recall having ever laughed as heartily and unrestrainedly as I did when watching funny scenes in these pleasure palaces. In fact, watching the movies thus carried me away so that I was no longer quite myself. Instead, we were part of the world of the moving picture. I was lifted out of my shell into a world where what I felt and did no longer had any relation to the real me and to reality."[1]

This brief reminiscence by the eminent psychologist Dr. Bruno Bettelheim captures the magic of moviegoing and explains why it has been such a favorite scapegoat of moralists. He speaks for all ages and generations, and for a medium whose influence is probably deeper and more durable than the stage or television. And he defines what may be lost to future kids whose first encounter with the movies will come in a home video center that — however sophisticated the choice and presentation — will lack the sense of a shared culture that only a public theater can provide.

The first, crude movies were shown in the 1890s in vaudeville houses and penny arcades. Soon after, they found a home in storefront theaters, dubbed "nickelodeons." A nickel bought an hour of short subjects that were influenced by vaudeville, Wild West shows, and dime novels. Melodramas and moralities both contained a strong dash of realism. A pianist would accompany the movies and possibly a sing-along. Jack Warner's first movie job was singing — so badly that he chased one audience out to make room for the next. Nickelodeons were as common as saloons in the poorer neighborhoods of large cities; their primary appeal was to immigrants and their families. Indeed, they drew customers away from the saloons, but social reformers were not to be appeased.

Thundered the *Chicago Tribune* in 1907, "[Movies are] without a redeeming feature to warrant their existence . . . ministering to the lowest passions of childhood . . . proper to suppress them at once." The city authorities established the nation's first censorship board for "those classes whose age, education and situation entitle them to protection against the evil influence of obscene and immoral representations."

Behind these righteous pronouncements was a middle-class fear that the movies were subverting traditional values and encouraging the lower orders to acquire ideas beyond their station. A 1913 article in the *American Magazine* took a more positive view: "For a mere nickel, the wasted man, whose life hitherto has been toil and sleep, is kindled with wonder. He sees alien people and begins to understand how like they are to him; he sees courage and aspiration and agony, and begins to understand himself. He begins to feel a brother in a race that is led by many dreams."

Other cities and states followed Chicago in setting up local censorship boards, especially after a 1915 Supreme Court ruling that denied motion pictures protection under the First Amendment, declaring that they were "a business pure and simple . . . not to be regarded as part of the press of the country or as organs of public opinion." The industry lobbied against local censorship and established its own self-regulatory boards, beginning in 1909 with an organization that evolved into the National Board of Review, which has survived to this day.

Chaplin look-alike competition in Bellingham, Washington, ca. 1917.

Nickelodeon marquee display, 1917. Gloria Swanson, "Fatty" Arbuckle, and Charlie Chaplin got their start in Mack Sennett's slapstick comedies.

Around 1912, ambitious showmen began importing European feature-length movies — *Quo Vadis* from Italy; a French production of *Queen Elizabeth*, starring Sarah Bernhardt — and attracted a more respectable audience by showing them in legitimate theaters at increased prices. Middle-class enthusiasm for the movies was boosted by the prestigious success of D. W. Griffith's *The Birth of a Nation* in 1915. The first movie palace was built in New York in 1913, and gentrification proceeded apace. By the 1920s, major companies were competing to build chains of ever larger and more luxurious showcases, each seating several thousand patrons. The movie palace was the cathedral of a secular society, a foretaste of paradise for as little as 65 cents admission, and a stage for such earthly delights as the gala premiere and the mighty Wurlitzer.

As Hollywood broadened its appeal, it came under closer scrutiny, from church and women's groups, a once-adoring press, and outsiders who resented its affluence and hedonism. The Fatty Arbuckle scandal of 1921 (in which the popular actor was falsely accused of raping a starlet) was orchestrated from San Francisco by the sensation-hungry Hearst press. Without waiting for the verdict (Arbuckle was acquitted with an apology from the jury), the industry banned the actor from the screen and appointed Will Hays as its official moral guardian, a task he performed zealously for twenty-three years.

Hays bade the tide of censorship recede — and it did. He introduced a voluntary code of "don'ts" and "be carefuls" that producers were expected to observe. Director Raoul Walsh recalls how easily the proscriptions could be flouted:

"Everybody had battles with the censors. They went out of their way sometimes to make it pretty tough for us. A kiss could only last three seconds. You weren't allowed to take any love scene if there was a bed visible, even if it was a mile away down the road. Every state had its own censors and Pennsylvania was the toughest. Whenever anybody took a scene that was the least bit off, everybody would yell: 'It won't be shown in Pennsylvania!' But we battled on. Sometimes we'd take maybe six or seven risqué scenes, hoping they'd leave two.

"I remember an instance in a picture I made, The Cockeyed World (1929), *with [Edmund] Lowe, [Victor] McLaglen, and El Brendel. McLaglen as captain was standing outside his tent in Nicaragua and Brendel went by with a very pretty*

French poster of "Fatty" Arbuckle, ca. 1920, whose popularity rivaled that of Chaplin. American theaters withdrew Fatty's movies when the comedian was embroiled in scandal; Parisian exhibitors ordered extra prints.

Nicaraguan girl and McLaglen yelled, 'Hey, where are you going?' Brendel gathered himself together and said, 'Captain, I'm bringing you the lay of the land.' He took out a card from his pocket and said, 'Here is where all the enemy is for you.' Well, when the picture opened and Brendel told the captain, 'I'm bringing you the lay of the land,' the audience nearly laughed the roof off the theater. That got by the censors because in the projection room when the censors ran it [they heard] that 'I'm bringing you the lay of the land and here is the map . . .' — but they never heard that in the theater.

"On What Price Glory? (1926) [a silent picture], I had about a hundred Marines that I got at the base down at El Toro. And of course McLaglen and Lowe, when they got talking to each other, they'd say, 'You dirty son-of-a-bitch, you lousy bastard, you prick' — and then, of course, we'd put on the title, 'I don't want nothing more to do with you. You're not a pal of mine.' Well, after the picture ran two or three weeks at the Roxy Theater, they got thousands and thousands of letters from lip-readers that said it was the most disgusting picture they ever saw, and the most terrible language that these men were talking. Now, that also sent back people who saw it. They became lip-readers. So the picture grossed over $700,000 in four weeks and it cost $360,000."[2]

In the economic and social chaos of the early Depression, from 1930 to 1933, producers ignored the code in their desperation to sell tickets. Violence and sexual innuendo flourished as never before. Sound gave the gangster a voice, and Hollywood turned him into a folk hero who defied authority and achieved his version of the American dream. Fifty gangster movies were made in 1931 alone. Director Howard Hawks describes the genesis of the most controversial of the genre, *Scarface* (1932):

"I asked Ben Hecht whether he'd like to do a gangster picture . . . [based on the] idea that the Borgia family is alive in Chicago today, and Caesar Borgia is Al Capone. We wrote the script in 11 days and wrote it for sheer entertainment. We had darn good sources of information about how things happened. Gangsters would come in and say, 'Do you want to know how such a killing was done?' I'd say, 'I'd love to know, thanks,' and we'd do it that way. There wasn't any idea of having any social significance at all."[3]

The Hays Office read the script and told producer Howard Hughes that it

Headlines from the *Los Angeles Examiner*, September 1921. A jury acquitted "Fatty" Arbuckle of charges that he had caused the death of a starlet during a debauched weekend, but he was relentlessly defamed in the tabloids, and his career was ruined.

VOL. XVIII—NO. 274   Official Forecast—*Fair*   LOS ANGELES, SUNDAY, SEPTEMBER 11, 1921

ARBUCKLE HELD FOR MURDER!

Fatty's Smiling Gaiety Turns to Sullen Gloom

FATTY ARBUCKLE, known the world over for his grin and his antics, is smiling no more. In his cell and in court at San Francisco, where he faces a first degree murder charge following the death of Virginia Rappe, pretty film actress, Arbuckle is living in gloom. Here are extracts from the story of his appearance yesterday in court proceedings that show how life has changed for for the debonair comedian:

Arbuckle came into court, faultlessly groomed, but unable to conceal under a mask of "well dressed leisure" the concern written largely on his features.

Dressed in a natty blue suit, freshly barbered and wearing a new tie and fresh shirt, he arrived at the inquest room at 2:15. A detective walked on either side of him and he was seated in the rear of the room with other witnesses.

• • •

He tried to avoid the court order to stand trial, begging that he be allowed to remain in his cell and away from the crowds, but the court was obdurate.

• • •

As he entered the courtroom through a side door a battery of flashlights opened up on him, the popping of flashlight guns having something of the staccato cadence of a machine gun battery.

• • •

Arbuckle was unmindful of this, but when the court advised him that he would have to stand trial on a charge of murder, his head dropped, and he could not keep his hands from trembling.

must not be made and that, if it was made, it would not be shown. Hughes cabled Hawks: "Screw the Hays Office. Start the picture and make it as realistic, as exciting, as grisly as possible." *Scarface* was released after a year's delay, with new scenes; a subtitle, "The Shame of a Nation"; and an exhortation, "This is an indictment of gang rule in America, and the careless indifference of the Government. What are you going to do about it?"

The gangster movie portrayed crime with token retribution; Mae West played sex for laughs and without guilt. Moralists moved in for the kill. A series of pseudo-scientific studies, supported by the Payne Fund, were published from 1933 on. A popular summary, *Our Movie-Made Children,* argued that movies were an incitement to juvenile delinquency. A new Production Code, authored by Catholic publisher Martin Quigley, had been promulgated in 1930. In April 1934, Catholic bishops established the Legion of Decency, and 10 million Catholics pledged to boycott movies that "offend decency and Christian morality." A trial boycott in Philadelphia persuaded Hays to enforce the Code. He created the Production Code Administration, headed by Joseph Breen, with authority to insist on script changes or cuts in a picture. Member companies agreed to release a film only after it had received a Seal of Approval; fines and the ever-watchful Legion guaranteed compliance. It was ironic that this

James Cagney and Jean Harlow in *Public Enemy* (1931). Violence and sexual innuendo flourished in the early 1930s.

minority regulation of majority behavior was launched just as the "noble experiment" of Prohibition was being abandoned.

Arthur Schlesinger, Jr., remarked:

"The Motion Picture Code imposed on film-making a set of rigid requirements and taboos which would have destroyed Shakespeare, Ibsen and Shaw, and which the lesser talents of Hollywood could not overcome. However satisfying the Code might have been to the guardians of public morality, it began the process of cutting films off from the realities of the American experience."[4]

Others would argue that the better talents of Hollywood obeyed the letter and ignored the spirit of the Code. Hays's greatest achievement was to take censorship out of the public arena for the next twenty years: the debate now took place behind closed doors, and the audience was shown the result of a consensus. Joseph Breen was a tireless vigilante, as this letter of April 1941 to Jack Warner demonstrates:

"We have read with great care the final script, dated as of April 13th, for your proposed production titled Kings Row, *and I regret to be compelled to advise you that the material, in our judgement, is quite definitely unacceptable under the provisions of the Production Code and cannot be approved. A picture, following along the lines of this script, would, necessarily, have to be rejected. . . .*

"Before this picture can be approved under the provision of the Production Code, all the illicit sex will have to be entirely removed; the characterization of Cassandra will have to be definitely changed; the mercy killing will have to be deleted; and the several suggestions of loose sex, chiefly in the attitude of Drake [Ronald Reagan] with reference to the Ross girls, will have to be entirely eliminated. In addition, the suggestion that Dr. Gordon's [Charles Coburn] nefarious practices are prompted by a kind of sadism will have to be completely removed from the story.

"You will have in mind, also, I am sure, that a picture of this kind could not be released in Britain, where any suggestion of insanity is always entirely eliminated from films.

"In this same connection, I throw out for consideration the very important question of industry policy, which is involved in an undertaking of this kind. Here is a story based on a so-called best-selling novel, which is identified in the public mind as a

New York City, 1941: a photo by Helen Levitt of kids playing gangsters that dramatizes the pervasive influence of movie stars.

© Helen Levitt. Courtesy Daniel Wolf, Inc. New York

definitely repellent story, the telling of which is certain to give pause to seriously thinking persons everywhere. . . . To attempt to translate such a story to the screen, even though it be rewritten to conform to the provisions of the Production Code *is, in our judgement, a very questionable undertaking from the standpoint of the good and welfare of this industry. Such a production may well be a definite* disservice *to the motion picture industry for, no matter how well the screenplay is done, the fact that it stems from so thoroughly questionable a novel is likely to bring down upon the industry, as a whole, the condemnation of decent people everywhere. . . ."*[5]

It is a myth that Hollywood was Depression-proof. Theater attendance soon recovered from the slump of the early 1930s, boosted by cheaper tickets, double bills, and "dish-night" giveaways. But business fluctuated throughout the decade, and the threat of crisis was a spur to efficiency. Moviegoing in the 1930s offered an affordable escape from reality for all but the most indigent. Even John Dillinger, who headed the FBI's Most Wanted list, was, in his own words, "nuts about Clark Gable." In 1934, agents shot him dead as he was leaving a performance of *Manhattan Melodrama* — in which Gable played a gangster on Death Row.

Artists such as Reginald Marsh and Edward Hopper celebrated the democratic inclusiveness of the movie theater. It was a favorite subject for the photographers who were commissioned by the Farm Security Administration to record contemporary American life. And Arthur Schlesinger, Jr., wrote of the time "When the Movies Really Counted":

"[In the 1930s,] Hollywood possessed the nation. It formed our images and shaped our dreams. . . . The announcement of new movies created anticipation and suspense. The art was bursting with ideas and vitality and point. Young men sauntered down the street like James Cagney, wisecracked like William Powell, cursed like Humphrey Bogart and wooed like Clark Gable; young women laughed like Lombard, and sighed like Garbo and looked (or tried to look) like Hedy Lamarr.

"In 1937, 61 per cent of the population went to the movies each week (today it is about 23 per cent). The film had for a moment a vital connection with American emotions — more, I think, than it ever had before; more certainly than it has had since. The movies were near the operative center of the nation's consciousness.

TEXT OF THE PRODUCTION CODE

tent of the Code appear in two parts—first, a working abstract of the Code which has been widely accepted as the complete Code, and, second, the Code proper, which has been referred to as "Reasons Supporting a Code".

GENERAL PRINCIPLES

1. No picture shall be produced which will lower the moral standards of those who see it. Hence the sympathy of the audience should never be thrown to the side of crime, wrongdoing, evil or sin.
2. Correct standards of life, subject only to the requirements of drama and entertainment, shall be presented.
3. Law, natural or human, shall not be ridiculed, nor shall sympathy be created for its violation.

PARTICULAR APPLICATIONS

I. CRIMES AGAINST THE LAW

These shall never be presented in such a way as to throw sympathy with the crime as against law and justice or to inspire others with a desire for imitation.

1. **Murder**
   a. The technique of murder must be presented in a way that will not inspire imitation.
   b. Brutal killings are not to be presented in detail.
   c. Revenge in modern times shall not be justified.
2. **Methods of crime** should not be explicitly presented.
   a. Theft, robbery, safe-cracking and dynamiting of trains, mines, buildings, etc., should not be detailed in method.
   b. Arson must be subject to the same safeguards.
   c. The use of firearms should be restricted to essentials.
   d. Methods of smuggling should not be presented.
3. **Illegal drug traffic** must never be presented.
4. **The use of liquor** in American life, when not required by the plot or for proper characterization, will not be shown.

II. SEX

The sanctity of the institution of marriage and the home shall be upheld. Pictures shall not infer that low forms of sex relationship are the accepted or common thing.

1. **Adultery,** sometimes necessary plot material, must not be explicitly treated, or justified, or presented attractively.
2. **Scenes of passion**
   a. They should not be introduced when not essential to the plot.
   b. Excessive and lustful kissing, lustful embraces, suggestive postures and gestures, are not to be shown.
   c. In general, passion should so be treated that these scenes do not stimulate the lower and baser element.
3. **Seduction or rape**
   a. They should never be more than suggested, and only when essential for the plot, and even then never shown by explicit method.
   b. They are never the proper subject for comedy.
4. **Sex perversion** or any inference to it is forbidden.
5. **White slavery** shall not be treated.
6. **Miscegenation** (sex relationships between the white and black races) is forbidden.
7. **Sex hygiene** and venereal diseases are not subjects for motion pictures.
8. Scenes of **actual child birth**, in fact or in silhouette, are never to be presented.
9. **Children's sex organs** are never to be exposed.

III. VULGARITY

The treatment of low, disgusting, unpleasant, though not necessarily evil, subjects should be subject always to the dictate of good taste and a regard for the sensibilities of the audience.

IV. OBSCENITY

Obscenity in word, gesture, reference, song, joke, or by suggestion (even when likely to be understood only by part of the audience) is forbidden.

V. PROFANITY

Pointed profanity (this includes the words: God, Lord, Jesus, Christ—unless used reverently—Hell, S.O.B., damn, Gawd), or every other profane or vulgar expression however used, is forbidden.

VI. COSTUME

1. **Complete nudity** is never permitted. This includes nudity in fact or in silhouette, or any lecherous or licentious notice thereof by other characters in the picture.
2. **Undressing scenes** should be avoided, and never used save where essential to the plot.

3. **Indecent or undue exposure** is forbidden.
4. **Dancing costumes** intended to permit undue exposure or indecent movements in the dance are forbidden.

VII. DANCES

1. Dances suggesting or representing sexual actions or indecent passion are forbidden.
2. Dances which emphasize indecent movements are to be regarded as obscene.

VIII. RELIGION

1. No film or episode may throw **ridicule** on any religious faith.
2. **Ministers of religion** in their character as ministers of religion should not be used as comic characters or as villains.
3. **Ceremonies** of any definite religion should be carefully and respectfully handled.

IX. LOCATIONS

The treatment of bedrooms must be governed by good taste and delicacy.

X. NATIONAL FEELINGS

1. **The use of the flag** shall be consistently respectful.
2. **The history,** institutions, prominent people and citizenry of other nations shall be represented fairly.

XI. TITLES

Salacious, indecent, or obscene titles shall not be used.

XII. REPELLENT SUBJECTS

The following subjects must be treated within the careful limits of good taste:
1. **Actual hangings** or electrocutions as legal punishments for crime.
2. **Third Degree** methods.
3. **Brutality** and possible gruesomeness.
4. **Branding** of people or animals.
5. **Apparent cruelty** to children or animals.
6. **The sale of women,** or a woman selling her virtue.
7. **Surgical operations.**

REASONS SUPPORTING CODE

Reasons supporting a code to govern the making of motion and talking pictures formulated by Association of Motion Picture Producers, Inc., and The Motion Picture Producers and Distributors of America, Inc.

REASONS SUPPORTING PREAMBLE OF CODE

1. Theatrical motion pictures, that is, pictures intended for the theatre as distinct from pictures intended for churches, schools, lecture halls, educational movements, social reform movements, etc., are primarily to be regarded as entertainment.

Mankind has always recognized the importance of entertainment and its value in rebuilding the bodies and souls of human beings.

But it has always recognized that entertainment can be of a character either helpful or harmful to the human race, and in consequence has clearly distinguished between:

a. Entertainment which tends to improve the race, or at least to re-create and rebuild human beings exhausted with the realities of life; and

b. Entertainment which tends to degrade human beings, or to lower their standards of life and living.

Hence the moral importance of entertainment is something which has been universal-

They played an indispensable role in sustaining and stimulating the national imagination. That is why those who went to the movies in the thirties remember the movies they saw with so much greater vividness than those who went earlier and those who went later — why scenes and faces and lines and credits still linger in our minds with a peculiar exactness and intensity. . . .

"The thirties represented America's first great crisis of confidence. For nearly a century and a half, the republic had lived and grown without serious doubts about its future. 'All the conditions of American life,' as Herbert Croly wrote in 1909, 'have tended to encourage an easy, generous and irresponsible optimism.' The rivers could always be forded, the mountains climbed, the wilderness domesticated, the Indians subdued. The national belief was in the omnipotence of the happy ending.

"The First World War disturbed this confidence for a moment, but only for a moment. Then came the crash of 1929, and suddenly the party was unmistakably over. Instead came the collapse of a supposedly infallible system, unemployment and misery, an unprecedented series of blows to the national morale, dwindling belief in the national capacity to deal with the future. The birth rate precisely registered the decay of national faith; the country's population increase in the thirties was only half what it had been in the twenties.

"Doubt, discouragement, despair generated the psychological imperatives which gave the movies a new role in the nation's emotional economy. It was not just a need for distraction and entertainment. It was a need for reassurance and hope. With the American dream in apparent ruins, with the American people struck down by circumstances beyond their individual control, with the very idea of the individual threatened by anonymous and impenetrable economic forces, people longed to hear again an affirmation of individual identity, to see again a chance for individual possibilities, to feel again a sense of individual potency.

"The movies were by no means the only method of therapy. The deeds which began to restore the national confidence took place, first of all, in Washington, where a strong President showed that the nation did not have to lie down and take it, the impotent victim of inexorable economic fatality. The combination of the Depression and the New Deal gave the Hollywood of the thirties its particular audience — an audience which was at once demoralized by the downfall of the

Poster of Mae West. Her playful attitude toward sex delighted audiences in 1933; the following year, she became the first victim of the newly enforced Production Code.

During World War Two, theaters stayed open until early morning for factory workers coming off the swing shift. Photo by Marjorie Collins, 1943, for the Farm Security Administration.

system, exhilarated by the promise of action and deeply responsive to images of purpose and freedom."[6]

On the eve of Pearl Harbor, this freedom was challenged by isolationist senators, who alleged that Hollywood was manipulating public opinion in favor of the Allies in the European war, and that the growing number of anti-Nazi films represented interventionist propaganda by a clique of foreigners. At a committee hearing, Jack Warner rebutted all the charges and declared: "The only sin of which Warner Bros. is guilty is that of recording on the screen the world as it is or as it has been." *Life* magazine characterized the hearings as "the funniest political circus of the year."

Nobody laughed when, six years later, the House Un-American Activities Committee began hearings in Washington. The mood of the country had shifted decisively. Many were angered by strikes at home and Soviet intransigence abroad. Communism was seen as a cancer that threatened America's very survival. Hollywood, with its enormous influence, was as convenient a scapegoat for domestic unrest as was the state department for troubles overseas. It was ". . . the greatest hotbed of subversive activity in the U.S.," claimed Mississippi Congressman John Rankin in 1945. HUAC Chairman J. Parnell Thomas had declared, back in 1938, that the New Deal was communistic, and the HUAC hearings were a thinly disguised attack on liberalism.

In October 1947, the committee subpoenaed nineteen witnesses. Hollywood liberals formed a Committee for the First Amendment to defend the rights of the accused. Eric Johnston, Will Hays's successor as President of the Motion Picture Association of America, reassured the defense lawyers: "Tell the boys not to worry. There'll never be a blacklist. We're not going to go totalitarian to please this Committee. As long as I live, I will never be a party to anything as un-American as a blacklist."[7]

At the hearings, ten of the witnesses were deliberately provocative, embarrassing some of their supporters and alienating public opinion. Friendly witnesses agreed that there were Communist Party members in Hollywood (about 200, most of them writers) and that they had tried to introduce their ideas into pictures, but had been foiled by the vigilance of the front office. In November, the "unfriendly ten" were cited for Contempt of Congress; they

would later be jailed for a year. Industry leaders met in New York the same day and issued the Waldorf Declaration, agreeing to dismiss the ten and any other Communists or fellow travelers as damaging to the industry. A secret blacklist was instituted and was enlarged with helpful suggestions from the American Legion, movie columnists, and professional red-baiters. The burden of proof was placed on the accused. Thousands of careers were stunted; the fresh ideas the industry so desperately needed were snuffed out in a climate of fear. Not until 1960 was the blacklist ended.

It was Hollywood's darkest decade. In the past, its leaders had always put business ahead of politics. Before HUAC held its hearings, Columbia chief Harry Cohn was asked to fire a contract writer, John Howard Lawson (a noted activist who was then scripting *Counter-Attack*). Responded Cohn: "I ain't going to louse up a picture that's going to do three million two domestic." In 1948, Lillian Hellman wrote witheringly about the industry's moral turpitude: "Naturally, men scared to make pictures about the American Negro, men who only in the last year allowed the word Jew to be spoken in a picture, who took more than ten years to make an anti-fascist picture, these are frightened men and you pick frightened men to frighten first. Judas goats, they'll lead the others to the slaughter for you."[8]

Ironically, as political censorship flourished, moral controls were challenged. In 1947, producer Jerry Wald had complained that "the Breen Office is narrowing our range of properties to where we can either make a musical or a comedy. . . . Censorship is what is making our pictures empty and running along with a competent mediocrity." In 1952, the Supreme Court reversed its 1915 ruling by giving movies First Amendment protection, and in subsequent opinions stripped the conceptual and moral justification from obscenity rulings by the six state censorship boards. Otto Preminger successfully challenged the Breen Office by releasing *The Moon Is Blue* without a Seal of Approval — and getting away with it. Other challenges followed, and the Code was extensively revised, and finally — in 1968 — abolished.

The ending of movie censorship (aside from local action against pornography) reflects a liberalization of public opinion — and a lessening of the movies' impact on society. Television is now the mass medium and takes the heat. It is

Hollywood on trial: J. Parnell Thomas, Chairman of the House Un-American Activities Committee (HUAC), conducts hearings on alleged subversion within the movie industry, November 1947. Photo by Francis Miller for *Life*.

Gary Cooper took the stand at HUAC and declared himself against communism, because, "from what I hear . . . it isn't on the level." Photo by Leonard McCombe for *Life*.

Poster for *Beau Geste* (1939), starring Gary Cooper. As legionnaire or cowboy, Cooper epitomized the laconic American hero.

even more vulnerable to commercial and social pressure than Hollywood was. And this gives moviemakers an opportunity they can exploit — for good or bad. A few individuals have seized that chance and have created pictures that have an honesty and a maturity that Joseph Breen would never have permitted.

Quotations

1. Bruno Bettelheim, Patricia Wise Lecture at The American Film Institute, Washington, D.C., February 3, 1981; unpublished (copyright Bruno Bettelheim).

2. Raoul Walsh, quoted in *The Men Who Made the Movies,* edited by Richard Schickel (New York: Atheneum, 1975), page 33.

3. Howard Hawks, interview in *Take One,* November–December 1971; reprinted in *Voices of Film Experience,* edited by Jay Leyda (New York: Macmillan, 1977), page 190.

4. Arthur Schlesinger, Jr., "When the Movies Really Counted," *Show,* April 1963; reprinted in *The Movies in Our Midst,* edited by Gerald Mast (Chicago: University of Chicago Press, 1982), page 426.

5. Joseph I. Breen, letter of April 22, 1941, to Jack Warner; reprinted in *Inside Warner Bros.,* edited by Rudy Behlmer (New York: Viking-Penguin, 1985), pages 136–137. (Copyright Warner Bros.)

6. Arthur Schlesinger, Jr., pages 419–421.

7. Stefan Kanfer, *A Journal of the Plague Years* (New York: Atheneum, 1973), page 42.

8. Lillian Hellman, "The Judas Goats," *Screenwriters Guild of America,* ca. 1948; reprinted in *Journal of the Plague Years,* page 83.

Other sources

Edward de Grazia and Roger K. Newman, *Banned Films: Movies, Censors and the First Amendment* (New York: R. R. Bowker, 1982).

Ben M. Hall, *The Best Remaining Seats* (New York: Clarkson Potter, 1961).

Swedish poster for *The Great Dictator* (1940), in which Chaplin played Hitler as a clown.

"Movies . . . meet man's need to escape from his anxieties; they help assuage his loneliness; they give him vicarious experiences beyond his own activities; they portray solutions to problems; they provide models for human relationships, a set of values and new folk heroes. . . . All entertainment is education, more effective than school because it appeals to emotion, not intellect." — Hortense Powdermaker, 1950.[1]

Movies are too complex a phenomenon to be evaluated by scholars of any one discipline. Hortense Powdermaker was an anthropologist who studied Hollywood for a year, using the same techniques she had applied to South Seas islanders. Historian Arthur Schlesinger, Jr., is a less detached observer — he has been the movie critic of the *Saturday Review*. In this excerpt from a 1984 lecture, he explores the impact of the movies:

"Movies work their magic through suggestion and subliminal infiltration. Film is above all a duplicitous art. The movies are simultaneously an industry that lives by stereotype and an art that lives by undermining stereotype. Manifest and latent meanings are often at war with each other. The unique technical triumph of film is verisimilitude — the capacity to reproduce the physical surfaces of life. Yet the cultural function of film has been to serve as the instrument, not of realism, but of dream and myth.

"The very nature of fiction film as a supremely popular art guarantees that it is the vehicle of deep if enigmatic truth. Individuals embody private truths in novels, poems, plays, landscapes, sonatas. But the creation of a movie is a mass undertaking, and the truth, such as it is, is a public, a collective truth. Making a movie involves directors, producers, writers, cinematographers, actors, set designers, an army of other technicians, all fleetingly remembered in interminable credits; and the artifact is delivered by the complex assembly line to a vast, varied and anonymous audience.

"In short, the cinema, while accepting restriction, defies control. The uplifting moral denouements demanded by the Production Code were often too perfunctory to overcome the powerful and subversive images in the earlier reels. The visions thrust into circulation — visions of diversity, spontaneity, beauty, aspiration, irreverence, passion — prevailed in the end over such requirements as the prohibition of swearing and of the double bed or the punishment of transgressors in the

last five minutes. Movies proved at once unifying and disruptive — another example of duplicity. The film has provided a common dream life, a common fund of reference and fantasy, for a society driven by economic disparities and ethnic tensions. At the same time, it gave the insulted and injured a disquieting sense of the abundance and fulfillment presumably available to more fortunate citizens. What is anodyne for some may be incitement for others.

"If, as Emerson said and cultural historians have always assumed, 'no man can quite emancipate himself from his age and country, or produce a model in which the education, the religion, the politics, usages, and arts of his time shall have no share,' how much truer this must be in the case of models created by a crowd for a crowd. The film production process, an unstable merger of commerce and art, dependent on collective initiative and collective response, is intimately interwoven with the mentalité of society. What succeeds at the time in the movies, what is remembered later (often two separate things) obviously offer historians significant clues to the tastes, hopes, fears, myths, interior vibrations of the age.

"Yet, some may object, do films really offer much more than clues to the tastes and preferences of film producers? Are not audiences passive assemblages, seated expectantly in shrouded theaters, systematically manipulated to like whatever the producer chooses to give them?

"No doubt the producer tries to control the audience. But it is evident that in the end the audience controls the producer; for it is the audience that decides which films, stars, directors, themes, genres will endure. The audience is far from passive. It seizes from the movie what it needs for its own purposes of tutelage and fantasy. It responds to each film, not as an isolated event, but as reverberant with memories of other films, reverberant with knowledge of the private lives of stars, who themselves carry burdens of meaning, reverberant too with sad awareness of their own private lives. The mystery of the audience remains the permanent challenge to the filmmaker."[2]

In the same lecture, Schlesinger cites D. W. Griffith as a director of "messianic zeal" who set out to convert the audience to his point of view. In *The Birth of a Nation* (1915), Griffith and author Thomas Dixon sought (in Dixon's words) "to revolutionize Northern sentiments by a presentation of history that would transform every man in my audience into a good Democrat!" Drawing on

D.W.
GRIFFITH'S
- AMERICAN INSTITUTION -
THE BIRTH OF A NATION
"THE SUPREME PICTURE OF ALL TIME"
NEW YORK MAIL
MAY 2ND 1921

their own prejudices as loyal sons of the Confederacy and on the writings of some revisionist historians, they portrayed Reconstruction as an assault on the dignity of the South and the virtue of its women by negrophile Northerners and vengeful blacks (played in the film by white actors in blackface).

There were many at the time who shared such a distorted view of history and the racist views that underlay it. By its cinematic brilliance and the impact of its images, *The Birth of a Nation* brought these prejudices to the attention of a wider public and sparked a furious controversy that resurfaces whenever the picture is shown.

More than any other film, it established movies, until then derided, as a respected form of entertainment. It was widely shown and frequently banned. It sparked protests by white liberals and the NAACP — and a ten-year surge in Klan membership. And the controversy it aroused helped keep blacks from important screen roles for three decades or more: positive images would have offended the South, negative portrayals would have stirred resentment in Northern cities. Hollywood preferred to avoid the issue.

In his next picture, *Intolerance* (1916), Griffith made an impassioned plea for peace and tolerance, cutting back and forth between four historical epochs. The structure was too demanding for contemporary audiences; the tone excessively preachy. Worse, it was released on the eve of America's entry into the European war, during which pacifists and dissenters were considered as traitors. Its failure was a setback for Griffith — and for movies as an instrument of shaping history.

Sam Goldwyn is supposed to have said, "If you have a message, send it by Western Union." Hollywood has discouraged the production of message pictures, unless the message has been sugar-coated, and the audience has failed to support more than a handful of such movies. Director Frank Capra had a shrewd approach: "I don't say, 'now I'm going to tell you a moral tale and you'd better like it.' No, first I entertain them. I get them in a spirit of laughter and then, perhaps, they might be softened up to accept some kind of a moral precept. But entertainment comes first. Without it, it's very heavy and . . . you can't sell the American people anything."[3]

Poster for *The Little American* (1917), a demonstration of Hollywood's jingoism in the First World War.

In Tune with the Times

There have always been exceptions. *I Am a Fugitive From a Chain Gang* (1932) pulled no punches, and its unrelenting portrait of a cruel and vindictive system of justice drew audiences and spurred reform. *The Grapes of Wrath* (1940) preserved the spirit and candor of John Steinbeck's account of migrant farm workers. Producer Darryl Zanuck commissioned his own investigation of California migrant camps and discovered they were even harsher than the novel had suggested, but he prodded screenwriter Nunnally Johnson to rearrange the material and to end on an upbeat note. Ma Joad's last words leave the audience chastened but hopeful: "Rich fellas come up, an' they die, an' their kids ain't no good, an' they die out. But we keep a comin'. We're the people that live. They can't wipe us out. They can't lick us. And we'll go on forever, Pa, 'cause we're the people."

Timing is important. *Fugitive* was released in the darkest year of the Depression, when Americans were questioning established institutions; *Grapes,* at the end of the Depression and on the eve of war, when an affirmation of the nation's moral strength found a ready audience. *Drums Along the Mohawk* (1939) dramatized the struggle of colonists to survive during the War of Independence; in the same year, *Gone With the Wind* offered a similar lesson from history. Both resonated with the spirit of the times.

In every era, certain pictures have expressed contemporary concerns and helped shape a response — for contemporary audiences and for us, looking back.

In the 1920s, America became an increasingly urban society, and the shift from rural themes is evident in the decade's movies. Three examples from the end of the decade express the ambivalence that so many must then have felt toward the bustle and impersonality of city living; together, they sound as a requiem for lost innocence.

Sunrise (1927) is a moody expressionist drama, scripted by Carl Mayer and directed by F. W. Murnau, in which a young couple from an idealized countryside visit the city and are overwhelmed by its scale. *The Crowd* (1928), directed by King Vidor, is a harrowing portrait of a clerk who works in an intimidatingly huge office, who later loses his job and his child and is swallowed up in the

crowd. In *Applause* (1929), director Rouben Mamoulian combines the mobile camera of silent films and the crackling energy of early sound to express the shock experienced by a sheltered young woman on her first visit to New York.

A 1937 *Fortune* magazine article described Warner Bros. as "the only major studio that seems to know or care what is going on in America besides pearl-handled gunplay, sexual dalliance, and the giving of topcoats to comedy butlers."[4] Warners made an aesthetic out of tightfistedness; even its Busby Berkeley musicals and Errol Flynn swashbucklers had a hardboiled quality that captured the mood of the decade.

The studio specialized in dramas "torn from the headlines." But attempts to deal with the realities of the Depression — its poverty and despair, its injustice and violence — foundered on the enormity of the problems and the public's resistance to paying for what they could see all around them. The solution was melodrama: every problem could be solved by identifying and eliminating a villain or two. But, despite the simplifications and evasions, many of the movies produced by Warners and the lesser studios powerfully evoke the drab and bitter feel of being hard up in the 1930s.

The more Hollywood tries to be literal, the more it falsifies; only when it trusts its instincts to entertain a broad audience does it capture the inner truth of the subject matter. Misguided attempts at direct propaganda reinforce this conclusion. Warners' contribution to America's short-lived alliance with the Soviets in World War Two was *Mission to Moscow* (1943), which looks as though it was made more to please Stalin than to win over Americans. It's as stiff and lifeless as the Soviets' own films about their heroic leader, and the account of the 1937–38 Moscow trials is straight party line — though the information was supplied by U.S. Ambassador Joseph E. Davies.

A few years later, Hollywood was grinding out anticommunist melodramas, made without stars or conviction as a ritual gesture of appeasement for its ideological errors. In *Red Nightmare* (1949), Jack Webb describes what would happen if an ordinary God-fearing American town were taken over by Communists! Decent citizens are dragged away by commissars and there — unchanged — is the same courtroom footage that had been used in *Mission to Moscow* to whitewash Stalin's purges.

The Hilton family, Selznick's model for the fictional characters in *Since You Went Away* (1943).

None of these cynically contrived pictures sold many tickets, which suggests that public concern with the red menace was less widespread than the vigilantes claimed. But tough subjects could draw crowds as well as critical acclaim. Sam Goldwyn's production *The Best Years of Our Lives* (1946) was sparked by a *Time* magazine story about the difficulties that returning veterans would have in adjusting to peacetime society. Goldwyn (like Darryl Zanuck with *The Grapes of Wrath*) wanted to make a statement on an important topic, one that would combine criticism and affirmation. "Don't knock America" was his advice to screenwriter Robert Sherwood. (His caution was well-merited: in the HUAC hearings the following year, one character's criticism of bankers as hard-hearted was cited as evidence of radical infiltration.)

Director William Wyler was himself a newly returned veteran, for whom the war had been "an escape into reality." To achieve a sense of the real world, the picture was shot on unfamiliar locations — in Cincinnati; clothes were worn ahead of time to give them a used look; cinematographer Gregg Toland used deep-focus shots to establish links between different groups of characters; best of all were the performances, including that of an armless veteran, Harold Russell. In retrospect, it is easy to criticize the film's balancing act, but at the time it seemed to express the national mood and to dramatize key issues.

The red scare silenced many and stilled candor in the movies. The 1950s was a decade of coded entertainments, analogous to those made to outwit political censorship in repressive societies. *Viva Zapata!* (1952), Elia Kazan's first major picture, reflected the liberal confusion of the period. Producer Darryl Zanuck kept watering down the script to avoid offending the military (Zanuck was a strong supporter of Eisenhower for president), the Mexican government, and the American right. Eventually, he turned the revolutionary of history into a liberal reformer calling for free elections.

On the Waterfront (1954) also proved controversial. Inspired by the report of the Kefauver Committee on Organized Crime, it dramatized the personal crisis of a longshoreman driven to fight corruption in his union despite the opposition of his fellow workers. Union leader Roy Brewer persuaded Columbia that the picture was un-American because none of his fellow labor leaders would ever tolerate corruption. (Shortly after, the president of the International Longshoreman's Union was jailed, and the union was expelled from the

AFL — partly as a result of the movie, which was taken over by independent producer Sam Spiegel.) But the film was also an apologia by director Elia Kazan and writer Budd Schulberg, both of whom "named names" to HUAC after disclosing that they had been members of the Communist Party. Their moral dilemma of whether to betray former associates in the name of a higher principle parallels that of the character played by Marlon Brando in the film.

High Noon (1952) was, still more, a tract for the times that proved very popular. Conceived by writer Carl Foreman and producer Stanley Kramer in 1948 as an affirmation of the principles of the United Nations, it was finally made as an allegory of Hollywood's isolation and timidity during the witch-hunts — in which Foreman was blacklisted. (A similar story, of a beleaguered sheriff and the woman who loves him, served as the basis for McCabe and Mrs. Miller, 1973, directed by Robert Altman. If High Noon is an affirmation of traditional values in the midst of crisis, McCabe, released at the end of the Vietnam war, is resolutely antiheroic: the sheriff is a drunk, the woman a prostitute hooked on opium.)

In the 1950s, political significance was found in the least-expected places. Cecil B. De Mille, in his spoken prologue to The Ten Commandments (1956), drew a clear parallel between the Egyptian pharaohs and the rulers in the Kremlin. The Invasion of the Body Snatchers (1956) had a similar message: "Only when we have to fight to stay human do we realize how precious our humanity is." And in a spate of such movies about alien invasion, we discovered that "they" have superior intelligence and an ability to organize, contaminate, and multiply; and that even when they look like us, they have been brainwashed and are out to steal our souls. Just like the Reds!

President Eisenhower's farewell speech, warning of the growth of the military-industrial complex, and the trauma of the 1962 Cuban Missile Crisis heralded a shift away from unquestioning faith in the armed forces. President Kennedy gave quiet encouragement to the production of Seven Days in May (1963), in which a peace-seeking U.S. president is overthrown in a military coup. The following year, Fail Safe (1964) suggested that a nuclear strike might be launched as a result of computer error, stimulating public debate on the subject. Dr. Strangelove (1964) went further, treating the nuclear holocaust as black

farce, the product of human folly and pretension. It was the forerunner of *M*A*S*H* (1970), which used the Korean conflict as a mask for an anti-Vietnam burlesque.

Bonnie and Clyde (1967) was inspired by *Breathless* (1960) and other French New Wave movies that treated American "B" thrillers as the stuff of myth. The script had, in fact, been offered to François Truffaut. He passed it on to Warren Beatty, who, with director Arthur Penn and writers Robert Benton and David Newman, transformed the story of two Depression-era petty hoodlums into a mythical saga for the counterculture. It had enough of the 1930s to prompt nostalgia and to launch a fashion wave, but its roots were in the violence of the late 1960s. It spoke to those — especially blacks in the audience — who shared the movie's rejection of the establishment, and who saw banks as symbols of the system.

It was a time for rebels. In *The Graduate* (1967), Dustin Hoffman escaped his family, the older woman, and a career in plastics to abduct his true love. In *Easy Rider* (1969), Dennis Hopper, Peter Fonda, and Jack Nicholson rode out on their Harley Davidsons in search of the real America. *Butch Cassidy and the Sundance Kid* (1969), like *Bonnie and Clyde,* ennobled outlaws.

The Bicentennial year of 1976 was a watershed. The war in Vietnam had ended; America was slowly healing, and the celebration was an occasion for taking stock. *Rocky* proposed that hard work and a personal commitment can bring success against the odds; that a bum can be a contender. Its gritty, blue-collar setting gave it an air of integrity and broad appeal. Said Sylvester Stallone of the audience: "When they're cheering for Rocky, they're cheering for themselves."

Taxi Driver, directed by Martin Scorsese, drew on news accounts of Arthur Bremer's attempted assassination of George Wallace, and in turn inspired John Hinckley's attempt on the life of President Reagan. More explicitly than the movies of the late 1920s, it shows the violence and pressure of the city and suggests how frustration finds release in rage. Behind its theatrical imagery and operatic rhythms lurks a documentary portrait of a character and a city on overload.

The Bicentennial year also yielded *All the President's Men,* in which the account by reporters Bob Woodward and Carl Bernstein of how they unmasked the Watergate conspiracy became an inspirational tale of David defeating Goliath.

The most timely of recent productions was *The China Syndrome* (1979). Jane Fonda pointed out to an interviewer: "*The China Syndrome* preceded Three Mile Island by two weeks, and we now have a government that wants to build more nuclear plants." But she remained hopeful:

"Films, novels and television all play a significant role in slowly altering people's perceptions of themselves and their society. Catcher in the Rye *and* Rebel Without a Cause *were two cultural turning points that altered young people. They mobilized their unrest and rebelliousness. They were very important to me personally. These movies we've made are just pieces in a puzzle."*[5]

Unearthing hidden messages requires a historical perspective; it is harder to determine which films of the last decade will endure and be seen as signposts to contemporary thinking. Candidates include a succession of films that offer an escape from present realities into the past (*American Graffiti, Reds, Chinatown*), where the issues seemed more clear-cut; or into a world of make-believe (*Close Encounters of the Third Kind, Raiders of the Lost Ark, E.T., Starman*). Like earlier examples, many of these films comment on the present while seeming to evade it. And the discouraging portraits of future dystopias (*Blade Runner, Escape From New York, Sleeper, Road Warrior*) also reflect our current thinking about human imperfections and the misuse of technology.

Perpetuating Stereotypes

Hollywood reveals itself as much through its omissions as its emphases, notably in its portrayal of women and minorities. These are complex and controversial topics that have been extensively explored in recent books, from which the following brief observations are derived.

In her pioneering study of women on the screen, *From Reverence to Rape*, Molly Haskell suggests that their role during the studio era was more significant than it appears today:

"Through the myths of subjection and sacrifice that were its fictional currency and the machinations of its moguls in the front offices, the film industry maneuvered to keep women in their place; and yet these very myths and this machinery cata-

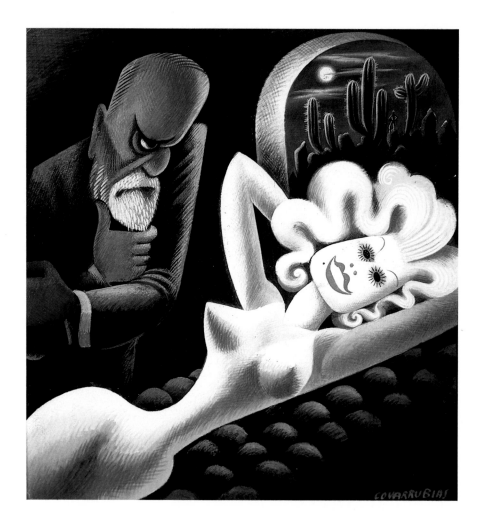

Sigmund Freud vs. Jean Harlow, 1935, gouache by Miguel Covarrubias, one of his "improbable conversations" series for *Vanity Fair*.

pulted women into spheres of power beyond the wildest dreams of most of their sex. . . .

"Indeed, the Production Code, for all its evils, was probably at least as responsible as the Depression for getting women out of the bedroom and into the office. . . . Women were no longer able to languish in satin on a chaise longue and subsist on passion; they were forced to do something, and a whole generation of working women came into being. . . .

"Whatever the endings that were forced on Bette Davis, Joan Crawford, Carole Lombard, Katharine Hepburn, Margaret Sullavan or Rosalind Russell, the images we retain of them are not those of subjugation or humiliation; rather we remember their intermediate victories, we retain images of intelligence and personal style and forcefulness. These women far surpass women in movies today. . . .

"In the 1930s and early 1940s . . . movies seemed to be saying that because men are secure, women can outsmart them without unsexing them, and because women are secure, they can act smart without fearing reprisals or the loss of femininity.

"The growing strength and demands of women in real life [in recent years] obviously provoked a backlash in commercial film. . . . With the substitution of violence and sexuality for romance, there was less need for exciting and interesting women."[6]

That was written over ten years ago, and little has changed, despite an abundance of skilled actresses and a discernible advance of women as producers, directors, and studio executives. In composition and outlook, Hollywood remains a predominantly male preserve. Male and white: minorities are still underrepresented, behind the camera and on screen.

Substantial progress has been made since Sidney Poitier first walked on the Twentieth Century Fox lot in 1950 and discovered that he and the shoeshine boy were the only blacks there. And shortly before that the movies cast every black as cheerful and submissive; Italians as waiters or gangsters; Swedes as sailors; and so on. The attitude is well captured in this description of how Hollywood responded to the shared experience of World War Two, creating

"a world of patient, waiting women; chipper, energetic factory girls; snappy secre-taries; eager chorus girls . . . a Noah's Ark of ethnicity — a Jewish soldier from Brooklyn, an Italian GI, a tough palooka with an Irish name; . . . a legion of understanding but gruff sergeants; sympathetic and lovely Red Cross nurses; wise, tender, waiting families; and suffering European victims of the Hun."[7]

The movies did not invent stock types, but borrowed them — from the stage, cartoons, popular literature, and folklore — and used them as a convenient shorthand, to telescope or evade character development. Hollywood smoothed the rough edges, and in doing so ensured the survival of these stereotypes into a time when the crude originals had been rejected. With the rise of ethnic consciousness in America, and the emergence of pressure groups, Hollywood has often chosen to blur racial or national characteristics to avoid giving offense.

At best, this leads to blandness; at worst, to the wholesale elimination of blacks, native Americans, and others from the screen. The traditional Western declined around the time it became unacceptable to cast Indians and Mexicans as villains. Italian-American pressure groups initially opposed the making of The Godfather, out of concern that society might think of all Italians as Mafiosi. Chinese-Americans angrily protested what they perceived as racial slurs in Year of the Dragon.

Blacks have suffered more than most races from derogatory casting. In the wake of The Birth of a Nation, black production companies were established to produce "race" movies with all-black casts for exhibition in the segregated theaters of the South and for black audiences in Northern cities. By the late 1920s, there were 700 such theaters; business had become profitable, and control of production had passed to whites. A few race movies spoke out boldly on prejudice and other important issues; most were cheaply made copies of Hollywood genres. Thus Lorenzo Tucker was billed as "the black Valentino," and Ethel Moses as "the black Jean Harlow." And even black producers such as Oscar Michaux perpetuated the caste system, by which lighter-skinned blacks played leads, and darker-skinned, the heavies.

Blacks enjoyed some exposure in early talkies — their voices were reported to record better — but only in supporting roles. The superb talent that played the jazz clubs and the theaters of Harlem — Duke Ellington, Billie Holliday, the

A segregated theater in Leland, Mississippi. All-black "race" movies, which parodied the conventions of Hollywood, were made for the South and for black neighborhood theaters in Northern cities. Photo by Marion Post Wolcott for the Farm Security Administration, 1939.

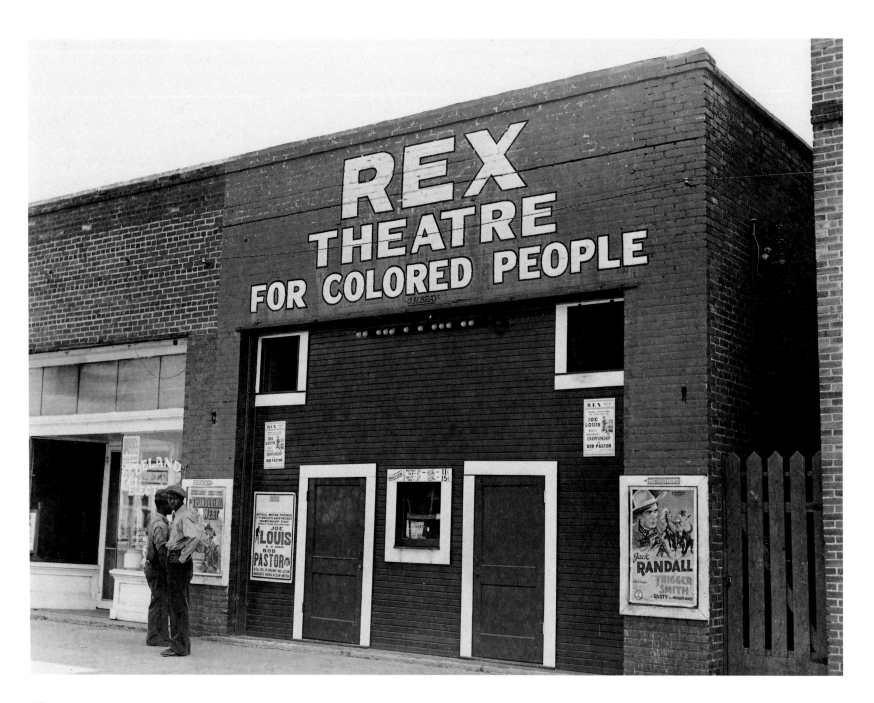

Poster for *Gone Harlem*, 1939. One of a series of "race" movies with all-black casts that mimicked the conventions of Hollywood.

Nicholas Brothers, Clarence Muse — was largely ignored; the electrifying tap dancing of Bill "Bojangles" Robinson was relegated to novelty routines with little Shirley Temple. Stepin Fetchit played (or parodied) a shuffling, easily frightened comic servant. Paul Robeson, an actor and singer of superb quality, proved too big a challenge for Hollywood and made his few movies abroad.

Gone With the Wind (1939) contained the expected stereotypes of faithful Negro slaves but, out of such limited material, Hattie McDaniel (who won the first Oscar awarded a black) and Butterfly McQueen created memorable characters. During the war and after, Hollywood made a small effort to give blacks more and better roles. Actor Paul Winfield (*Sounder*) recalls a childhood experience in Seattle in the late 1940s:

"All the blacks would sit in the movie theater balcony. Nigger heaven, they used to call it. Then one night we saw Stanley Kramer's Home of the Brave, *the first picture we'd seen in which a black was not a Stepin Fetchit, and we resolved never to sit in the balcony again. The power of seeing a black face in a real role affected the whole city as I knew it."*

Sidney Poitier's growing popularity with audiences of every color in the 1950s and 1960s laid the groundwork for others — though for twenty-five years he was the only bankable black star. Often his roles were impossibly noble, but at least he won respect and came out ahead. With the growing militancy of the late 1960s, younger black audiences turned away from Poitier toward bolder, angrier portrayals, and to "blaxploitation" — action dramas, often set in the urban ghetto, that pitted black heroes against white villains.

Blaxploitation soon faded, leaving blacks with greater respect but little employment. The popularity of Richard Pryor, Eddie Murphy, and Diana Ross did not open doors for serious actors. As Charles Fuller, author of *A Soldier's Story*, remarked: "Americans trust black people when we sing, dance or tell jokes. It's when we stop laughing that people get itchy."

Defining America to the World

"HOLLYWOOD, THE MAGIC EMPIRE OF THE TWENTIETH CENTURY! THE MECCA OF THE WORLD!" — opening title on *The Last Command*, 1928

Hollywood is a microcosm of America, luring established talent and eager

Bill "Bojangles" Robinson as Shirley Temple's partner in *The Little Colonel* (1935). A legendary star of black vaudeville, Bojangles came late to Hollywood and was limited to a few supporting roles.

hopefuls, diffusing its products and its influence around the world. The influx began in the 1920s and shows no signs of abating. Moviemakers have "gone Hollywood" for money, political asylum, and creative opportunities. It is estimated that a third of Hollywood's directors in the late 1920s were foreign-born. Today, the competition is fiercer and, as a result, there are fewer foreigners, but some of these few have enjoyed notable success.

Early immigrants included Chaplin and Erich von Stroheim, Josef von Sternberg and Ernst Lubitsch, F. W. Murnau and Victor Seastrom. With the rise of Hitler, the pace accelerated: Billy Wilder and Fritz Lang, Max Ophuls and Jean Renoir, Alfred Hitchcock and Douglas Sirk, Robert Siodmak and René Clair. And those are just some of the star directors; the finest European writers, actors, designers, and cinematographers also enriched Hollywood. The first wave of immigrants had created an industry; later arrivals fostered an art form.

Unfortunately, few of these early arrivals enjoyed the creative opportunities they had had back home. The studio system was inflexible: these "strangers in Paradise," as a recent book has characterized the prewar exiles, often came out of necessity and left by choice. Recent immigrants have been more fortunate. Those who have been able to adapt to the American way of making movies have flourished, and have given us a distinctive perspective on their adopted country. The decline of Hollywood as the dominant center has encouraged them to range freely through the United States.

Sergio Leone, who directed a trio of "spaghetti Westerns" in his native Italy, remarked: "I love the vast spaces of John Ford and the metropolitan claustrophobia of Martin Scorsese, the alternating petals of the American daisy" (*American Film*, June 1984). Drawn by that love, he made a legendary Western on location, and, in New York, *Once Upon a Time in America* (1984), an epic gangster movie that rivals the best work of an Italian-American, Francis Coppola.

Bruce Beresford made *Tender Mercies* (1983) in Texas, because it reminded him of the Australian outback, its vast distances enhancing the value of human relationships. Another Australian, Peter Weir, turned to the Amish country of rural Pennsylvania for *Witness* (1985).

French poster of Charlie Chaplin, ca. 1919. Chaplin came to America as a penniless immigrant and, within a few years, became Hollywood's best-known export.

None of these moviemakers was playing tourist; in each case they captured the essential qualities of their characters and locations. Louis Malle has repeatedly caught the spirit of place, in *Pretty Baby, Atlantic City*, and *Alamo Bay*. Other Europeans have explored the quirkiness of people that Americans take for granted: Alex Cox with *Repo Man* (1984), John Schlesinger with *Midnight Cowboy* (1969), Milos Forman with *One Flew Over the Cuckoo's Nest* (1975), and Peter Yates with *Breaking Away* (1979).

What drew these talented mavericks to work here was, in most cases, a love affair with Hollywood. In the ferment of the Russian Revolution, the model for the young Soviet directors was D. W. Griffith. A print of *Intolerance* was sneaked through the blockade, dissected, and studied with as great avidity as a purloined computer today. Later, Sergei Eisenstein tried unsuccessfully to direct Theodore Dreiser's *An American Tragedy* in Hollywood. Mary Pickford and Douglas Fairbanks enjoyed such popularity in Russia that a million people turned out to greet them in Moscow in 1925, and a feature film — *The Kiss of Mary Pickford* — was inspired by the visit.

In Italy in the 1930s, Mussolini's ban on American films encouraged native moviemakers to develop their own versions of Hollywood genres; Vittorio De Sica made his reputation playing a charmer modeled on Leslie Howard and Fred Astaire. In the 1950s, the props made for Hollywood costume epics were recycled in Italian productions. Even the neo-realist films of the 1940s (*Open City, Paisan, The Bicycle Thief*), which so inspired young Americans, were based on Hollywood's dramas of the Depression, which contrasted so sharply with the decorative escapism of fascist Italy.

Federico Fellini recalled the impact they had on him as a child:

"In the small movie house of my village — with two hundred seats and five hundred standing room — I discovered through your films that there existed another way of life; that another country existed — of wide-open spaces, of fantastic cities which were like a cross between Babylon and Mars. Perhaps, thinking about it now, the stories were simplistic. However, it was nice to think that despite the conflicts and the pitfalls there was always a happy ending. It was especially wonderful to know that a country existed where people were free, rich and happy, dancing on the roofs of the skyscrapers, and where even a humble tramp could become President.

Perhaps, even then, it wasn't really like this. However, I believe that I owe to those flickering shadows from America my decision to express myself through film."[8]

The French have long prided themselves on discovering the best of American cinema before Americans realized its significance. French critics of the 1950s acclaimed the films of Orson Welles and Fritz Lang, of Howard Hawks, Alfred Hitchcock, and Raoul Walsh when these directors were regarded merely as hired guns in Hollywood. The same critics praised "auteurs" Americans had scarcely heard of — Nicholas Ray, Sam Fuller, Edgar Ulmer — and when these critics (François Truffaut, Jean-Luc Godard, Claude Chabrol, and others) turned to directing in the 1960s, they incorporated references to favorite Americans in their own work. Godard dedicated *Breathless* (1960) to Monogram Pictures, a poverty-row studio that was a joke in Hollywood.

Americans have anxiously debated how foreigners must judge them from the movies we export. In 1939, producer Walter Wanger wrote in *Foreign Affairs* magazine "[The American cinema is] a perpetual epic of the ordinary, unregimented individual — who chooses a profession, travels at will, outguesses the boss and wisecracks the government."

In 1945, Jan Kouwenhoven wrote in *Harpers*: "[Movies] have been among the most appealing representatives of our civilization . . . because they were uninterested in putting our best foot forward. They were made to please American movie fans, and everyone else liked them too." And, in the same year, *Look* reported: "In every country liberated by Allied arms, the first civilian demand was for food; the second was usually for American movies."

Frank Capra suggests why, when he recalls the agitation to suppress *Mr. Smith Goes to Washington* (1939), the story of an idealistic young senator defying corruption in that august body. The American ambassador in London, Joseph P. Kennedy, warned that *Mr. Smith* would be used as propaganda by the Nazis and would lower the morale of the Allies — at the time the Germans had overrun Poland and were threatening Western Europe. Capra pleaded with Columbia not to listen to the politicians and they went ahead with the release. The picture was one of the last American films to be shown in France before the German occupation — and audiences cheered when Jimmy Stewart made his speech about liberty.

Fashions and Myths

Hollywood has always helped to shape public taste and behavior. As the First World War ended, Paramount's head office in New York cabled director Cecil B. De Mille in Hollywood: "What the public demands today is modern stuff, with plenty of clothes, rich sets and action." He did everything they asked — and more. In *Male and Female* (1919), adapted from J. M. Barrie's play *The Admirable Crichton*, he developed a formula that he was successfully to recycle through the 1920s: combining a modern story with a flashback to ancient times, depravity and titillation with a highly moral ending. Gloria Swanson played a shipwrecked heiress and a Babylonian slave, cowering beneath a snarling lion.

De Mille's films were the stuff of fantasy. But they were also instructive, providing lavish and intimate details of how the upper classes lived. *Male and Female* marked the first appearance of the nude bathing sequence that was to become a De Mille signature. (In later years, the director was to claim that he had made a wholesome contribution to American life by encouraging the creation of clean and comfortable bathrooms!)

Sixty years later, *Flashdance* offered a less exotic but equally calculated recipe to its appreciative young audience. In place of haute Babylonian couture, it showed them what trendsetters were wearing (new wave Japanese, punk rock, athletic chic) and launched an overnight fad for torn sweatshirts. It helped move break dancing from the urban ghetto to suburban malls, as *Saturday Night Fever* had boosted disco a few years before.

Writer-director Peter Bogdanovich observed: "The influence that the movies have had on every generation since 1910 is amazing. They have told us what to think, how to dress, what to say and do, how to cry, move, fall from a gunshot, act drunk, draw a gun, swoon, kiss."[9]

As tastemaker, the movies are today much less influential than television, but in its heyday, Hollywood was unchallenged at speeding the acceptance of new fashions. Designers accelerated the spread of white-on-white decor and the differing versions of art deco that movies used as shorthand for rich and fashionable — even if the fashion generally went no further than bakelite lamps and a relentless jazz pattern on every available surface. In the 1940s, the movies boosted the Latin American look and musical beat, and they introduced surrealism and psychoanalysis to a mass audience.

Hollywood put words in our mouths: "Take him for a ride"; "Frankly, my dear, I don't give a damn"; "You must remember this"; "I made him an offer he couldn't refuse." The words were all-pervasive. Complained the Chief Constable of Wallasey, in the north of England: "I cannot refrain from commenting adversely on the pernicious and growing habit of . . . youths to use Americanisms, with nasal accompaniment, in order to appear, in their own vernacular, 'tough guys.' 'Lay off, cop,' and 'Oh, yeah?' are frequent in answer to charges. . . ."[10]

Movie titles are employed as shorthand: Star Wars defense, Big Chill generation, and Death Wish vigilante are recent examples of how popular movies are a part of our shared culture. In 1933, the song "Who's Afraid of the Big, Bad Wolf" (from Walt Disney's cartoon *The Three Little Pigs*) became a popular echo of President Roosevelt's defiance of the Depression: "We have nothing to fear but fear itself." Forty years on, *The Graduate* made Simon and Garfunkel balladeers of the counterculture. *The Sting* marked the rediscovery of Scott Joplin; *Amadeus* vastly enlarged the audience for Mozart.

These are a few examples of how the surface attributes of movies have made their mark. But Hollywood's greatest and most durable achievement has been the making of myths. Scale is a factor: Western man's substitute for tribal ritual is watching large, hypnotic moving images in a darkened room, in silent communion with a crowd of his fellows.

Hollywood improves on reality. "In actual history, many of the great moments were undoubtedly dramatic flops: unimpressive, badly lighted and acted, cluttered with irrelevant detail," commented the authors of *Life Goes to the Movies*. And David Thompson observed: "Hollywood stylishness makes conservatives of us all. There is a certainty and serenity in the balance of light and shadow, and an implicit commitment to order and stability in the neatness of the compositions."[11]

Dr. Bruno Bettelheim spoke eloquently of myth and the deeper purpose of cinema:

"The Western . . . gave us the feeling of wide open spaces, of the unlimited oppor-

John Wayne, 1969, sculpture by Harry Jackson in painted bronze for *Time* magazine cover, inspired by Wayne's role in *True Grit*.

tunities this wilderness offered to man, and the inherent challenge to bring civilization to places where there had been none. The same movies also suggested the danger of chaos; the wagon train symbolized the community of man, the community man must form for such a perilous journey into the untamed wilderness which also referred to all that is untamed within ourselves.

"The Western gave us a vision of the need for cooperation and civilization because, without it, man would perish. . . . But although most of us continued to enjoy this myth, by now it has lost much, or all, of its vitality. We have become too keenly aware of the destruction of nature, and of the American Indian, that were part of the reality of opening the West. And the myth was based on an open frontier that no longer exists.

"Our nostalgic infatuation as a motive for the Western suggests how much we are in need of a myth about our past, which would not be invalidated by the realities of today.

"Science fiction movies can serve as myths about the future, and thereby give us some assurance about it. Whether it was 2001 or Star Wars, such movies tell about tremendous progress which will expand man's powers and his experience beyond anything now believed possible. But they assure us, on the other hand, that all these advances will not obliterate man or life as we now know it. Thus one great anxiety about the future, that it will have no place for us as we now are, is allayed by such films. Equally important, the promise of even the most distant future in spite of progress that will have occurred in all aspects of the material world, man's basic concerns will be the same, and the struggle of good against evil, the central moral problem of all times, will not have lost its importance."[12]

Quotations

1. Hortense Powdermaker, *Hollywood: The Dream Factory* (Boston: Little, Brown, 1950), page 15.

2. Arthur Schlesinger, Jr., "Film and History: An Equivocal Relationship," Patricia Wise Lecture at The American Film Institute, Washington, D.C., February 8, 1984; unpublished.

3. Frank Capra in *The Men Who Made the Movies*, edited by Richard Schickel (New York: Atheneum, 1975), pages 74–75.

4. "Warner Bros.," *Fortune*, December 1937.

5. Mike Bygrave and Joan Goodman, "Jane Fonda: Banking on Message Movies," *American Film*, November 1981.

6. Molly Haskell, *From Reverence to Rape* (New York: Holt, Rinehart & Winston, 1973), pages 30–31.

7. Barbara and Nancy Lynn Schwartz, *The Hollywood Writers' Wars* (New York: Alfred Knopf, 1982), page 179.

8. Federico Fellini, address to Film Society of Lincoln Center, New York City, June 1985.

9. Program note for New Yorker Theater, ca. 1965.

10. Quoted by Leo Rosten in *Hollywood: The Movie Colony, the Movie Makers* (New York: Harcourt, Brace, 1941), page 361.

11. David Thompson, *America in the Dark* (New York: William Morrow, 1977), page 85.

12. Bruno Bettelheim, Patricia Wise Lecture at The American Film Institute, Washington, D.C., February 3, 1981; unpublished (copyright Bruno Bettelheim).

Other sources

Donald Bogle, *Toms, Coons, Mulattoes, Mammies and Bucks* (New York: Viking, 1973).

Thomas Cripps, *Slow Fade to Black: The Negro in American Film 1900–42* (New York: Oxford University Press, 1977).

Daniel Leab, *From "Sambo" to "Superspade"* (Boston: Houghton Mifflin, 1975).

Randall M. Miller, editor, *The Kaleidoscopic Lens: How Hollywood Views Ethnic Groups* (Englewood, N.J.: Jerome S. Ozer, 1980).

Nora Sayre, *Running Time: Films of the Cold War* (New York: Dial, 1982).

David E. Scherman, editor, *Life Goes to the Movies* (New York: Time-Life Books, 1975).

Robert Sklar, *Movie-made America* (New York: Vintage, 1975).

John Russell Taylor, *Strangers in Paradise: The Hollywood Emigres 1933–50* (New York: Holt, Rinehart & Winston, 1983).

Walter Wanger, "120,000 American Ambassadors," *Foreign Affairs*, October 1939.

No movie role has been so idolized, denigrated, or misrepresented as that of the producer. Scott Fitzgerald transformed Irving Thalberg of MGM into the mythic Monroe Stahr of *The Last Tycoon*. In *What Makes Sammy Run?*, Budd Schulberg (himself the son of a former Paramount studio chief) created an unflattering portrait of a mercenary hustler, Sammy Glick. A favorite image is the cigar-chomping philistine, fondling flesh and spouting figures, fawned upon by acolytes as he takes a meeting beside a pool in Beverly Hills. It is a durable cliché, in cartoons and fiction — even movies — because the real function of a producer is mysterious and changeable.

David O. Selznick, producer of such pictures as *Dinner at Eight, David Copperfield, Gone With the Wind,* and *Rebecca,* described his approach in a 1937 lecture at Columbia University, from which these excerpts are taken:

"At some studios the producer is purely a creative producer, and has nothing to do with the business end. Many of these producers would be helpless without a big studio behind them. On the other hand, a producer like [Samuel] Goldwyn is in charge of the creative and business end. . . . Then there is the very able factory head who is a mass-production expert, able to keep the wheels turning and boss a great number of projects effectively by dividing his time among them. In that field I suppose the best examples are [Darryl] Zanuck [of Twentieth Century Fox] and [Hal] Wallis [of Warner Bros.].

"The producer . . . must be able, if necessary, to sit down and write the scene, and if he is criticizing a director, he must be able — not merely to say 'I don't like it,' but tell him how he would direct it himself. He must be able to go into a cutting room, and if he doesn't like the cutting of the sequence . . . he must be able to recut the sequence.

"A picture is usually born in two or three different ways. Either the producer gets a conception that he would like to make such and such a picture . . . buy a play, or create an original . . . or the idea comes from one of the staff, a director or a star. But more often than not, the idea is born in the Story Department or in the producer's mind.

"He starts from that, to select the people who are going to make the picture with him. Now the casting of the people who are going to make the picture is an even more important factor than the casting of actors, because you can take the best

writer in the world, and if he is misassigned, you will get a bad job. Take the best director in the world, and if it does not happen to be his particular type of picture, you are also defeated.

"The first step in either the creation of an original story or the adaptation of a book or play is usually the preparation of an adaptation, which is simply a narrative outline told in synopsis form. I like to be able to look at the outline and analyze where it seems weak, dull or slow. Or where it misses its climax, its opportunities for showmanship, for only in such naked form are you able to determine what the picture will be like. . . . I find it terribly important to get down to the bones of the story, before we start putting flesh on it in the way of scenes, business, dialogue and the dressing.

"Sometimes you go through as many as six, nine, ten or fifteen treatments before you get the outline that satisfies you in its basic elements. That process may see the demise of half a dozen writers or more before you get to the point that satisfies you. More often than not, you are forced by the exigencies of contracts and dates to start a picture before you are ready, or to rush your preparation . . . and you may have to start the picture before your script is complete. For that reason alone, it is a great satisfaction to have your treatment sound, because if you know the direction that your story is taking, you are not worried so much about writing the script as the picture is in progress as you would be if you didn't have that outline and just hoped to stumble through. . . .

"The other functions of the producer include the costuming. . . . It starts with a conference with the head of the Costume Department, an explanation of your needs, an indication of what point, dramatically, you want to make with each costume, and subsequent acceptance or rejection of sketches.

"With the sets you go through the same process: meetings with the designer of the sets, the head of the Art Department, and with the head of the Trick [special effects] Department, because today, a large part of the business of making sets is in trick work. In almost all pictures of importance, there are from ten to a hundred shots that are either glass or matte shots, which means that some part of them is painted in by one process or another, with only part of the set being built.

"Now, the day finally comes when your picture starts and you get that first-day nervousness, waiting impatiently for the first rushes. Rushes is a term for the film

as it comes straight from the laboratory. Each scene is photographed from several angles, varying all the way from one angle to ten . . . long shots, pan shots, close-ups of the individual actors, medium shots and so on, all of which come through in the rushes. . . . The producer and the director jointly select which of these takes is the best, after seeing it on the screen . . . from which the film editor roughly assembles the sequence.

"The putting together of those rough sequences means your rough picture. The only things that will be missing will be the trick shots, which take longer, and the sound effects, which are a separate process. Music doesn't come in until the final step. You then start your cutting conferences, far into the night, on getting the picture into shape for preview.

"Then, after you have completed your final editing, while the negative is being cut and the sound effects are being put in, the score, which has been in the process of composition in the weeks preceding, is then recorded by a thirty-, forty-, or sixty-piece orchestra [following] a series of conferences with the composer, the exact laying out of where music is required, what type of music, etc."[1]

Selznick was a special case. Among his contemporaries, only Goldwyn had the taste, passion, and obsessiveness to hire the finest creative talent and to supervise every aspect of every film he produced, from conception to exhibition. Rudy Behlmer's *Memo from David O. Selznick,* from which the above excerpts are taken, portrays a man who was half genius, half fanatic, driving himself and his colleagues to a pitch of excellence and a pit of exhaustion. *Gone With the Wind* justified such pains; Selznick's attempt to top that epic with *Duel in the Sun* (1946) failed — in part from too close an involvement, which stifled creativity.

Hollywood's pioneers had an easier task: such directors as D. W. Griffith and Cecil B. De Mille were their own producers, and much of what they did was improvised on the set. Mack Sennett wrote and acted for Griffith at Biograph in New York, became a director, and, in 1912, brought his Keystone comedy troupe to Los Angeles:

"We heard our picture before we saw it, although sound didn't arrive in motion pictures until 15 years later. A Shriners' parade, stepping to oom-pah and brass, was marching up Main Street. . . .

ITEM	METRO GOLDWYN MAYER	WARNER BROTHERS
RHETT	Gable	Flynn
SCARLETT	None	Bette Davis, if we wish.
OTHER PLAYERS	None obligatory	Entire stock company available, including de Havilland if desired.
COST OF RHETT	$150,000.	$50,000.
TIME OF STARTING	Feb. 15th, if Gable sells his vacation time, which is unlikely; otherwise Apr. 1st guaranteed.	October, or any time on 10 wks. notice.
FINANCE	50-50 up to $2,500,000.	$400,000. SIP. Up to $2,100,000. W.B.
RISK OF LOSS	50-50	Identical
OVERAGE COST	Advanced by SIP and recouped by SIP only out of its own profits.	Advanced by W.B. up to $250,000. on same basis as $2,500,000. limit, and recouped out of 82½% of gross; beyond $250,000. overage, identical with MGM.
COST OF DISTRIB.	20%	17½%
PROFITS	50%	40% of gross beyond cost to include profit and distribution; equivalent of 27 7/10% of profits.
ROAD SHOWS	Gross computed after deduction of cost.	Identical.
BILLING	Joint presentation SIP and MGM	SIP picture.
CONTRACT APPROVAL	None. Protective clauses only.	Complete approval as under UA contract.
ADVERTISING	Consultation, but final MGM approval.	Complete approval as in UA con.
TRAILERS	Pays for cost and retains profits	SIP pays cost and retains profits.
PRINT COST	Entirely out of SIP's share.	Out of SIP's share up to limitation, then paid partially by WB as in UA contract.
TECHNIC. OPTIONS	All remain with SIP	Identical.
NEW TALENT	Remains with SIP (not yet agreed to by Schenck and Mannix)	Remains with SIP except one picture to WB if use new personality as Rhett or Scarlett.

In planning the production of *Gone With the Wind* (1939), producer David O. Selznick noted the competing offers from MGM and Warner Bros. To secure Clark Gable for the role of Rhett Butler, Selznick had to meet MGM's stiff terms.

David O. Selznick on the *Gone With the Wind* set of Atlanta at his Culver City studios. Photo by Edmund Bert Gerard for *Life*.

"The parade was a whopper and it would take a long time to pass a given point. A given point in my mind was a free lunch or wherever I could set up the camera and shoot unpaid actors.

"'We got us a spectacle, kids,' I said. 'Bauman and Kessel are always hollering about costs. Look at that crowd scene — all free! . . .'

"'What's the story, boss?' Pathé [Lehrman] asked.

"'Got no story. We'll make it up as we go along,' I said. 'Pathé, run over there to the department store and buy a baby doll. . . . Jim, you get the camera set up on the corner. Ford [Sterling], you put on a tall overcoat and make like an actor.'

"Mabel Normand could throw herself into any part instantly, even into a part that didn't exist. . . .

"Mabel put on the comicalest act you ever clapped eyes on, pleading, stumbling, holding out her baby — and the reactions she got from those good and pious gentlemen in the parade were something you couldn't have caught on film after six days of D. W. Griffith rehearsals. Men were horrified, abashed, dismayed. One kind soul dropped out and tried to help Mabel.

"'Move in, Ford,' I told Sterling. Ford leaped in and started a screaming argument with the innocent Shriner, who didn't know he was being photographed to make a buck for Keystone.

"The police moved in on Ford and Mabel. Ford fled, leaping, insulting the police, and they — God bless the police! — they chased him. I helped the cameramen and we got it all.

"The Shriners were good, but the best scenes we nabbed were the running cops. . . . They were the original Keystone Kops."[2]

As an independent from 1919 on, Chaplin established his own studio, where he could write, produce, direct, and star in movies that might take a year to complete. His popularity allowed him such an indulgence; other artists were cut down to size. Pandro S. Berman, whose credits as producer include *Top Hat*, *Gunga Din*, and *The Blackboard Jungle*, recalls the changes that occurred during his forty-plus years in Hollywood:

"My greatest contribution was to find the story material, develop it into a screenplay, get a director, cast it, and make the picture, usually using other studio personnel for all these jobs. To make a distinction between the producer I am describing and the producer of today, the producer of today is more of an agent, a packager, a promoter, or a financial man who will put things together and take them to a studio, a distribution company, or a bank and get financing. That method has had a very great effect in that the producer has abdicated his function as the creative man in the setup. He has gone to other business activities, leaving the director as the creative influence.

"Today in the industry the director is the boss. He is the one who decides what he is going to make, how it should be written and by whom, who is going to star and other key talent. Then he makes the picture having virtually no one over him. Whereas in my day, under the Louis B. Mayer system, which was not just Mayer but was prevalent throughout the whole industry, the producer had that function. Strangely enough, the long period in which the producer had these duties was the second phase in the industry because originally it was the director who did all these things. If you go back far enough to the old boys like D. W. Griffith, you see that the director was the first creative influence in the making of motion pictures. They ran the show then, as now. It was only at a certain time when directors began to get extravagant that Mayer, or somebody, dug up the concept of putting a supervisor in charge who could hold the director down in terms of budget. Little by little that developed to where the producer became the important cog in the wheel. He made the decisions or approved of all decisions, both artistically and financially.

"Louis B. Mayer used to say, 'Give me a screenplay that I like, and you've done your job as producer.' He thought everything that was to be film footage should be on paper, and that was the movie. His filmmaking factory took over from there. He had a stable of actors, directors, and technicians. If you didn't use one, you'd use another. Sometimes you'd have one director on a picture for a while, and if he got sick, instead of calling the picture off for a week as they would do now if Mike Nichols took ill, they'd say, 'Jack Conway isn't well. Let him rest. We'll put Harry Beaumont on it for a week, and he'll pick up where Jack left off.' That's the way we made pictures. Of course, it's not the way it's done now."[3]

The best of today's producers do enjoy creative control, but never to the

Louis B. Mayer, MGM studio chief, and his top stars celebrating the company's twentieth anniversary in 1943. Photo by Walter Sanders for *Life*.

same extent as the legendary production chiefs of the studio era. Here is an account by *Fortune* magazine of a day in the life of Darryl F. Zanuck in 1935 — just after he had become the first head of Twentieth Century Fox:

"Wherever Zanuck goes, there are dictaphones: in his bedroom, in his office, in the projection rooms where he sees what he has wrought. His genius is one of self-expression: he talks incessantly of whatever comes into his head. . . . At ten-thirty he rolls in through the gates of Movietone City [the new Fox studio in West Los Angeles], impatient for his dictaphone.

"First there are treatments and synopses to be read. Synopses of novels, magazine stories, plays, and original screen stories come to the studio office at a rate of 150 a week from New York and Hollywood; and of these he reads the best dozen or so himself. If he likes [the story] he sends it to Will Hays's office; and if Will Hays sees no harm in it, Zanuck buys it. It then goes to a scenario writer for a treatment, about thirty-five pages long. But if Zanuck doesn't like any of the synopses, he dictates an idea of his own. A Zanuck idea is so fertile that it often turns out to be a treatment.

"At eleven-thirty there is a story conference. One of Zanuck's secretaries ushers in the scenario writer and the associate producer assigned to supervise the production. Zanuck stands behind his desk, silhouetted against a zebra skin. He mentions what pleases him about the script or treatment. Then he dismembers it. For twenty minutes, through the fluent tide of his conversation, you see the characters in the story dissolve and change, the scene fade and resolve itself into another setting, the conflict ebb and flow with the shift of opposing forces. It is like watching the tortured spirit of a motion picture in the body of a medium. Zanuck utters brief snatches of dialogue. Striding up and down, he lets his invention run free until it tires him. Then there is some discussion, and there are suggestions from the writer and producer.

"He goes to lunch at one o'clock with his executives. . . . At two there may be a conference with Lew Schreiber, the casting director. Three months before a film goes into production, Zanuck will have made up his mind about the featured players and altered the script to fit them. Six weeks in advance, he must assign players from his own studio, negotiate for players from other studios, so that he will have a full cast ready when filming begins.

"Zanuck goes to the projection room at three. There the rushes are run off for his inspection: scenes taken the day before. About two-thirds of the film has already been edited out by the cutter before Zanuck sees it. There is a dictaphone at Zanuck's elbow, and a telephone on the table in front of him. To the dictaphone he makes comments for the benefit of the director. With the telephone he talks to the cutter in the projection booth, editing the scenes while they are run off before him."[4]

Zanuck was a benevolent dictator, whose authority within the studio was unchallenged and who answered only to the Board of Directors in New York — and to the theatergoers who passed judgment on each movie. The power of such moguls was matched only by the stress they endured, but most enjoyed extraordinary longevity, buoyed by unflagging enthusiasm for movie-making and the gamble on public taste.

With the decline of the studio system, power has fragmented. Studio heads play musical chairs every few years, and each tries to use such a position as a springboard to become an independent producer with financial and distribution guarantees from a studio. Every studio in Hollywood will bid for a Ray Stark or a Steven Spielberg; the measure of George Lucas's success is that he can afford to turn his back on Hollywood, just as (on a more modest budget) Woody Allen can maintain his creative independence in New York. Even Darryl Zanuck — as later his son, Richard — became an independent producer, back in 1956.

But independence is an illusory state: Lucas is perhaps the only major movie-maker who can finance production out of his own resources, and even he must depend on another organization to handle distribution. The studio remains closely involved in key decisions, as this discussion of the making of *The Godfather* (1972) indicates. (Peter Bart supervised the project for Robert Evans, Paramount Pictures' production chief; Albert S. Ruddy produced the picture.)

*"**Bart:** [Paramount] bought the rights to* The Godfather *after seeing fifty or sixty manuscript pages and an outline of the rest of the book. That was a case where one took a piece of material which, at the beginning, a lot of people were very unsure about and seeing it through the various stages over a period of years,*

Producers David Brown and Richard Zanuck flanking director Steven Spielberg on the set of *Jaws* (1975). Zanuck and Brown helped launch Spielberg's career with *The Sugarland Express* in 1974.

seeing it through the obstacles. I was responsible for optioning the basic material, I worked on the screenplay with Mario Puzo, I brought in Al Ruddy as producer, and later, Al and I brought Francis Ford Coppola in as director. Mario Puzo was always going to do our first-draft screenplay. The basic decision we faced in terms of developing the screenplay was whether to make a relatively inexpensive action-gangster picture, or whether to tell it from the point of view of a family chronicle. It was the decision of all of us to try for the bigger, more substantial film, not just a rip-off Mafia picture. . . .

"A lot of the idea for making it a family chronicle came from discussions that I had early on with Francis. It wasn't any brilliant brainstorm I had; it grew out of our discussions. . . . That idea of doing the film as a period piece was Al's, it was Evans's, it was mine, it was Francis's. When the decision was made to do it as a substantial picture, to spend the money on it, then we decided to make it a period rather than a contemporary film. . . . Once the picture started shooting, it was very much Francis's ball game.

"**Ruddy:** . . . There is a moment when the director takes it over. And that is why you've got to hire the right director. You must build a wall around him so that he can address the greatest possible amount of his creative energies to the execution of the film and not be concerned with a lot of the other pressures. However, that must always be within the framework of sharing. As I share, in a sense, his job in that his reputation is riding on the film, so I insist that he have a concern for my job and my reputation. In the case of The Godfather, there were areas where the creative judgment had to be placed against or counterpointed to the dollars we had to spend, making for problems that Francis and I had to solve together on a moment-to-moment basis. That's the area where the two jobs overlap and you both share the same concern. If we're shooting on Fifth Avenue, as Michael [Al Pacino] and Kay [Diane Keaton] come out of Best & Co., I want to have enough period cars on the street so that it looks real and Francis wants enough. But the budgetary demands may restrict how many cars you can have.

"I would say that the movie was very tightly controlled as to how the money was spent. There were a lot of bright, young people who worked on it in a production capacity, in assisting Francis, in assisting the production designer, Dean Tavoularis, who really made great contributions. They did research and got certain things that were critical to the film — secured certain locations — and it was not done by dint of a lot of money. 'I don't care what you want for this place, we'll pay you!' — it was never done that way.

"When production started the budget was locked at somewhere between $5.4 and $5.5 million. The film came in at $6.1 million, but the film never slipped. It was things we had no control over: Al Pacino got hurt, it started snowing. Filming in New York in the winter, with a $5.5 million budget, the expenditure of an additional half million or so does not represent a slide. A real slide on a film on that scale could bring it up to, maybe, eleven million. That's because the cost of making a film, at certain points, increases not arithmetically but geometrically. You have the various departments — camera, sound, wardrobe, Teamsters — and if you lose, or start sliding, in one department it affects every other department. If the set you've constructed is not staying up, then you can't proceed with set dressing; and everybody else is not working, literally, but is being paid nevertheless.

"**Bart:** I would say that the front office does not make, despite allegations to the contrary, creative contributions while a film is before the cameras.

"**Ruddy:** As the film started to generate an enormous amount of publicity and the dailies indicated to the studio that there was quality . . . there arose a very expansive feeling about the potential success of The Godfather. We were going to do the scene where Jimmy Caan is killed at the tollbooth — in one day, on a real highway out near Jones Beach. Paramount said, 'Don't worry about the money, do a spectacular job.' So we went out to a deserted airstrip at Floyd Bennett Field which would be much easier to control than an actual location, and dressed it up to look like a highway. Dean Tavoularis designed two tollbooths, and we shot there almost three days. I would say that scene cost $100,000, but that was a conscious choice. It reflected the feeling of all of us that we could keep reaching for a little more quality — at moments — and that every dollar we spent would be money well spent both in terms of the creative return on the film and the financial return on the film.

"I worked on the various stages of the editing and I was in on the mixing from the first minute to the last minute. Francis has a facility in San Francisco — American Zoetrope — and a wife and kids and a house in San Francisco. When we wrapped in Sicily he had been gone from San Francisco for about eight or nine months. He wanted to do the first assembly of the film in San Francisco at American Zoetrope, and I thought it was not only fair, but I felt that we would probably get through that maze much more rapidly by letting Francis live at home and work at his own facility. We had two cutters up there with him, I went up once a week, but, basically, the first assembly of the film was done in San Francisco by Francis. Then we started refining, taking out certain things, Francis came down here, we moved the cutters down here, and we worked in Los Angeles. Francis and I worked on the first cut basically without anyone from Paramount looking in. When we finished our cut it ran two hours and fifty-five minutes, we showed it to Bob Evans and — as a result of our anxiety, because we knew that Paramount wanted a two-hour-and-twenty-five-minute movie — we cut it down to two-twenty-five.

"**Bart:** . . . In postproduction, there have been instances where the front offices of the different studios have been extraordinarily astute. Bob Evans makes very insightful suggestions at the postproduction stage. I think that many directors are extremely shortsighted in that they aren't open to ideas when they're editing. If you go to people you respect and solicit their advice, you might get, out of ten ideas or suggestions, one that really makes it better.

"**Ruddy:** I must say, to Bob Evans's credit, and Paramount's, he said, 'It's better at two-fifty-five, it played faster at two-fifty-five.' And so, again, you had a corporation that was going against what you'd call standard studio procedure."[5]

Every producer and studio head has similar concerns, and they have changed little over the past sixty years. Irving Thalberg, who asserted his authority as MGM's first production chief in 1924 by taking the eight-hour cut of Greed from Erich von Stroheim and slashing it to two — Thalberg, the master of retakes and happy endings, could have anticipated the January 1983 declaration of MGM production head Freddie Fields: "We're going to make pictures for what they should truly cost, and the emphasis is on adventure, action and romantic pix hyphenated to comedy. We're not making any downbeat, subjective, introverted, negative character studies."

Quotations

1. David O. Selznick, "The Functions of the Producer and the Making of Feature Films," excerpts from a lecture given by Selznick to a Columbia University extension film-study group, in conjunction with the Museum of Modern Art, November 1, 1937; reprinted in *Memo from David O. Selznick,* selected and edited by Rudy Behlmer (New York: Viking, 1972), pages 474–479. (Copyright Selznick Properties, 1972)

2. Mack Sennett with Cameron Shipp, *King of Comedy* (New York: Doubleday, 1954); reprinted in *The Voices of Film Experience,* edited by Jay Leyda (New York: Macmillan, 1977), pages 427–428.

3. Pandro S. Berman, quoted in *Hollywood Speaks,* edited by Mike Steen (New York: G. P. Putnam, 1974), pages 176–177.

4. "Twentieth Century–Fox," *Fortune,* December 1935.

5. Peter Bart and Albert S. Ruddy, quoted in *Filmmaking: The Collaborative Art,* edited by Donald Chase for The American Film Institute (Boston: Little, Brown, 1975), pages 21–27.

Other sources

Steven Bach, *Final Cut* (New York: William Morrow, 1985).

John Gregory Dunne, *The Studio* (New York: Farrar, Straus & Giroux, 1969).

Scott Fitzgerald, *The Last Tycoon* (New York: Scribner's, 1940).

Hugh Fordin, *The Movies' Greatest Musicals* (New York: Frederick Ungar, 1984).

Philip French, *Movie Moguls* (New York: Penguin, 1971).

Ronald Haver, *David O. Selznick's Hollywood* (New York: Alfred Knopf, 1980).

Garson Kanin, *Hollywood* (New York: Viking, 1974).

Samuel Marx, *Mayer and Thalberg: The Make-Believe Saints* (New York: Random House, 1975).

Lillian Ross, *Picture* (New York: Rinehart, 1952).

Budd Schulberg, *What Makes Sammy Run?* (New York: Random House, 1941).

Anita Loos, the most celebrated (and durable) of early screenwriters, with her husband, director John Emerson, in 1918. They collaborated on the social comedies that launched Douglas Fairbanks.

4 SCREENWRITING

Hollywood writers were treated as second-class citizens from the start. In the 1910s, directors usually worked from a story outline or a loose scenario, improvising scenes as they went along; there was no script for Griffith's early masterpieces, let alone routine comedies and Westerns. Title cards were added to the edited footage, making it easy to adapt the movie to different audiences and languages.

Anita Loos sold her first story to Griffith in 1912, while she was still a teenager; and she wrote many of Douglas Fairbanks's early comedies in conjunction with her husband, director John Emerson. In later years she wrote the novel and screenplay of *Gentlemen Prefer Blondes*, and coscripted *San Francisco*. In 1916, she was working for D. W. Griffith:

"'I'm running my new picture tonight,' said D.W., 'and I'd like you to see it with me. You're to write the subtitles.' . . . That night I sat alone in the projection room with D.W., the first viewer ever to see Intolerance. *I must be honest and say I thought D.W. had lost his mind. It is difficult to realize in these days of non-sequitur film technique what a shock* Intolerance *provided. In that era of the simple, straight-forward technique for telling picture plots, Griffith had crashed slam-bang into a method for which neither I nor, as was subsequently proved, his audiences had been prepared. The story of* Intolerance *jumped back and forth between four different periods of time with nothing to tie the pieces together except its theme of man's inhumanity to man.*

"I went to work writing the subtitles for Intolerance *and for weeks went about the studio nursing that mighty secret. I spent every day alone in the projection room, running the picture over and over and fitting it with words. D.W. bade me put in titles even when unnecessary and add laughs whenever I found an opening. I found several. At one point I paraphrased Voltaire in a manner which particularly pleased D.W.: 'When women cease to attract men, they often turn to reform as second choice.' Recently, when* Intolerance *was shown at the New Yorker Theatre on Broadway, that subtitle cribbed from Voltaire was still getting a big laugh."*[1]

Griffith was his own master, but producer Thomas Ince instructed his directors — as early as 1915 — to "shoot the script as written," to ensure they would make the movie (within the budget) he had approved. In their quest for status, early moguls would have imported Shakespeare if he had still been around; lesser but well-established writers who did accept an invitation to Hollywood included Maurice Maeterlinck and Rex Beach, Elinor Glyn and Michael Arlen. None achieved anything of significance, but they lent cachet and gave a hook to the publicists.

By the mid-1920s, Hollywood was a powerful lure to New York wits and Chicago reporters. Herman Mankiewicz was both. His career in Hollywood was celebrated more for brilliant conversation than great scripts, though he coauthored two of the finest: *Dinner at Eight* and *Citizen Kane*. Once settled in, he cabled Ben Hecht, a former colleague on the *Chicago Tribune*, who was now in New York — unemployed and flat broke: "Will you accept three hundred per week to work for Paramount Pictures. All expenses paid. The three hundred is peanuts. Millions are to be grabbed out here and your only competition is idiots. Don't let this get around."[2]

In his autobiography, *A Child of the Century*, Hecht recalled:

"Mankiewicz's telegram had told the truth. Hollywood, 1925, was another boom town, and my nerves were alive to its hawker's cry an hour after I had left the train. It reminded me happily of that other El Dorado — Miami. Miami had run up the price of its real estate. Hollywood was doing the same thing for talent, any kind of talent, from geese trainers to writers and actors.

"For many years Hollywood held this double lure for me, tremendous sums of money for work that required no more effort than a game of pinochle. Of the sixty movies I wrote, more than half were written in two weeks or less. I received for each script . . . from $50,000 to $125,000. I worked also by the week. My salary ran from $5000 a week up."[3]

In *Talking Pictures*, Richard Corliss remarks that "Hecht personifies Hollywood itself: a jumble of talent, cynical and overpaid; most successful when he was least ambitious; often failing when he mistook sentimentality for seriousness; racy, superficial, vital and American."[4]

Few achieved such heights of fame or fortune. Hecht was one of a small band who combined a prolific output with dependable quality. His credits included *Scarface, The Front Page, Twentieth Century, Gunga Din, Wuthering Heights, His Girl Friday,* and *Notorious*, alone or in partnership with Charles MacArthur. He worked on many others without credit:

"One of my favorite memories of quickie movie writing is doing half of the Gone With the Wind movie. Selznick and Vic Fleming appeared at my bedside one Sunday morning at dawn. I was employed by Metro at the time, but David had arranged to borrow me for a week.

"After three weeks' shooting of Gone With the Wind, David had decided his script was no good and that he needed a new story and a new director. The shooting had been stopped and the million-dollar cast was now sitting by collecting its wages in idleness.

"The three of us arrived at the Selznick studio a little after sunrise. We had settled on my wages on the way over. I was to receive fifteen thousand dollars for the week's work, and no matter what happened I was not to work longer than a week. I knew in advance that two weeks of such toil as lay ahead might be fatal.

"Four Selznick secretaries who had not yet been to sleep that night staggered in with typewriters, paper and a gross of pencils. Twenty-four-hour work shifts were quite common under David's baton. David himself sometimes failed to go to bed for several nights in a row. He preferred to wait till he collapsed on his office couch. Medication was often necessary to revive him.

"David was outraged to learn I had not read Gone With the Wind, but decided there was no time for me to read the long novel. The Selznick overhead on the idle Wind stages was around fifty thousand dollars a day. David announced that he knew the book by heart and that he would brief me on it. For the next hour I listened to David recite its story. I had seldom heard a more involved plot. My verdict was that nobody could make a remotely sensible movie out of it. Fleming, who was reputed to be part Indian, sat brooding at his own council fires. I asked him if he had been able to follow the story David had told. He said no. I suggested then that we make up a new story, to which David replied with violence that every literate human in the United States except me had read Miss Mitchell's book, and we would have to stick to it. I argued that surely in two years of preparation someone must have wangled a workable plot out of Miss Mitchell's Ouïdalike flight into the Civil War. David suddenly remembered the first 'treatment,' discarded three years before. It had been written by Sidney Howard, since dead. After an hour of searching, a lone copy of Howard's work was run down in an old safe. David read it aloud. We listened to a precise and telling narrative of Gone With the Wind.

Form 73—20M—4-38—K-I Co.

SELZNICK INTERNATIONAL PICTURES, INC.

9336 WASHINGTON BOULEVARD   CULVER CITY, CALIFORNIA

Inter-Office Communication

TO   Mr. David O. Selznick   **DATE**   October 12, 1938

FROM   Val Lewton   **SUBJECT** SUGGESTED WRITERS FOR
                                                 "GONE WITH THE WIND"

         Naturally you understand that the field of good writers is limited, especially for an assignment of this sort. This is not so much an apology for the shortness of my list as for some of the choices, which at first blush, might strike you as rather odd.

CLEMENCE DANE   No one can quarrel with the worth of her dialogue and it is my feeling that she can give the character of Scarlett an intangible quality of life and fire. She's always been good with rebellious women characters. If you are going to Bermuda she could go straight there from England. The fact that she is an English woman should not deter you. "Abraham Lincoln," the best play ever written on an American historical character, was written by John Drinkwater. I think the English know and love our Civil War period even better than we do.

BEN HECHT   This seems the wrong assignment for him, but I think he can do anything he sets his mind to.

THORNTON WILDER   I don't know how much screen experience he has had, but he has a good quality of mind and it seems to me enough real intelligence, rare enough in writers, to be able to pick it up quickly from you. From all accounts he is a very pleasant person and I have a hunch that you might get on very well with him. His dialogue and its range over periods, peoples and countries, is exceptionally good.

LOUIS BROMFIELD Here again I am not certain as to whether or not he has had enough screen experience. I know that he has had some, but how much I've been unable to find out in this brief time. He has nice structure sense and is such a good story teller that his limited experience as a screen writer might not count against him.

LAURENCE STALLINGS His dialogue, to judge from his last picture, is pretty bad, but that may have been the fault of a collaborator or producer. He has a lot of feeling for this period and might work out, although I would not strongly recommend him to your attention; just a slight possibility.

LYNN RIGGS   He's good on dialogue, a little vague and poetical in his plays, but you might be able to keep this tendency in leash as you did in "Garden of Allah."

O.H.P.GARRETT.   If only structural changes are needed, cuts of scenes and general rearrangement, he might be a good man. As to dialogue, much as I love the man, I, personally, wouldn't let him write dialogue for a "Mickey Mouse." I think visualization of scenes and general plot carpentry are his field, and he excels in it.

(more suggestions to come.)

Sweerling?
Lillian Hellman?

Form 73—20M—4-38—K-I Co.

SELZNICK INTERNATIONAL PICTURES, INC.

9336 WASHINGTON BOULEVARD   CULVER CITY, CALIFORNIA

Inter-Office Communication

TO   MR. DAVID O. SELZNICK   DATE   January 18, 1939

FROM   F. Scott Fitzgerald   SUBJECT "GONE WITH THE WIND"
                                               MELANIE HAMILTON
                                               RING EPISODE - SC. 133

I believe you are unnecessarily worried about Melanie. We
have seen actors and actresses created by one or two strong
scenes in the end of a picture, and dozens fading out in
padded, hollow parts. As an instance: the women who play
in men's pictures -- criminal and sporting and war pictures --
how it bores the audience when they have empty things to say.
I believe this is one of the great current mistakes in
pictures.

Melanie will develop in her strong scenes -- the murder of the
soldier, etc. -- will develop better if we haven't made her a
shadowy, goody-goody with speeches that are little more than
Maureen O'Sullivan "Oh's" and "Ah's" no matter how many words
they contain. I would rather see her out of scene than
annoying us by delaying action -- the audience will detest her
for that. I know your problem there, but I would like to see
it solved the right way.

One more word about Rhett's returning the ring in Scene 133.
I have just talked to Miss Keon, who tells me it was once in
the scene where Rhett gives Scarlett the bonnet. Believing
firmly that it belongs there, I have tried a little scene to
that effect -- not so long as what is cut in scenes 133-136.

                                 Scott Fitz
                         Scott Fitzg-----

FSF:cs

Memo to Selznick from Scott Fitzgerald, one of fourteen writers who contributed to the script of *Gone With the Wind*.

Scott Fitzgerald during his short-lived stint as a Hollywood screenwriter on the set with actor Richard Barthelmess.

Opening titles by Ben Hecht for the domestic (left) and foreign release prints of *Gone With the Wind*.

Title 1

There was a land of Cavaliers and Cotton Fields called the Old South...

Here in this pretty world Gallantry took its last bow..

Here was the last ever to be seen of Knights and their Ladies Fair, of Master and of Slave...

~~Beyond its happy borders the Age of the Machine and the Time of Science had already begun~~

~~But in this land Yesterday still ruled..~~

Look for it only in books for it is no more than a dream remembered, a civilization gone with the wind.

Opening Title for FOREIGN USE.

Preview dummy title has 143 words
    This has 122 words..)

        - - -

~~xIn 1861xthexien~~
This is a story of the War that once threatened the existence of the United States of America....

In 1861 ~~the~~ ten Southern States Seceded from the Great Union, and formed ~~the Union~~ a new nation, the Confederate State of America.

~~They Ixx~~
The Southerners were a romantic-minded folk who raised cotton, believed in Honor and owned slaves..

Abraham Lincoln's cry that a nation could not exist half free and half slave struck at their pride and their pocketbook.

They answered that each state had the right to decide its destiny for itself, and they sent their chivalrous sons gayly to battle for this right...

Among the commonwealths to challenge the great Union was the State of Georgia...

And this story begins with the laughter of the easy-going, aristocratic Georgians awaiting a new adventure- WAR...

"We toasted the dead craftsman and fell to work. Being privy to the book, Selznick and Fleming discussed each of Howard's scenes and informed me of the habits and general psychology of the characters. They also acted out the scenes, David specializing in the parts of Scarlett and her drunken father and Vic playing Rhett Butler and a curious fellow I could never understand called Ashley. He was always forgiving his beloved Scarlett for betraying him with another of his rivals. David insisted that he was a typical Southern gentleman and refused flatly to drop him out of the movie.

"After each scene had been discussed and performed, I sat down at the typewriter and wrote it out. Selznick and Fleming, eager to continue with their acting, kept hurrying me. We worked in this fashion for seven days, putting in eighteen to twenty hours a day. Selznick refused to let us eat lunch, arguing that food would slow us up. He provided bananas and salted peanuts. On the fourth day a blood vessel in Fleming's right eye broke, giving him more of an Indian look than ever. On the fifth day Selznick toppled into a torpor while chewing on a banana. The wear and tear on me was less, for I had been able to lie on the couch and half doze while the two darted about acting. Thus on the seventh day I had completed, unscathed, the first nine reels of the Civil War epic."[5]

When the talkies arrived, studios signed up playwrights and novelists by the score in their anxiety to secure that exotic commodity: spoken dialogue. These new recruits considered themselves artists, whose words were sacrosanct. In the theater, the Dramatists Guild prohibited unauthorized changes in their work; out West, the producer's word was law. Jack Warner dubbed his contract writers "schmucks with Underwoods" and treated them like assembly-line workers. At Paramount, writers had to deliver eleven pages every Thursday or face dismissal.

Scripts were routinely torn apart and rewritten, at the whim of a supervisor, a director, or a star. "The last one I wrote was about Oakies in the Dust Bowl," remarks the screenwriter played by William Holden in *Sunset Boulevard*. "You'd never know because, when it reached the screen, the whole thing played on a torpedo boat."[6]

Writers have always complained long and loudly at the indignities heaped upon them. Some had little choice; during the Depression and into the 1940s, serious writers were unable to live on their income from book royalties. For Scott Fitzgerald, William Faulkner, Nathanael West, and John Steinbeck, Robert Sherwood and Clifford Odets, Hollywood spelled survival. In his account of such writers, *Some Time in the Sun*, Tom Dardis suggests that their years in Hollywood were less a humiliating waste of time and talent than has been supposed. Fitzgerald drew on his experiences at MGM to create, in *The Last Tycoon*, what remains the finest insider's account of a studio in its prime. West was as unfortunate in his career as a screenwriter as he had been in securing a readership for his mordant novels. But his years there provided the material for *The Day of the Locust*, as dazzling an account of the underside of Hollywood as Fitzgerald's is of its mythic dimensions.

For William Faulkner, Hollywood and the work he did for hire was a thing apart from his personal writing in Oxford, Mississippi. But he succeeded much better than Fitzgerald and West, becoming an intimate friend and professional associate of Howard Hawks, and helping him develop the scripts for *To Have and Have Not* (adapted from a Hemingway story) and *The Big Sleep* (adapted from Raymond Chandler). A later arrival, James Agee, was passionate about the movies and turned in two of Hollywood's most distinguished scripts: *The African Queen*, cowritten with John Huston; and *The Night of the Hunter*, for Charles Laughton.

Writers with fewer literary pretensions benefited—and gave—even more, as long as they were willing to work within a collaborative system and fight for their views. One of Jack Warner's workhorses, Norman Reilly Raine, fired off this blast to producer Hal Wallis, contesting director William Keighley's desire to add a spectacular tournament to his script for *The Adventures of Robin Hood* (1938)—and won his point:

"The jousting tournament never can be anything but a prologue which, if done with the magnificence Mr. Keighley sees, will have the disastrous effect of putting the climax of the picture at the beginning—and I'll be goddamned if that is good construction dramatically in fiction, stage or screen, because the only way you could ever top it would be to have a slam-bang battle or something equally spectacular—and expensive—at the end. Maybe I'm crazy—but what we set out to tell was the story of Robin Hood . . . the swashbuckling, reckless, rakehell type of character who, by his personal adventures has endeared himself to generations. . . .

"I maintain that it is the human element that makes great drama and great entertainment . . . the conflict, and growing of love between boy and girl; the characterization of Robin in his scenes with his men so we understand why this great human story came down through the ages . . . and if these things are entertainingly told . . . we'll get all the spectacle naturally we want in the archery tournament as now written. But the archery tournament will certainly suffer pictorially if we stick a jousting tournament in the beginning. Christ's second coming in a cloud of glory would seem tame if we showed the creation of the world first. . . ."[7]

The procedure during the 1930s differed little from one studio to another. A writer (sometimes a pair) would first be asked to prepare a synopsis of an idea or property; then a treatment; and, if that was approved, a script. At each stage, the producer, director, and others could propose changes. Nunnally Johnson, who scripted *The Grapes of Wrath, The Prisoner of Shark Island, Jesse James,* and other important projects for Twentieth Century Fox, took a positive view of the system and of studio chief Darryl Zanuck:

"Zanuck was the master of the story conference. When the first draft of a script was finished he sent copies to, I don't know, half a dozen, maybe eight, of the people who advised him, and Casting, and so on. Then he'd call me, and the director, if there was a director assigned to it, and we'd discuss the parts he wasn't satisfied with, or his dissatisfaction with the whole, and we'd also take up each point that was made in these notes from his advisors. He'd say, 'Well, I don't believe what this fellow says. I had no confusion about it, so forget it.' Or he'd say, 'He's got a good point here. Now that I look back at it, it seemed that way to me too. Now what can we do to reconcile these differences?' Eventually, after I'd done a number of scripts for him and he had some trust in me, he would get to a point where he would begin to improvise. As often as not his improvisation was not to my liking. (He was inclined to the cornball stuff.) I wasn't going to say that to him, but I'd say, 'Will you let me work on that a little longer?' He'd say, 'Okay.' When I came back in with the revised version, and I'd altered that, rewritten that particular part of the picture that Zanuck had 'improvised' on, it didn't matter to him whether I'd followed anything he suggested or not. Not as long as it made dramatic sense. He never made another mention of it. I don't even know if he remembered. But if it fit and felt right, it went.

"When I'd bring him back the first revised script, he'd say, 'Well, this looks pretty good. I like the way you straightened out so-and-so, and could we get a little stronger ending?' Now it was just between him and me, and we'd discuss two or three endings until we found something that looked like it might fade out properly and satisfactorily. Then, after the second revised script was done, we would discuss it, and he would say, 'I haven't got but two notes here. One, I don't think that the fellow ought to wear a beard,' or something. He would mention some tiny thing like that. 'And two, the guy's a little too harsh with the woman. I don't think he would be that harsh with her.' I would say, 'All right, that's easily fixed.' He would say, 'All right. Do those. Send it to Mimeograph and we'll go to work.'"[8]

Many of the better writers directed their own scripts (Preston Sturges and Billy Wilder are classic examples) or worked in partnership with a favorite director (Samson Raphaelson with Ernst Lubitsch, Robert Riskin with Frank Capra, Frank Nugent with John Ford). Ernest Lehman, whose credits include *West Side Story* and an underrated picture, *The Sweet Smell of Success,* authored three scripts for Alfred Hitchcock. He writes of their association:

"You got a lot more attention paid to every little thing you did and said in a Hitchcock picture. It's amazing, you know, how he could manipulate an audience. Take North by Northwest, for example: the beginning of the crop-duster sequence, in particular, when Cary Grant is standing alone by the roadside waiting for a man he has not met (but has been mistaken for) to show up. Most directors would have had maybe one or two cars whiz by, and figure that that was about all an audience could tolerate. But Hitchcock knew better than that. He had a car come from one direction, zoom by and disappear in the distance; then he held on a long interval in which nothing was happening; then he had a car come from the other direction, and zoom by and disappear in the distance; and then another long interval of silence with nothing happening; and then a truck came by and merely blew dust all over Cary Grant and disappeared in the distance. And still nothing had really happened. Hitch knew how to milk that sequence in a way that no other director would have known how to do, or would have had the guts to do. There was an awful lot of ominous nothing going on for a long time before the stranger appeared on the other side of the road. That was just one aspect of Hitchcock's unique style. . . .

"I remember Hitch kept talking about a cyclone, and how it menaces Grant from the sky. I said, 'Hitch, that's not good.' He said, 'Oh, that would be wonderful. It's

easy to do.' I said, 'Yeah, but they're *trying to kill him. How* are they going to work up a cyclone?' Anyway, now we are up in the sky with a cyclone, right? And I just can't tell you who said what to whom, but somewhere during that afternoon, the cyclone in the sky became the crop-duster plane. Before the day ended, Hitch and I were acting out the entire sequence. The plane making its passes, Grant seeing the cornfield, ducking into the cornfield, the various passes of the plane with a gun; then he sees a car, tries to wave it down, it ignores him, and he races into the cornfield. Crop-dusting poison is going to drive him out. He sees a diesel truck. I remember all that stuff. The next day I went to my office and wrote it, naturally with the greatest of ease. I had already seen it all."[9]

By the late 1950s, the contract system was dead. Writers, who had begun to freelance back in the 1940s, were now free agents — unless they had been blacklisted, in which case they had to use another writer as a front or write under a pseudonym, and always at cut rates. In 1957, *The Bridge on the River Kwai* won several Oscars, including Best Screenplay. The script had been written by Michael Wilson and Carl Foreman — both blacklisted. The Academy Award went to the author of the novel on which the film was based — Pierre Boulle — who could barely speak English. Only in 1960 did the blacklist end, and not until 1985 were Foreman and Wilson given (posthumously) the award they had earned.

Over the past twenty years an increasingly sterile debate has been waged over the authorship of movies. Directors have achieved greater public recognition than writers; books on directors are legion, on writers few. Some writers get quite angry thinking about it; Gore Vidal is one:

"Ever since that dread moment, when Al Jolson said, 'You ain't heard nothin' yet' — which I think is the most sinister line in all of world drama — it's been a writer's medium. But nobody ever knew this. The directors know it. Cecil B. De Mille, that gorgeous ego-maniac, said, 'You know, it's all the script.' Kurosawa said, 'It's the script.' I think even Delmer Daves would say it's the script. The script is all-important. But the director has got to get it away from the writer because he must be an auteur du cinéma.

"Almost anybody can do what a director does. I've worked on about fifteen movies; I've done 150 live television plays; I've done eight plays on Broadway — I never saw

a director yet who contributed anything. When I got to Cannes for The Best Man [1964] — I got the critics' award for the best script — there on this banner was the title in French and: Un film de Franklin Schaffner. Well, I just hit the ceiling. I mean, this was my play, my movie. I had helped put the thing together; I had hired Frank. 'Un film de Franklin Schaffner'! That's when I first ran into the auteur theory, in 1964. The French are always wrong, remember that."[10]

Writer-director Billy Wilder takes a calmer view:

"Directing is a pleasure because you have something to work with: you can put the camera here or there; you can interpret the scene this way or that way. But writing is just an empty page; you start with nothing, absolutely nothing, and, as a rule, writers are vastly underrated and underpaid. It is totally impossible to make a great picture out of a lousy script; it is impossible, on the other hand, for a mediocre director to screw up a great script altogether."[11]

Andrew Sarris, who popularized the French critics' theory that the director was the author of a movie, and applied it to a wide range of American moviemakers, offered this definition: "As a screenplay is less than a blueprint and more than a libretto, so directing is less than creating and more than conducting."[12]

Increasingly, screenwriters try to become involved with a project at the outset and to stay close to it until the movie is in the can. Writers, recognizing the limitations of their own profession, are more frequently insisting upon producing or directing their own scripts. An example is Robert Towne. Acclaimed as a "doctor" of others' scripts (*Bonnie and Clyde* and *The Godfather* among them), and for his original work (*Chinatown, The Last Detail,* and *Shampoo*), he secured an agreement from Warners to direct his Tarzan script, *Greystoke.* But first, he decided to hone his skills on a more modest undertaking, *Personal Best.* The film ran over budget, and to secure the funds to complete it, Towne was forced to sell the *Greystoke* script.

In conversation with John Brady in *The Craft of the Screenwriter,* Towne describes his experience as director and as script doctor:

"When you are writing you are alone and can confine your foolishness to a room; but when you work with people, when you're directing, it's quite possible to feel

like the biggest idiot on earth. Here is this elaborate machine, this infernal machine — it's out of Rube Goldberg — and you're there. Trucks. Maniacs carrying things running all over the place. Lunch wagon. Everything. Suddenly you are this guy that everybody is looking at, and it's intimidating too. Directors all have to feel like idiots. I know I do.

"One feeling I'm experiencing as a director is that it's like rewriting standing up. The actors do the scene, you are looking at the take, and then real fast you've got to figure out how to rewrite that take before the next one. You've got to watch it as though the writing had nothing to do with you — as though they are the writers. Forget that you are watching your own stuff. You are watching this Thing coming out from the actors, the screenwriter, and everybody else, and you've either got to figure out how to rewrite the scene immediately, or be able to tell that it's good enough and doesn't have to be rewritten. Doing that as a writer in your own room — 'This doesn't look quite right; I'll go out and think about it for half an hour' — is one thing; on the set, you've got to do it right away, or not do it at all, or run the risk of going up to a producer and saying, 'Jeez, I've been looking at that scene, and I think we should reshoot that.' And you get a very unhappy producer. The necessity of having to do it fast under that special kind of pressure is a different kind of discipline than what I've known as the discipline of writing.

"Writing is creating something out of nothing. Rewriting is creating something out of what is there — but doing it with fifty-five thousand people and trucks and equipment standing around staring at you, wondering what you are going to do next, or if you know what the hell you're doing, and somebody asking you, 'Do we break for lunch at twelve-thirty or at one?' and, 'When do you want to look at dailies?' and, 'We can't get this actor for that. Do you want to see So-and-So?' and, 'Do we this?' and 'Do we that?' and trying to clear your head and think: Did I really like that take or didn't I? . . .

"Filmmaking is dictated by fear. By financial pressures, temporal pressures, career pressures. You really have to be with people who are close friends, who have the proverbial grace under pressure (and it's easier with friends), and that's one reason why some movies turn out better than others. I don't know that anybody's ever bothered to investigate, but you go down and look at the number of films that have been made and pick out what you consider are the good films. I'll bet you in

almost every case that the major people involved in the making of every good film — the cinematographer, the costume designer, set designer, director, actors, screenwriter — had worked together on several films and were close to each other. Strangers coming together for the first time rarely make anything good. . . .

"On The Godfather, *Francis was perplexed. In the book there wasn't any resolution between Vito Corleone and his son Michael — their relationship. He needed a scene between the two of them. Francis kept saying, 'Well, I want the audience to know that they love each other.' He put it that way. But you couldn't do a scene about two people loving each other. So I wrote a scene about the succession of power, and through that it was obvious that the two men had a great deal of affection for each other. Through Brando's anxiety about what would happen to his son, and his anxiety about giving up his power — his ambivalent feelings about, in effect, forcing his son to assume his role, and having to give up his role — that was the key to that scene.*

"If you want to use the 'script doctor' analogy, it wasn't a major operation — just spot surgery in a highly specific area. That creates all sorts of problems by itself. I wasn't rewriting the script from beginning to end, which I've done most often. Instead, I was adding outside material and had to fit it in with what existed, make it consistent — and this meant knowing everything that had been shot, and everything that the director had in mind. An interesting problem. Usually you're rewriting right along with the director as you know where you're going. On The Godfather *it was a case of someone saying, 'This is where I think I'm going, but I don't know where to go anymore. You help me make up my mind where I want to go next.' And yet I hadn't been in on any of the original process. They'd been shooting for five or six weeks before I even got there. So I had to look at the footage and say either, 'This is terrific' or, 'This is so bad, I can't possibly fix it.' Which, of course, was the last thing in the world from the truth. . . .*

"That was the scariest situation I've ever been in, because I knew they were going to lose Brando within twenty-four hours. It was a tense situation at that particular point because no one figured that the film was going to be the big hit that it was. I saw about an hour of assembled footage, and I thought it was brilliant. Francis was troubled. There was a lot of backstabbing on the set, and he was constantly being undermined. So I couldn't get over it: The footage was so extraordinary. I felt that I was going to make a contribution to a film that was virtually assured of being a major hit, although that was not the prevailing opinion on the set.

"I worked on a few minor scenes. I remember restructuring Michael's speech for the scene where he tells how he is going to kill the cop. I just did a simple thing there. The way that Francis had originally written the speech, Michael says at the beginning he's going to kill the cop, and then he tells about the newspaper story and other things to justify it. But it was much more dramatic for him to withhold what he was going to do until the end of the speech. I just reversed it. There were a few other little things like that. . . .

"What seems to be a kind of absentmindedness on the part of Vito Corleone as far as protective measures are concerned is really his unwillingness to accept the position he's placed his youngest son in.

"But the two men in the course of the scene really accept the dictates of fate. It's sort of a perverse noblesse oblige: Vito is obliged to pass the cup, and Michael is obliged to take it. He does, and through that you see that the two men love each other very much, rather than my writing a scene about love, which wouldn't have worked in that movie. It's illustrative in a way of writing in general. Most scenes are rarely about what the subject matter is.

"But mainly Francis was concerned about having a scene between Michael and his father. So we sat down with Marlon and Al Pacino, got their feelings, and began writing about eight o'clock that night and did a scene about the transfer of power: Uneasy lies the head that wears the crown. I don't know if you remember the scene at all, but that's the gist of it. The don is saying, 'We've got to see about this,' and Michael is saying, 'Dad, I told you I'd take care of it, and I'm taking care of it.'"[13]

William Goldman is a writer with outspoken views on everyone and everything. He is the author of scripts for *Butch Cassidy and the Sundance Kid*, *Marathon Man*, and *All the President's Men*. He has stuck to the craft he practices so well:

"Ideas come to you in very different ways. Some people occasionally will ask, 'Why didn't you do Butch Cassidy as a novel?' Because it came to me as a movie. The feel of it was a movie. Movies do some things wonderfully well that novels don't do. There's a marvelous narrative thing that movies have: they do size and scope.

They aren't really very good at interpreting. I don't think they are much on complexity. But movies are marvelous in terms of a story's size and sweep that you can hardly do in a novel unless you are Tolstoy, but most of us aren't Tolstoy. So they are entirely different forms. The only similarity is that very often they both use dialogue. Otherwise, the way that one handles a scene in a movie and the way one handles a scene in a book have nothing to do with each other. . . .

"You always attack a movie scene as late as you possibly can. You always come into the scene at the last possible moment, which is why when you see a scene in a movie where a person is a teacher, for instance, the scene always begins with the teacher saying, 'Well, class . . .' and the bell rings. And then you get into another scene because it's very dull watching a man talk to people in a room. This interview, if you had a camera on it, would have put people to sleep already — whereas in a book you could have a scene. There's a teaching scene in the book Marathon Man that must run three, four, five, seven pages where Babe goes to class. Well, that scene in the movie is very short. You truncate it somehow, as much as you can. In a book you might start with some dialogue, and then describe the room, and start with some more dialogue, and then describe your clothing, and more dialogue. The camera gets that in an instant. Boom, and you're on. Get on, get on. The camera is relentless. Makes you keep running.

"The average screenplay, as you know, is very short. Rule of thumb: a page a minute. The ideal length for a screenplay is a hundred and thirty to a hundred and thirty-five pages because that lets everybody be creative when they get it. That means that the producer will be able to say, 'Well, we must cut fifteen pages out of this.' No matter what you give them, ultimately you end up with a hundred and fifteen pages, because that is how long the movie is. But if you gave somebody a first draft of a hundred and fifteen pages, they would say, 'What's this, television?' So you have to give them a little extra to work with. . . .

"Most people think that screenwriting is only dialogue, and that we're those people who write those dreadful lines that all those nice, wonderful actors have to say. And the reality is that the single most important thing contributed by the screenwriter is the structure. It's a terrible thing for a writer to admit, but in terms of screenwriting, dialogue really doesn't matter as much as in plays and books — because you have the camera. The camera gives you the actor's eyes. If you have

a speech or a couple of lines that an actor feels awkward saying, and he can feel more comfortable changing your dialogue, and you get his emotion that way, then by all means that must be done, because what really works in a film is the actor's emotion. Movies are a group endeavor. We live in a world where people think the director is this giant genius 'having dreams,' as Robert Altman would say: 'I woke up with a dream, and there it was.' But basically there are seven people who are essential to a film, and if the film's going to be really any good, all seven have to be at their best . . . the director, the producer, the players, the cinematographer, the production designer, the editor, and the writer. Now sometimes the composer is essential, absolutely essential. But that varies from film to film. Sometimes the special-effects man is absolutely essential. The most important single thing in Jaws, for instance, was the shark, and the most important single thing I think in The Exorcist was Dick Smith's makeup on the girl. If you hadn't had that fabulous makeup, the reality that picture had for that vast audience would have gone out the window. Really dazzling makeup is hard to do.

"Same is true of the cinematographer. The director doesn't look through the camera except to see if the shot is showing. Are the corners correct? Is it framed properly? Is that what they want to see? But the lighting — in other words, how it looks on film — is the province of the cameraman. One of the reasons cameramen have much better lives than writers is because nobody says to a cameraman, 'I'll fix the lighting,' because nobody knows how to do it. But everybody knows words.

"Really dazzling production design is hard to do, too. The production designer is the person who is responsible for everything that you see on the film, what is there and how it looks, what's the reality of it. A good production designer can carry a weak director. Does it look like a room? Is it interesting? The director doesn't say to a production designer, 'Put this here and that there.' He hires a production designer and prays. Nobody messes with their work.

"The only one who gets screwed around with basically is the writer, because, as I say, everybody knows the alphabet. And the producer makes contributions, and so does the actor's mistress, and so does the agent, and all that. That's why I say the first draft of the screenplay is all that gives me pleasure. The rest of it is basically dealing with exigencies that you know are going to happen. I am making this up now, but suppose you have a part in your script and suddenly someone says to you,

'I hear Ali MacGraw wants to go to work. If we can build up the girl's part we have a shot at getting Ali because I know she wants to do a movie in the jungle.' So that part balloons. Or this happens, and that happens, or Jack Nicholson doesn't want to play a loser, or . . . you get the idea. . . .

"When people say, 'Is it like the book?,' the answer is, 'There has never been a movie that's really been like the book.' Everybody says how faithful Gone With the Wind *was. Well,* GWTW *was a three-and-a-half-hour movie, which means you are talking about a two-hundred-page screenplay of a nine-hundred-page novel. The novel has, say, five hundred words per page; and the screenplay has maybe forty, maybe one hundred and fifty words per page, depending on what's on the screen . . . you're extracting little, teeny essences of scenes. All you can ever be in an adaptation is faithful in spirit."*[14]

Quotations

1. Anita Loos, *A Girl Like I* (New York: Viking, 1966), pages 102–104.

2. Ben Hecht, *A Child of the Century* (New York: Simon and Schuster, 1954), page 466.

3. Ben Hecht, pages 467, 477.

4. Richard Corliss, *Talking Pictures* (Woodstock, N.Y.: Overlook Press, 1974), page 5.

5. Ben Hecht, pages 488–489.

6. *Sunset Boulevard*, original screenplay by Charles Brackett, Billy Wilder, and D. M. Marshman, Jr. (copyright Paramount Pictures, 1950).

7. Norman Reilly Raine, quoted in *Inside Warner Bros.*, edited by Rudy Behlmer (New York: Viking-Penguin, 1985), pages 47–48.

8. Nunnally Johnson, quoted in *Filmmaking: The Collaborative Art*, edited by Donald Chase (Boston: Little, Brown, 1975), pages 48–49.

9. Ernest Lehman, interviewed in *The Craft of the Screenwriter*, by John Brady (New York: Touchstone–Simon & Schuster, 1982), pages 183–184.

10. Gore Vidal, quoted in *Filmmakers on Filmmaking, Volume 1*, edited by Joseph McBride for The American Film Institute (Los Angeles: J. P. Tarcher, 1983), page 186.

11. Billy Wilder, quoted in *Filmmakers on Filmmaking, Volume 1*, page 59.

12. Andrew Sarris, preface to *Talking Pictures: Screenwriters in the American Cinema, 1927–1973*, by Richard Corliss (Woodstock, N.Y.: Overlook Press, 1974), page xv.

13. Robert Towne, interviewed in *The Craft of the Screenwriter*, pages 373–374, 430, 398–399, 401.

14. William Goldman, interviewed in *The Craft of the Screenwriter*, pages 88–89, 97–98, 149, 163, 168–169.

Other sources

Tom Dardis, *Some Time in the Sun* (New York: Charles Scribner's Sons, 1976).

William Goldman, *Adventures in the Screen Trade* (New York: Warner Books, 1983).

Harry Haun, *Movie Quote Book* (New York: Harper Colophon Books, 1980).

Screenplays: a few of the more celebrated have been published. Extensive collections of unpublished screenplays can be consulted in major film reference libraries.

D. W. Griffith, detail of *Way Down East*, 1979, a construction by Red Grooms that recreates the off-screen drama of Griffith's 1920 classic.

"What is directing? It's trying to use a lot of people and some very, very heavy apparatus and give it the lightness of a pen while you are writing." — David Lean (*The Bridge on the River Kwai, Lawrence of Arabia, A Passage to India*)[1]

"The most important thing about directing [is] to be in good physical shape. . . . It's the most enormously grueling physical exercise . . . partly because there is so much emotional strain. . . .

"For every moment that it takes you to solve the artistic problem, it's costing millions of dollars. And millions of dollars make people behave badly. Grown men behave like five year olds. They cry. They threaten you. They get hysterical. Actors, who . . . believe that you are going to destroy their careers, will get crazy at three in the morning and call you, and fight with each other, and won't come out of the trailer, and so on. Everybody comes to you every minute with a decision. . . .

"You start at six a.m. and you're wired all day. If you produce your own pictures, then after you see the dailies at seven p.m. and you finish at eight, you go in a production meeting about how much over budget you are. The trucks are costing money, and they won't give you permission to shoot on the street the day after tomorrow. . . . Anybody who tells you that he isn't scared to death directing a $10 million movie with major stars is a liar." — Sydney Pollack (*They Shoot Horses, Don't They?; Tootsie; Out of Africa*)[2]

"The ability to communicate with actors is the most important thing that a director needs. The second is a sense of where to put the camera. And the third is to know when to cut. And you should know all those things on the set. Otherwise you waste a lot of time.

"You can over-rehearse a picture. You have to rehearse to the point where nobody knows exactly what they're going to do but they think they know approximately. Then it's time to shoot. Almost everything that I'm happiest with in the pictures I've done, were first takes. John Ford said that the best things in pictures happen by accident. And Orson Welles said that a director is a man who presides over accidents." — Peter Bogdanovich (*The Last Picture Show, Paper Moon, Mask*)[3]

These observations by contemporary directors on their craft reveal the responsibility, the creativity, and the drudgery it involves. Reminiscences by directors of the studio era suggest the constraints within which they worked.

Erich von Stroheim shows Gibson Gowland
how to ravish ZaSu Pitts in *Greed* (1925), a
mutilated masterpiece as uncompromising as
its title.

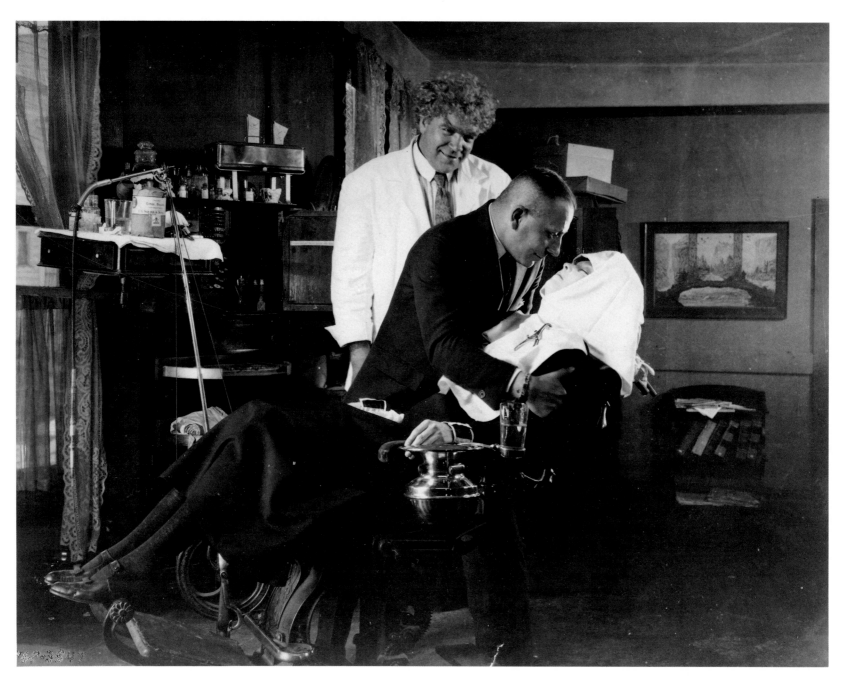

"When the movie industry was young, the filmmaker was its core and the man who handled the business details his partner. . . . When he finally looked around, he found his partner's name on the door. Thus the filmmaker became the employee, and the man who had time to attend to the business details became the head of the studio." — George Stevens *(Gunga Din, Shane, Giant)*[4]

One of the great mavericks of cinema, Erich von Stroheim, director of *Foolish Wives, The Merry Widow,* and *The Wedding March* in the 1920s, recalled the moment when — for him — the system changed:

"At the time when I began [work on Greed, in 1924] the slogan of the Goldwyn Company was 'the author and the play are the thing,' and I was given [full authority] to make the picture as the author might have wanted it. However, when — during the time I was cutting the film — the Goldwyn Company became Metro-Goldwyn-Mayer, with Irving Thalberg as the new general manager, their new slogan was 'the producer is the thing.'. . . When I got through making the film as written and okayed by Goldwyn, I found myself with 42 reels [about eight hours in running time]. Even if I wanted the film to be shown in two parts, it was necessary to cut half of it. This I accomplished myself. When I arrived at 24 reels I could not, to save my soul, cut another foot. But the new company insisted on cutting it down. Unknown to them I sent one print to my friend Rex Ingram [director of The Four Horsemen of the Apocalypse], *and begged him to cut it if he could. . . . He returned it in 18 reels . . . [and] sent me a telegram: 'If you cut one more foot I shall never speak to you again.' I showed the telegram to Mr. [Louis B.] Mayer who told me that he did not give a damn about Rex Ingram or me, and that the picture would be a total loss to the company anyway and must be cut to 10 reels. . . . It was given to a cutter, a man earning $30 a week who had never read the book nor the script, and on whose mind was nothing but a hat. That man ruined my work of two years."*[5]

But, as Andrew Sarris has noted, "the studio system victimized the screenwriter more than the director. . . . A producer was more likely to tamper with a story line than with a visual style." And the director — unlike the writer — was guaranteed sole credit on the screen, with all the implications of authority that went with it. But "to look at a film as the expression of a director's vision is not to credit the director with total creativity. All directors, and not just in Hollywood, are imprisoned by the conditions of their craft and their culture."[6]

The most talented and/or forceful directors functioned effectively in spite of — even because of — the constraints. They duelled with their bosses, sometimes winning, often conceding. As Richard Schickel suggested:

"They seemed rather to have enjoyed sneaking stuff past the producers, [who] once they accepted a director as a competent craftsman, tended to leave him alone to do his work — the ins and outs of which were largely mysterious to producers anyway. . . . They were proud of their ability to efficiently bring forth — often from unpromising material — solid commercial entertainments, on time, on budget, often with more verve, more sheer fun, than one would have thought could be infused into the banalities they were given to work with. At their best, they created masterpieces, works that created standards by which we judge later movies of the same genres. The weight of the ages, the opinion of future generations did not weigh on them.

"The studio chiefs created a magnificent support system for directors, [who] functioned best with a familiar stock company of actors, with crews that worked with them picture after picture. . . . [Veteran directors] compared the present system — where a man can spend a year or two packaging and financing a project and then must do it with strangers — most unfavorably with the old way, which permitted a man to do what he did best — direct films — efficiently, without fuss."[7]

The system did not prevent a director from realizing his personal vision or from making pictures in an idiosyncratic fashion. Here is testimony from three of the masters.

Rouben Mamoulian was a leading theater director in London and New York before making one of the most adventurous of the early talkies *(Applause,* 1929). Highlights of his career in Hollywood include *Dr. Jekyll and Mr. Hyde, Love Me Tonight,* and *Queen Christina.* He observed:

"I believe that film is primarily a graphic medium. Sound is secondary. You can have all the philosophy you like; if a film doesn't come across in graphic terms, it falls short. It is closer as a medium to painting than to the stage. And it should, to achieve greatness, be divorced from realism and naturalism. Obviously, poetry cannot be realistic; it's a lot of foolishness really. 'The dawn came up like thunder'. . . Absurd! But beautiful. Sculpture and painting are at their finest unreal. Film should be poetic, integrating all the components of art. And it should show the

inner truth, not merely the 'realistic' truth, in a stylized manner. It must also have rhythm. When I was a child, our teacher of elementary physics said: When a regiment of soldiers crosses a stone bridge, it is always ordered to break step, because if it walked in step, the power of its rhythmic vibration would destroy the bridge. It stuck in my mind that rhythm can have great power: if it can destroy, it can also build. And it can build great tension and excitement in a film."[8]

Alfred Hitchcock made over twenty suspense dramas in England before coming to Hollywood in 1940 to direct *Rebecca* for producer David O. Selznick. He remained there until his death in 1980. Each of his films was meticulously preplanned.

"So, one reads a book, and, providing all the story elements are there and the characters are there, it's best then to lay the book aside and start with scene one in cinema terms. The rectangular screen in a movie house has got to be filled with a succession of images. And the public aren't aware of what we call montage or, in other words, the cutting of one image to another. It goes by so rapidly that they [the public] are absorbed by the content on the screen. But such content is created on the screen and not necessarily in a single shot.

"For example, devising, in a picture like Psycho, the murdering and the stabbing of a girl in a bath — in a shower in a bathroom: this scene is forty-five seconds long, but was made up out of seventy-eight pieces of film going through the projector and coming onto the screen in great rapidity. In fact, in the scene itself, the knife stabbing at the camera never touched the flesh of the woman at any time. You went to her face, you went to her feet, you went to the assailant in quick, rapid shots. But the overall impression given the audience is one of an alarming, devastating murder scene.

"I would prefer to write all this down, however tiny and however short the pieces of film are — they should be written down in just the same way a composer writes down those little black dots from which we get beautiful sound. So I usually start with the writer long before dialogue comes into it, and I get on paper a description of what comes on that screen. It is as though you ran a film on the screen and turned off all the sound so you would see the images filling the screen one after the other.

"These have to be described. If I'm describing the opening, say, of a film like Frenzy, it starts this way: The camera is high above the city of London. In the righthand corner is a heraldic arms device with the word LONDON on it. The camera descends lower and lower until it approaches Tower Bridge and the arms of the roadway have opened. The camera proceeds to go through the opening and is lost in a cloud of smoke from a passing tugboat. When the smoke clears, the camera is now approaching the terrace of what is known as County Hall. As it gets near we see a speaker addressing a group of people. Another angle shows that he is being photographed by press people and he is talking about the pollution of the river and how it has all been cleaned up. We then go to a scene of people leaning over the parapet, turning from the speaker and looking down. From their viewpoint, we see a body floating. There are immediate cries, and from another angle we see the whole listening crowd turn from the speaker and all rush to the parapet to look at this floating body.

"Now, you see the way I've described it — I've described what takes place. Of course, interspersed with it later will be the speech of the speaker about pollution and there will be cries of the crowd: 'Look, it's a body!' Another voice: 'A woman!' Another voice: 'She's been strangled! There's a tie.' Then another voice: 'A necktie murder again!' So these are the things that fill out later. But the early description is literally of the action and the picture.

"In a sense, I'm bringing the writer into the direction of the picture, letting him know how I'm going to direct it. So we end up with possibly seventy to a hundred pages of description of the film. I have a very strong visual sense, and while I'm going through this process I am absorbing all the visual side of the film. So what happens? By the time that the script is finished and the dialogue has been added, I know every shot and every angle by heart. So when I'm shooting the picture, I very rarely look at the script because I've now by this time learned the dialogue myself. I have to say I am equivalent to, though maybe not so good as, a conductor conducting an orchestra without a score.

"I could almost say I wish I didn't have to go on the stage and shoot that film because from a creative point of view one has gone through that process. That's why, you see, I never look through the camera. People say, 'You don't look through the camera?' I say, 'Why should I? I'm looking at a screen.' When we've been putting this thing down on paper, my mind and my eye are on a motion-picture

screen. The only reason one would look through a camera is that, having made a request to the cameraman for a shot, he takes it into his head to do something different."[9]

In 1919, Universal Studios head Carl Laemmle reportedly launched the career of John Ford by telling a producer, "Let Jack Ford direct it. He yells good." Other directors entered the business in just such a casual way: Raoul Walsh had been a cowboy, Howard Hawks a flier, Frank Capra a chemical engineer. In those years, movies were an unconventional way to earn a living. Now, film schools graduate thousands of aspiring directors every year; competition for the handful of jobs is ferocious. So insecure a profession has it become, so few the opportunities to make a statement, that too many directors are driven to assume the entire burden of production — from conception to final cut. The experience can be draining, often unmanageable.

There are, perhaps, only three contemporary producer-directors who have consistently achieved creative freedom and commercial success, and the ability to control their destiny: Woody Allen, Warren Beatty, and Steven Spielberg. (George Lucas has chosen to withdraw from directing.) All the rest are, to some degree, hired guns or have, like Stanley Kubrick, been forced into inactivity. Alan Pakula, director of *Klute, The Parallax View*, and *Sophie's Choice*, is a craftsman in the old-fashioned sense. Brought in by producer-star Robert Redford to direct *All the President's Men*, he describes how he heightened the drama (scripted by William Goldman from the true-life account by Bob Woodward and Carl Bernstein):

"What fascinated me about that story was the power of the typewriter, of words, to triumph over the most powerful people on earth. David and Goliath. The [image] and sound of typewriters is a theme through the whole film. There is a scene in which Nixon is on television — at the Republican Convention — and Bob is pounding away on one side of the screen. There is this huge television set and this one man; the sound of those keys against screaming, orchestrated cheers. The idea is being told cinematically.

"I said to [cinematographer] Gordon Willis, 'I want very deep focus in this film. Sharp and hard. It's about reporters who try to see everything, who are always looking.' Now we got lucky with the Washington Post *which, six months before*

Frank Capra and Gary Cooper on the set of *Mr. Deeds Goes to Town* (1936), one of Capra's Depression-era fables that exalted Everyman.

Rouben Mamoulian on the crane, lining up a shot with Jeanette MacDonald while directing *Love Me Tonight* (1932). Cameraman Victor Milner is bedside.

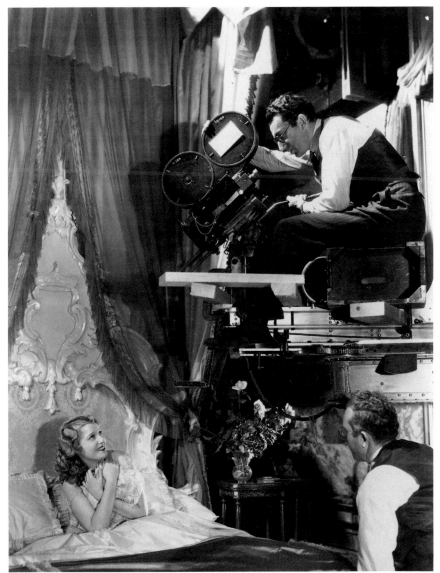

Francis Coppola (back to camera) directing *Apocalypse Now* (1979) on location in the Philippines. Cinematographer Vittorio Storaro is on the left. Photo by Nancy Moran.

Apocalypse Now sketch by Tom Wright for production designer Dean Tavoularis. This and other sketches were videotaped to pre-visualize the helicopter attack before it was filmed.

Barbra Streisand produced, scripted, directed, and starred in *Yentl* (1983), in order to put on film this story of a woman's struggle to succeed in a man's world. Photo by Dan Weaks.

Hal Ashby directing Jon Voight, who played a paraplegic Vietnam veteran in *Coming Home* (1978). Actors and crew worked closely with vets in an actual hospital. Photo by Nancy Ellison.

Czech emigré Milos Forman directing Jack Nicholson and cast in *One Flew Over the Cuckoo's Nest* (1975), a project that all the major studios declined to support, but which went on to win the top five Oscars. Photo by Peter Sorel.

Robert de Niro and director Martin Scorsese between takes on *Taxi Driver* (1976). Together they created a memorable portrait of a deranged Vietnam veteran and the pent-up violence of New York.

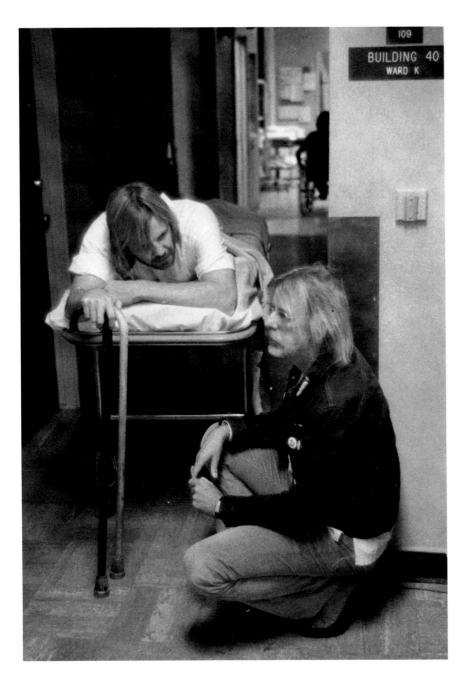

[Woodward and Bernstein] got on the story, had moved into a new building with a fluorescent white office — a world without shadows. And the world that our detective-reporters go through is a world in which the sun shines, the grass is mown, and the houses are bright and cheerful. And in the midst of all this orderliness, is decay. It was rather difficult for Gordon. He is known for his dark, moody photography; after Godfather II, a critic called him 'the Prince of Darkness.' But I wanted that counterpoint.

"There's a sequence with Jane Alexander which he shot in a little house in Maryland. She's the bookkeeper for the Committee to Re-elect the President — a key to a whole part of the cover-up — and she's terrified of talking. Bob Redford and Dustin Hoffman are interrogating her, and I said to Gordon, 'Can you give me a dappled green light, sunlight on a Sunday afternoon — almost Renoir — and very romantic?' The antithesis of what they are finding out about who did all these crummy things."[10]

Let John Huston have the final word. His career began with such studio productions as The Maltese Falcon and The Treasure of the Sierra Madre, and has since yielded such landmarks as The African Queen, The Man Who Would Be King, and Prizzi's Honor.

"Each picture with its particular environment and unique personal relationships is a world unto itself — separate and distinct. Picture makers lead dozens of lives — a life for each picture. And, by the same token, they perish a little when each picture is finished and that world comes to an end. In this respect it is a melancholy occupation."[11]

Quotations

1. David Lean, quoted in Filmmakers on Filmmaking, Volume 1, edited by Joseph McBride for The American Film Institute (Los Angeles: J. P. Tarcher, 1983), page 196.

2. Sydney Pollack, quoted in Filmmakers on Filmmaking, Volume 1, pages 194–195.

3. Peter Bogdanovich, seminar at The American Film Institute, Los Angeles, July 28, 1977; unpublished (copyright Peter Bogdanovich).

4. George Stevens, quoted in Andrew Sarris, The American Cinema, Directors and Directions, 1929–68 (New York: E. P. Dutton, 1968), page 21.

5. Erich von Stroheim, quoted in Peter Noble, Hollywood Scapegoat (London: 1950); reprinted in Voices of Film Experience, edited by Jay Leyda (New York: Macmillan, 1983), pages 446–447.

6. Andrew Sarris, The American Cinema, pages 30, 31, 36.

7. Richard Schickel, The Men Who Made the Movies (New York: Atheneum, 1975), page 6.

8. Rouben Mamoulian, interviewed in The Celluloid Muse: Hollywood Directors Speak, edited by Charles Higham and Joel Greenberg (Chicago: Henry Regnery, 1969), page 129.

9. Alfred Hitchcock, quoted in The Men Who Made the Movies, pages 283–285.

10. Alan Pakula, seminar at The American Film Institute, Los Angeles, July 11, 1978; unpublished (copyright Alan Pakula).

11. John Huston, quoted in Maureen Lambray, The American Film Directors, Volume 1 (New York: Rapoport Press, 1976).

Other sources

Eric Sherman, editor, for The American Film Institute, Directing the Film: Film Directors on Their Art (Boston: Little, Brown, 1976).

William Cameron Menzies made his debut as
one of Hollywood's greatest art directors by
designing the lavish sets for a Douglas Fairbanks
spectacle, *The Thief of Bagdad* (1924).

Poster for *The Black Pirate* (1926), another elaborate period spectacle. Hand-painted by Batiste Madalena for the Eastman Theater in Rochester, New York. The movie used the two-strip Technicolor process.

The earliest movie designers were theatrical scene painters, and a painted backdrop was the only decor. For a more elaborate setting, moviemakers would shoot in the streets, and the comedies of Chaplin and Harold Lloyd and the early shorts of D. W. Griffith offer a documentary record of urban — more precisely, of working-class — life in the 1910s. Italy and France were far ahead of America in visual sophistication. Such epics as *Quo Vadis* (1912) and *Cabiria* (1914) inspired the vast Babylonian set that Walter Hall designed for Griffith's *Intolerance* (1916). It towered 165 feet above the bungalows of Hollywood, and itself inspired the castle built for Douglas Fairbanks's *Robin Hood* (1922) and the Arabian Nights city in his *The Thief of Bagdad* (1924).

By 1920, the art director had begun to play an essential role in Hollywood. Extraordinary talents, lured from Broadway and the studios of Europe, created sets whose extravagance and finesse has seldom been excelled. William Cameron Menzies gave his definition of the art director in a 1929 lecture at the University of Southern California:

"He must have a knowledge of architecture of all periods and nationalities. He must be able to picturize and make interesting a tenement or a prison. He must be a cartoonist, a costumier, a marine painter, a designer of ships, an interior decorator, a landscape painter, a dramatist, an inventor, a historical and now, an accoustical expert."[1]

Menzies, who did outstanding work on Douglas Fairbanks's costume extravaganzas, the last films of Valentino and Griffith, and *Things to Come* (1936), won a new title — that of production designer — for his work on *Gone With the Wind* (1939). Gene Allen, President of the Art Directors Guild (and past president of the Academy of Motion Picture Arts and Sciences) explained the distinction between art director and production designer:

"A production designer is an art director who has an in with the director in the sense of having some authority. Otherwise an art director can be limited to doing sets and then he is kept in the background, and the cameraman and the director work together. Where you have a director who is professional enough to want some help in certain areas that he isn't trained for, allowing him more time to work with his actors behind the scenes, then he gives the production designer things to do. . . ."[2]

Monte Carlo in Universal City: Erich von Stroheim directing *Foolish Wives* (1922) on a set designed by Richard Day. In his fifty-year career, Day designed most of von Stroheim's movies; *Dead End, The Grapes of Wrath, A Streetcar Named Desire*, and many more.

Allen performed such a role on a series of movies directed by George Cukor, including *A Star Is Born, Les Girls,* and *My Fair Lady*:

"Early in the game, I learned that Cukor's apparent lack of knowledge about cameras, compositions, color et cetera, was a great hoax. By pretending not to be knowledgeable about such things he forced you to explain fully what it was you had in mind. Cukor is the expert on all elements of filmmaking. At times, he was the auctioneer allowing the production designer and the director of photography to bid against each other . . . to see who could come up with the best method of visualizing a particular segment of a film."[3]

Ideally, the production designer plans and coordinates every visual element in a picture, working from the script and in close association with the director, the costume designer, and the cinematographer. He plans sets, selects and adapts locations, coordinates colors and lighting, helps the director visualize camera angles and movements. On a major production, he may have an art director to execute his ideas, to turn his concepts into working drawings from which sets can be constructed. He supervises the artist who draws the cartoon strips (known as continuity sketches or storyboards) that block out each scene from the camera's point of view and are photocopied for the production team; also the draftsmen, set decorator, and a host of specialized craftsmen. An illustrator may be brought in to develop detailed renderings that will allow the producer and director to judge an effect before construction begins.

All of this work is preceded by research, as veteran Robert Boyle recounts:

"We're on our own to begin with — sometimes we have to make up our own stories about the characters — and we're off to another area when the glamorous business of shooting starts. We begin with the script: what economic bracket are the characters in? What educational level? Which ethnic background? Geographical location? Is the character influenced by his surroundings or does he influence them? For example, if you're a mining engineer, you influence the surroundings; if you're riding a dog sled in Alaska, the environment influences you. We like to think we can direct or control the relationship between that environment and the characters."[4]

From the mid-1920s to the mid-1950s, all of this work — from research to

The laboratory in *Frankenstein* (1931): sketch by Dutch-born theater designer Herman Rosse, who worked briefly in Hollywood.

special effects — was the province of the studio art department and its supervising art director, who reigned as God in his own universe. At MGM, Cedric Gibbons headed a department of up to 200 art directors and draftsmen, scenic and matte painters, in addition to running a model shop and prop and construction departments. For thirty years his name appeared on every MGM release. Cedric Gibbons designed the Oscar, and he personally collected eleven for Best Art Direction.

Like his counterparts at other studios, including Hans Dreier at Paramount and Van Nest Polglase at RKO, Gibbons was an administrator and an arbiter. He assigned each picture to an art director, changed or approved budgets and sketches, and ran interference for his department. Occasionally, he lost a battle:

"Because [Production Head Irving] Thalberg wanted pictures made where he could watch them, the art department had to design sets of foreign locales at a furious rate and paint backdrops of famous places, although Cedric Gibbons thought they should be photographed on their actual sites. His fine sense of authenticity was outraged when the scenario of Paris *(1925) called for a love scene in that city with a moonlit ocean in the background. He went to Thalberg with a sheaf of photographs to prove that no large body of water was anywhere in the vicinity. Thalberg was unmoved.*

"'We can't cater to a handful of people who know Paris,' he told the annoyed art director. 'Audiences only see about ten per cent of what's on the screen anyway, and if they're watching your background instead of my actors, the scene will be useless. Whatever you put there, they'll believe that's how it is.'"[5]

But Gibbons's authority was rarely challenged — least of all by his own department — and Thalberg backed his effort, from 1924 to the mid-1930s, to maintain a consistency of style that became MGM's hallmark. More than anyone else, Gibbons popularized art deco as a symbol of wealth and fashion, and the white-on-white decor first introduced by decorator Syrie Maugham. MGM's sets were larger and brighter than those of other studios — no matter how inappropriate such opulence might be to story or character. Thalberg's prestige pictures challenged the department's expertise, as art director Preston Ames recalled:

Robert Usher's sketch for Mae West's boudoir in *She Done Him Wrong* (1933). Usher helped make Paramount the most stylish and sophisticated of Hollywood studios through the 1930s.

Set sketch by Harold Grieve for *So This Is Paris* (1926), a risqué comedy directed by Ernst Lubitsch (bottom).

One of Boris Leven's atmospheric designs for *The Shanghai Gesture* (1941), directed by Josef von Sternberg, a master of moody lighting.

Parlor of the Butler House: concept sketch for *Gone With the Wind*; sketch by J. MacMillan Johnson (bottom).

Streamline-*moderne* nightclub, designed by
Lyle Wheeler for David O. Selznick's production *The Young in Heart* (1937). Movies helped
create a vogue for glass brick and blond
wood, formerly limited to a fashionable elite.

Sketch by Anton Grot for Max Reinhardt's sumptuous production of *A Midsummer Night's Dream* (1935).

Herman Rosse's sketch for *Murders in the Rue Morgue* (1932). Horror and fantasy enjoyed a vogue during the social turmoil of the early 1930s.

"In 1938 we did an expensive production called Marie Antoinette *with Norma Shearer. A great many architects came to Metro to see our sets and congratulated Cedric Gibbons on his authentic reproduction of French Renaissance architecture, with particular emphasis on what he did with Versailles. Mr. Gibbons looked at these gentlemen and said, 'If you will study very carefully what we did, you'll see we did everything except copy the architecture of Versailles, because if we had, photographically it would have been absolutely nothing. The molding and design are so delicate, so sensitive, they would never have come across on the screen. We had to redesign the entire thing so it would photograph properly!' That is what I mean by catching the spirit of what you are reproducing."*[6]

Paramount's Hans Dreier also achieved a distinctive studio style in the late 1920s and early 1930s, combining his own experience at the UFA Studios in his native Germany and the exotic tastes of immigrant directors. At their best, in the films of Lubitsch and Sternberg, of Mitchell Leisen and Billy Wilder, Paramount Pictures had a pictorial elegance, a shadow-veiled atmosphere, a Continental sophistication worlds away from the clean, brightly lit sets of MGM.

Remarked Ernst Lubitsch: "There is Paramount Paris and Metro Paris, and of course the real Paris. Paramount's is the most Parisian of all." Art director Robert Usher specialized in Parisian sets, bringing a flavor of the city to a dozen studio productions. Josef von Sternberg, an obsessive visual stylist and master of atmospheric lighting, visited China after making *Shanghai Express* at Paramount in 1932 and was bitterly disappointed by the real thing. Dreier selected from the pool of young architects left unemployed by the Depression, drove them hard, but gave them greater creative freedom than they would have had at MGM. Several — including Boris Leven and Robert Boyle — are still at work, fifty years after their debut.

Anton Grot, born and educated in Poland, was head of Warner Bros.' art department from 1927 to 1948, the years in which that studio became a major, and he achieved marvels of style on the tightest of budgets. Grot imposed his vision, less through supervision than by example. It is estimated that he personally designed eighty movies in twenty years, dashing off thousands of pencil or charcoal sketches, some only an inch or two across, but each infused with a sense of mood and structure.

The essence of swashbuckling adventure: concept sketch by Anton Grot for *The Sea Hawk* (1940), which starred Errol Flynn.

Battle montage: concept sketch for *Gone With the Wind* by Frank Powers, one of a team of designers who worked closely with William Cameron Menzies and art director Lyle Wheeler.

Grot had apprenticed on the costume spectacles of Fairbanks and De Mille. His work at Warner Bros. — notably on the Errol Flynn swashbucklers, the Busby Berkeley musicals, and the horror movies of the early 1930s — all draws on that experience and on the tradition of German expressionism that enjoyed a second life in Hollywood. Grot's drawings are characterized by single-view, forced-perspective sets, designed to be shot from a low angle. Actors are dwarfed by vast expanses of wall and ceiling. The Grot style reached its apotheosis in Max Reinhardt's production of *A Midsummer Night's Dream* (1935) — one of Warners' rare excursions into high art — and in *The Private Lives of Elizabeth and Essex* (1939). Yet he could scale down and subdue these visions in response to a producer's anguished protests, and achieve miracles with light and shadow when the studio's parsimony was reinforced by an official cost ceiling of $5,000 for sets during the war.

Each studio had its visionaries and magicians. RKO was second to none in invention and style. *King Kong*, the "Big White Sets" of the Astaire-Rogers musicals, *Gunga Din*'s recreation of India's northwest frontier (in central California), and *Citizen Kane*'s Xanadu were triumphs of production design and special effects. *Kane* cost under $800,000; over half the shots were enhanced by Linwood Dunn's optical effects. Even a poorer studio could afford the occasional splurge. Universal recreated Monte Carlo for von Stroheim's *Foolish Wives* (1921) and medieval Paris for *The Hunchback of Notre Dame* (1923); Columbia built a streamline-*moderne* Shangri-La for Frank Capra's *Lost Horizon* (1937). Producers like Goldwyn, De Mille, and Selznick commissioned the finest designers. In the case of De Mille, the sketches are often more impressive than the static Victorian tableaux of the movies.

The studios commanded such resources that art directors were often little more than decorators, adapting and dressing standing sets — on stage and on the back lot. The Welsh mining town built on the Fox ranch for *How Green Was My Valley* (1941) reappeared the following year, with a dusting of snow, as a Norwegian village in *The Moon Is Down*. Shangri-La, the streamline-*moderne* extravaganza of *Lost Horizon* (1937), long a landmark on the Columbia ranch, became Seville in *The Loves of Carmen* (1946). The staircase built for Orson Welles's *The Magnificent Ambersons* (1942) saw repeated service in every RKO haunted-house drama. The set from Universal's 1925 *Phantom of the*

Orson Welles's *Citizen Kane* (1941): sketch by
Claude Gillingwater for art director Perry
Ferguson. Xanadu was a triumph of illusion: to
save expense, many of the mansion's splen-
dors were simulated optically.

Cutaway set of house in Amsterdam, designed by George Davis for *The Diary of Anne Frank* (1959), on a stage at Twentieth Century Fox. Photo by Ralph Crane for *Life*.

Cel (hand-painted celluloid) from the first
major animated feature, Walt Disney's *Snow
White and the Seven Dwarfs* (1937).

SNEEZY

BASHFUL

DOPEY

SLEEPY

DOC

GRUMPY

HAPPY

Matte painting used in the filming of *The Wizard of Oz* (1939) to create the illusion of a fantasy city — little of which was actually constructed. Its inspiration was a futuristic German drawing of the 1910s.

Opera is still in use. The tradition survives: the New York streets at Twentieth Century Fox and the Burbank Studios have been endlessly recycled.

Everything could be recreated without leaving the lot: a glass painting or a hanging miniature conjured up a gorge or a viaduct, a skyscraper or a prairie. In *The Day of the Locust,* Nathanael West evoked the surreal juxtapositions of the back lot:

"He pushed his way through a tangle of briars, old flats, and iron junk, skirting the skeleton of a zeppelin, a bamboo stockade, an adobe fort, the wooden horse of Troy, a flight of baroque palace stairs that started in a bed of weeds and ended against the branches of an oak, part of the Fourteenth Street elevated station, a Dutch windmill, the bones of a dinosaur, the upper half of the Merrimac, a corner of a Mayan temple, until he finally reached the road."[7]

The constraints of early talkies compelled a retreat from outdoor sets to soundproof stages and gave birth to a studio aesthetic. A flash of neon and the scream of tires suggested the streets of Chicago; a stock shot of the Eiffel Tower or Big Ben transported us to a make-believe Paris or London. During the Depression, realism was anathema to moguls who had escaped from poverty and to an audience that stared it in the face. Louis B. Mayer used his influence to prevent the Academy from giving its Best Picture Award to King Vidor's *The Crowd* (1928): it was an MGM production, but one he would rather not have made. Sam Goldwyn objected to Richard Day's tenement set for *Dead End* (1936): "It cost me a lot of money, that slum; it doesn't have to be so dirty!"

By the mid-1940s, theatergoers had a bad case of cabin fever. Movies had become stale and airless, the repetition of familiar settings as limiting as in the 1910s when the same New Jersey landmarks recurred in every Western. The war had been at once a confining and a liberating experience; people were impatient for fresh experiences and broader horizons. Inspired by the verisimilitude of wartime documentaries, moviemakers began to return to the streets they had left thirty years before. The decline of the studios, the competition of television, and the development of lightweight equipment accelerated this quest for real worlds beyond the studio.

There was a brief flourish of street movies, such as *Panic in the Streets* and

Naked City, inspired by the neo-realist films of Italy, and a more durable cycle of scenic Westerns, which received a big boost with the coming of wide-screen formats. But Hollywood had its own notions of realism. Postwar Italy was starving: shooting in the streets was an economic and an ideological imperative. As prosperity returned, neo-realism ebbed. In America, poverty and social conflicts seemed inappropriate subjects — dangerously so in the red-baiting 1950s. But the spirit left its mark on such productions as *The Lost Weekend, House on 92nd Street,* and *On the Town* — all of which breathed an authentic air of New York.

Indeed, the Big Apple became the principal character in an increasing number of films, as it regained some of its former preeminence as a production center. Boris Leven designed *West Side Story* (1960), whose backgrounds were shot on West 68th Street — among tenements condemned to make room for Lincoln Center — and on matching sets in Hollywood. Leven wrote to director Robert Wise:

"I have been thinking about the prologue and the problem of using New York in daylight. As I mentioned to you before, each location must be selected for its color, shape and mood. The more I think about these exteriors, the stronger I feel that the problem is not the location or the daylight. The problem is that we presently lack the approach.

"There are many ways to photograph a street. Each photo will convey something different. I feel that we must have a definite conception which continues and develops. Each locale — real as real can be — should be photographed as a stage setting, as a drop. For example, the brownstone street with stoops, doorways etc. instead of being photographed at an angle should be photographed straight on, preferably in shadow, so that it will appear as a backdrop. Our people, as on a stage, work in the foreground. They are in light. Other locations are to be used in the same manner. By employing such an approach we shall have visual continuity, strength and simplicity.

"I have also been thinking about the people on the streets of New York. I would like to suggest the following idea. The people are there, but they are part of the architecture; they sit or stand, or move about, but they do not react to what takes place in the foreground. I believe that this can be done very effectively. Particularly

if the set and the people are some distance away and are in shadow while our group is in light. This is their world, others just exist."[8]

Harry Horner, another veteran designer, achieved a similar kind of stylized realism a year later:

"The idea for The Hustler, *which was directed by Robert Rossen, was to do it all on location, because it was necessary to make it very hard and very realistic in a sense. The story had a pool player (Paul Newman) and a girl, played by Piper Laurie, who falls in love with him. She is a lost soul, who has left a university and just lived around. The word 'hippie' wasn't existing then. How does a person like that live? The apartment must look believable for a person like that. So I went to places around universities and Carnegie Hall where students and younger dancers live. . . . I found one place which was very interesting. A dancer lived there. She was not home, and what I recall was how sloppily she had left her clothes around. But there was an interesting mixture. On the wall, for instance, she had prints which showed taste. . . . The books that she had, paperbacks were all piled up. The arrangement of the whole thing was very nice. You had to go through the kitchen. On one side was a toilet with bath, which was always open because she used it as a wardrobe. . . . The search for a character within the location that you must invent is a fascinating experience.*

"But ultimately it didn't work, because Rossen wanted to have total control of the locale. That means he wanted to take a wall out when he wanted to, which you can only do on stage. There were about eight or ten different poolrooms in which the picture played, so it turned out that it was easier to design them. We looked for locations in New York, and I found — particularly in Harlem . . . some marvelous, strange, dark rat-holes; poolrooms that were gray and dirty with those green pool tables. And these pool players standing or sitting in the shadows — a little angry, maybe, at some 'whitey' coming up in this area. They had the poetic quality that lies in ugliness.

"I made a very careful study of texture. . . . For instance, a cracked door or a wall that has the effect of humidity on it. It is very difficult and expensive to recreate. But there is one artist, Stan Cappiello, who is superb. When you say to him: 'I want a door in a cheap apartment where there is no upkeep. It should be cracked and has been painted over three or four times with different paints that now have cracked or peeled,' he will ask you, 'How old should it be, fifteen years, or seven-

teen years?' He is so skillful in cracking that it looks absolutely real. He puts acid and all kinds of things on it, and within a week it looks marvelous."[9]

By the end of the decade, moviemakers and audiences had become even more adventurous. *Los Angeles Times* film critic Charles Champlin praised *Midnight Cowboy* (1969) for its Times Square of "grifters, drifters, pawn shops and all-night coffee counters whiter and colder than icebergs . . . it evokes Manhattan's lower depths with a fidelity that recalls George Orwell's 'Down and Out in London and Paris.'" In *Taxi Driver* (1975), Times Square has a voluptuous theatricality; it is a painterly inferno of blood and neon, and steam gushing from street vents. The movies of Martin Scorsese *(Mean Streets, Taxi Driver, After Hours)* and Sidney Lumet *(Serpico, Dog Day Afternoon, Prince of the City),* and many others confront the harsh realities of the city or transform them into a savage poetry — the street and subway as an auto-da-fé. "You can't show New York from a Fifth Avenue bus," remarked Lumet.

It is rumored that Woody Allen wishes that everything — even the Rocky Mountains — could be within a block of Fifth Avenue. In *Manhattan* (1979; Mel Bourne, production designer), he shares his idyllic version of a New York in which lovers can sit unscathed on a park bench watching the sun rise over the East River, and the music of George Gershwin evokes a skyline of classic beauty. His is a world in which nobody takes the subway and graffiti are to be found only in a chic art gallery. By contrast, Allen's view of Los Angeles in *Annie Hall* (1975; Mel Bourne) is of a stage set — paper-thin facades and palm trees; a place "whose only cultural advantage is turning right on red."

Each of these directors has a personal vision of a city that has its own multi-faceted character, and the production designer labors to reconcile the two. Italian director Michelangelo Antonioni gave us a unique perception of Los Angeles as a pop-art kaleidoscope in the much-underrated *Zabriskie Point* (1970; Dean Tavoularis, production designer). And Louis Malle remarked, apropos of *Atlantic City* (1981; Anne Pritchard, production designer): "I felt visually inspired. The razing of the old and the new construction created an exciting metaphor for the story of an ageing gangster and a girl on the make."

The best designers can create a world of experience within a single set. In *Citizen Kane* (1941; Perry Ferguson) and *The Magnificent Ambersons* (1942; Mark Lee Kirk), in *Psycho* (1960; Robert Clatworthy and Joseph Hurley), and *Giant*

Chinatown (1974): sketch by Joe Hurley for production designer Richard Sylbert. This evocation of Los Angeles in the 1930s made use of stylized sets and a variety of locations.

(1955; Boris Leven), in *Sunset Boulevard* (1950; Hans Dreier and John Meehan) and *The Heiress* (1949; Harry Horner), a house is a principal character and a catalyst for the story. Horner describes his experience on *The Heiress* (directed by William Wyler):

"What I wanted to do with the house . . . was to give it many varied possibilities. When we photographed the house with the father in it, it was seen from the father's point of view. I wanted to establish that it would be very elegant, with large rooms and sliding doors. It was very beautifully furnished, with fine curtains and wallpapers. When one saw the house from the daughter's standpoint, it was a different house. It was a confining cage: the winter garden, the backyard where she would buy things from the travelling grocer. There were a lot of rain scenes that gave a kind of depressing feeling when she was around. To her, and to the camera in relationship to her, the house was supposed to look like a bird cage in which she was caught.

"The other person who has to see the house is the young adventurer who comes there and wants to marry her. From his standpoint, it should be a kind of castle, tempting, accentuating the wealth of the family. There should be gold and metal and glassware. . . .

"The staircase in The Heiress *was in the middle of this construction, and it went up three stories high. It was very useful as a kind of starting-off place, like a ski slope from which you get a swing and then the action goes on by itself. In one scene, the daughter comes down very excitedly to wait for her lover who is to come at midnight and take her away with him. You first see her come running down in the mirror, strategically placed so that you can see the rest of the staircase winding up to the third floor where her bedroom is. Then she turns and comes running down towards the camera. Later, when she's disappointed that the man doesn't come, the same staircase becomes a painful climb up. . . ."*[10]

Polly Platt describes a similar approach that yielded a very different result, for *What's Up, Doc?* (1973; directed by Peter Bogdanovich):

"In the old movies, the people who had money were always old and had great mahogany libraries with leather seats and all that. I just didn't think I could make a set like that; it's so old-fashioned. Young people are in control of money now. I felt that Austin's character was a pretentious, transparent rich guy. So I made every-

thing plexiglass [sic] — plexiglass staircase, plexiglass pillars. Since it was San Francisco and there were those beautiful narrow Victorian gingerbread houses, I thought what better example of the bad taste of the nouveau riche than to take a Victorian house, rip out the inside and put in plexiglass. That was built on the stage to the dimensions of a real house in San Francisco."[11]

Conscientious designers go to extraordinary lengths in the quest for authenticity. For *All the President's Men* (1976), George Jenkins recreated the *Washington Post* newsroom on two stages at the Burbank Studios and stocked each desk and wastepaper basket with replicas of the paperwork he had found during his research. On *Klute* (1971), he encouraged Jane Fonda to sleep overnight in the apartment he had created for her character on a stage. Each morning she carried out a little pile of furnishings and knick-knacks she felt were inappropriate to the hooker she played, and suggested substitutions.

Dean Tavoularis has a similar approach:

"Anything that can help the actor must be done. Little things. For example, why don't some directors or production designers put weights in a suitcase? I always insist that a suitcase be filled. You open a drawer, there should be shirts in it. You open cabinets in a kitchen, they should be stocked with groceries. And a kitchen should smell like a kitchen. For an Italian kitchen, which we created in The Godfather, *you'd have to go in and mash garlic all over the place, take tomato paste and throw it on the floor and mop it up so you'd have a little bit of last month's tomato paste spillage. And you should have the smell of oregano and paprika.*

"If you're on location, say at a house somewhere, then you should have real mail delivered to that house, addressed to the character who lives there. I remember we did that in The Conversation. *We had this apartment in San Francisco and we knew months ahead of time that we were going to have it for the making of the film. The Gene Hackman character was supposed to be an electronics wiz, and it seemed rather obvious to me to subscribe to all those magazines which cater to this kind of person. So we mailed off 30 letters and started getting all this stuff with the real character's name and address on it. This was a very important detail."*[12]

Perfectionism paid off for Tavoularis on these films and on *Apocalypse Now* (1979). In each, the ambience reinforces our belief in the characters and story.

Olivia de Havilland in *The Heiress* (1949), directed by William Wyler. Art director Harry Horner designed the staircase as a catalyst of mood and action.

If the latter are weak, or the designer plays prima donna, the settings can upstage the story and the costs can go through the roof. The Francis Coppola–Dean Tavoularis collaboration on *One From the Heart* (1982), which featured an $8 million studio version of Las Vegas, proved a ruinous extravagance. And stories are still told of how Erich von Stroheim lost the confidence of the industry, less through budget overruns than through such odd obsessions as outfitting palace guards with silk drawers, hand-embroidered with the royal coat-of-arms, which were never shown.

Richard Sylbert's credits include *The Graduate* (1967), *Rosemary's Baby* (1968), and *Shampoo* (1975). For *Reds* (1982), he designed 140 sets, which were built in several European countries. The movie is a masterpiece of disciplined imagination. Sylbert and producer-writer-director Warren Beatty developed the idea that the American interiors should be cluttered and claustrophobic, the Russian spaces vast and empty. It's a visual metaphor that echoes John Reed and Louise Bryant's sense of liberation from bourgeois restraints; a subjective reality buttressed by Sylbert's research on the actual sites of the revolution in Leningrad and in Reed's home in Provincetown.

For *Chinatown* (1975; directed by Roman Polanski), Sylbert captured the look of Los Angeles in the mid-1930s through such details as glass brick and highly polished wood, venetian blinds, and cradle telephones. The movie is about the importance of water during a drought, and so the movie emphasizes images of burnt grass and heat, achieving a sense of oppression that underlines the theme of greed and corruption more economically than if (like von Stroheim on *Greed*) the moviemakers had taken off to the desert in midsummer.

Robert Boyle put it well in a seminar on production design:

"Most of us can design a smashing set that will make the audience gasp and stop the story right in the middle. Occasionally, if you have the good fortune to have a Star Wars or a film that gives you a chance to do some extraordinary thing, fine. But most of the time you are dealing with real people and real situations. . . . There is one thing that has always interested me . . . the search for what I call 'dramatic truth.' This has nothing to do with photographic truth. . . . Any of you who have ever photographed anything know what a liar the camera can be. It is up to us to make the truth, and the truth can be very, very far from reality."[13]

Director Steven Spielberg plotting setups with a model of the archeological dig in *Raiders of the Lost Ark* (1981). Production designer: Norman Reynolds. Photo by Nancy Moran.

Quotations

1. William Cameron Menzies, lecture at the University of Southern California, April 1929; reprinted in *The Art of Hollywood,* by John Hambley and Patrick Downing (London: Thames Television, 1979), page 91.

2. Gene Allen, seminar at The American Film Institute, Los Angeles, October 13, 1971; unpublished.

3. Gene Allen, quoted in *Filmmaking: The Collaborative Art,* edited by Donald Chase (Boston: Little, Brown, 1975), page 162.

4. Robert Boyle, lecture at the Astoria Foundation, New York, 1984.

5. Samuel Marx, *Mayer and Thalberg, the Make-Believe Saints* (New York: Random House, 1975), pages 82–83.

6. Preston Ames, interviewed in *Hollywood Speaks!,* edited by Mike Steen (New York: G. P. Putnam, 1974), page 234.

7. Nathanael West, *The Day of the Locust* (1939; New York: New Directions Paperbook, 1962), page 131.

8. Boris Leven, memo to Robert Wise, 1960 (University of Southern California Special Collections).

9. Harry Horner, seminar at The American Film Institute, Los Angeles; reprinted in *American Film,* February 1977.

10. Harry Horner.

11. Polly Platt, *Filmmakers on Filmmaking, Volume 1,* edited by Joseph McBride for The American Film Institute (Los Angeles: J. P. Tarcher, 1983), page 132.

12. Dean Tavoularis, quoted in Ronald Varney, "Production Number," *TWA Ambassador,* March 1984.

13. Robert Boyle, seminar at the Academy of Motion Picture Arts and Sciences, 1981; unpublished.

Other sources

Leon Barsacq, revised and edited by Elliott Stein, *Caligari's Cabinet and Other Grand Illusions: A History of Film Design* (Boston: New York Graphic Society, 1976).

Mary Corliss and Carlos Clarens, "The Hollywood Art Director," *Film Comment,* May–June 1978. [A major book on production design by these authors is in preparation.]

John Kobal, *De Mille: The Man and His Artists* (to be published by Alfred Knopf).

Carrie Rickey, "Art Directors — Theatrical Realism," *Film Comment,* January–February 1982.

Mia Farrow and Robert Redford in *The Great Gatsby* (1974), in which designer Theoni Aldredge recreates the look of the Jazz Age. Photo by Steve Schapiro.

7 COSTUME DESIGN

"Today, designers don't have the time or the budgets they once had. In the past, the designer was much more important because everything for a film was made. If the star had to wear an old, ragged apron, we made it because she was a star. But today, partly because so many films are contemporary, instead of period, we buy blue jeans, sweaters, skirts.

"In earlier days I never knew what I had to spend. The designer would make a dress, and if the actress didn't like it, the designer would make another. But today, we are all so tightly budgeted that, in a way, the budget comes before the design. . . . In the old days I knew with whom I was working. I was at Paramount, and I knew I had Grace Kelly . . . Dorothy Lamour, Bob Hope and Bing Crosby. I could plan. I would order fabric. . . . At the moment, I'm doing a character named Aunt Sonya, who is between a size fourteen and a size sixteen. That's all I know about her. The actress is coming tomorrow, and she will probably start work on Monday. So things have changed."[1]

Thus did Edith Head, designer of Mae West's first pictures and Alfred Hitchcock's last, eight times winner of the Academy Award for Best Costume Design, review her fifty-year career at Paramount and Universal. She was the last of the great studio designers, bridging the era when the designer's chief concern was to glamorize the star and dazzle her fans, and the current obsession with authenticity. In recent years, the studio system has provoked nostalgia and criticism. Polly Platt (whose credits as costume and production designer include *Paper Moon* and *Tender Mercies*) recalled:

"When I went to the movies, I used to think, 'These clothes don't have anything to do with these characters. What is this tailored suit doing on every person Edith Head designs for? Why does everyone look like a Vogue *magazine person? Why don't people design the clothes to match the people?' I remember that* Charade *drove me crazy. Audrey Hepburn in those Paris fashions — she wasn't a real person at all. It hurt the film. I always thought the men's clothes fit too well. Clothes don't fit correctly. What's funnier than a guy with the shoulders down, or the sleeves too short? I think that is character. Character comes out of design, or vice versa."*[2]

In fact, Edith Head didn't design all those tailored suits — though, as head designer, she took the credit. And she believed strongly that clothes should express character, before the idea won general acceptance, notably on *The Heiress* (1949):

"Olivia de Havilland, in the early parts of the film, was an awkward girl. She was never an ugly duckling in terms of clothes, because her father was very wealthy, but you had the feeling she wasn't quite put together. That no matter how much money she had she never looked soignée. That's what we tried to get . . . that she wasn't at ease in her clothes.

"In the film this man, Montgomery Clift, betrayed her; she was ready to elope with him and he found out she didn't have as much money as he expected and left her. Years pass. Her father has died. She's now an heiress, a fantastically wealthy woman. The man comes back and she pretends to like him still. She is sure of herself. [Director William] Wyler said, 'I want her to look so beautiful, so feminine . . . she can have him now. She can have anything she wants. And she doesn't want anything anymore.' He wanted a light dress because it was evening and all you saw was a woman going up the stairs carrying a lighted oil lamp. I asked Olivia, 'What color would you like for this?' Any pastel would photograph a soft misty white in this black-and-white film. She said, 'I would love a soft mauve.' And Wyler said, 'Surely, why not?' because mauve is a lovely period color."[3]

Head contrasts that experience, and her equally conscientious work for Gloria Swanson on *Sunset Boulevard* and for Bette Davis on *All About Eve* (which both won her Oscars in 1951), with the typical practice of the time:

"I did a picture once in which a woman was crossing the prairie from the East to the gold rush. She had to face a buffalo stampede, three Indian attacks, and a prairie fire. But every morning the heroine came out of the prairie schooner wearing white ruffles and her hair done up in curls. But nobody cared, because then the public accepted motion pictures only as a fantasy and an amusement. . . . We did things then that were outrageous. But today, perhaps because the public is much smarter, or reads more, or looks at more television, I have to be more careful."[4]

Even in the era of fantasy, there was some concern with realism. Producer Hal Wallis launched this blast at director Michael Curtiz on the subject of *Captain Blood* (1935):

"I distinctly remember telling you, I don't know how many times, that I did not want you to use lace collars or cuffs on Errol Flynn. . . . I want the man to look like

a pirate, not a mollycoddle. I suppose that when he goes into battle with the pirates at the finish, you'll probably be having him wear a high silk hat and spats. . . . When the man divided the spoils you should have had him in a shirt with the collar open at the throat, and no coat on at all. Let him look a little swashbuckling, for Christ sakes!"[5]

Irene Sharaff came to Hollywood from Broadway in 1943 to design *Meet Me in St. Louis* and stayed on to design a succession of classic musicals, including *An American in Paris* (ballet only), *West Side Story*, and *Funny Girl*, in addition to Elizabeth Taylor's wardrobe for *Cleopatra* and *The Taming of the Shrew*. In her autobiography, she evokes the spirit of those times:

"For the actresses, the three most important departments were hairdressing, make-up, and costume — in that order. In the first two, face and hair were studied and analyzed. Compared to make-up in the theater, these men in the studio's make-up department worked like skillful miniaturists. They were, however, usually so intent on ironing out deficiencies, even the natural asymmetry of a face, that in most instances final results presented an unreal image, either too good to be genuine or emptied of individuality. The hairdresser reigned supreme. Disregarding whether a hairdo was appropriate or whether it went with the face, his main concern was to invent a hairstyle that would attract attention, lend glamour to his name, keep him in constant demand, and, he hoped, initiate a new fashion.

"One section of the make-up department dealt with character actors and had developed the art of make-up to an extraordinary degree. It was organized with such efficiency that, for instance, drawer upon drawer containing rows of differently shaped ears filled cabinets along one wall of a room; the exact cauliflower ear for an actor could be fished out pronto.

"The attitude which made actresses depend to such an extreme on make-up men and hairdressers, and which put such great value on youth, sometimes was exaggerated ridiculously. At one time children of stars were not mentioned or allowed to appear with their star parents in person or in photographs. Until Dietrich broke the taboo, no star would admit to being a grandparent. Motherhood, to say nothing of grandmotherhood, was associated with gray hair. In one of the first movies I watched being filmed, the star was dismayed over having an eight-year-old son in the picture. The hairdresser, leaving her face untouched by the years, sprayed her hair a silver gray so the audience would accept her as a mother.

Irene Sharaff with Elizabeth Taylor on the set of *Cleopatra* (1963). Sharaff has had a long and distinguished career on Broadway and in Hollywood.

Thomas Meighan and Gloria Swanson in Cecil B. De Mille's *Male and Female* (1919). The extravagant costumes and sets were by the celebrated Parisian designer Paul Iribe.

Suit of lights, by an unknown designer, worn by Rudolph Valentino in *Blood and Sand* (1922). This popular adaptation of Vicente Blasco-Ibañez's romantic novel boosted Valentino's reputation as "the Latin Lover."

"The hurdles set up by censorship then seem incredible today. There were strict rules decreeing exactly how much of the body could be exposed. Nudity in films being accepted now without a second thought, it seems unbelievable that even in the 1940's women's bathing suits could not be made without a skirt attached. With the emphasis on bosoms at the time, the amount of cleavage permitted was left to the discretion of a man from the censorship office, whose OK was necessary for every dress and costume before it could be shot. I was visiting on a set when a censor was on the job: a small gray man, serious and stern at his task, he stood in front of Lana Turner's well-padded bosom peering down her low-cut dress. Shaking his head, he turned to the designer standing anxiously beside him and said, 'You'd better cover the cleavage with net or tulle. It'll never pass the office.'"[6]

In Hollywood's first decade, even the stars supplied their own wardrobe for contemporary films, and period clothes were supplied from stock, or by the Western Costume Company, which was established in 1912. This remained the practice for most male actors and for extras; anyone with a dress suit could earn extra money (and higher status) in the 1920s. Cecil B. De Mille, whose influence on how movies looked was as great as Griffith's on how they were put together, quickly realized that extravagance could sell tickets. Paramount's boss was Adolph Zukor — formerly a fur dealer — and his partner, Samuel Goldwyn, had been a glove salesman. Such men appreciated luxury and its popular appeal.

For De Mille's landmark *Male and Female* (1919), Zukor brought artist-designer Paul Iribe from Paris to design the sets and Gloria Swanson's costumes; other costumes were created by Clare West (who had worked on Griffith's *Intolerance*) and Mitchell Leisen (who would turn to directing in the 1930s.) All three would work on other De Mille extravaganzas of the early 1920s, which featured lavish and revealing costumes from a decadent present and a largely mythical past. Insisted De Mille, "I want clothes that will make people gasp when they see them. Don't design anything that anyone could buy in a store." (As late as 1949, De Mille was supplying peacock feathers from his own birds to adorn Hedy Lamarr's Delilah!)

Until the rise of MGM in the mid-1920s, Paramount was the richest and most stylish of studios — in New York and in Hollywood. It led the way in hiring out-

Dress designed by Adrian for Jeanette
MacDonald in *Maytime* (1937).

Dress designed by Adrian for Norma Shearer
in *Marie Antoinette* (1938).

Adrian, chief costume designer at MGM from 1928 to 1942, with Garbo, whom he dressed in all her major pictures. Publicity still for *The Single Standard* (1929).

side designers and in building its own stars. Howard Greer and, after 1927, Travis Banton headed a costume department of 200 employees that was organized like a production line. Banton had apprenticed to New York society dressmakers and had designed extravagant costumes for the Ziegfeld Follies before coming to Hollywood as Greer's assistant. Like other head designers, he played a major role in defining the look of the studio's top female stars: Marlene Dietrich and Claudette Colbert, Carole Lombard, Mae West, and Kay Francis. Such luminaries encouraged him to range from subdued elegance to luxurious extravagance, to indulge in the costliest of fabrics and trim. No one in Hollywood made greater use of sequins and bugle beads, of maribou feathers and lace; few rivaled his talent for building and sustaining the personalities of his favorite stars, on- and offscreen.

His contemporary at MGM, from 1928 to 1942, was Adrian. Spotted in Paris by Irving Berlin, and hired to design Valentino's last movies, he was the ideal match for MGM production designer Cedric Gibbons. Both were strong-willed, capable administrators, possessed of superb taste and imagination. Adrian's stature was enhanced by the fact that, at MGM, everything was subordinated to glorifying the star. "Do it big, do it right, do it with class" was the motto, and in such movies as *Dinner at Eight, Grand Hotel, The Great Ziegfeld, Marie Antoinette, The Women,* and all but a few of the Garbo pictures, Adrian was given unlimited scope. He left when Garbo did, opened a highly successful couture house, and made one return visit to MGM, to design *Lovely to Look At* (1952), a showcase for his fashions.

If Banton was the master of texture and extravagance, Adrian excelled in line and restraint. He softened Garbo's angularity and dramatized Joan Crawford's broad shoulders. He responded to Gibbons's all-white sets with stark white or black-and-white costumes. For Norma Shearer, he designed one of the first clinging sheaths of bias-cut satin — which he later dubbed "Norma's night-gowns." For her, and still more for Jean Harlow, they became an erotic uniform, a symbol of the early 1930s, before the enforcement of the Production Code. Adrian popularized the V-shape torso, inspired by a hussar's tunic, and padded shoulders and inventive hats, all of which served to focus attention on the actress's face for the all-important close-up.

Travis Banton, chief costume designer at Paramount from 1924 to 1937, with Marlene Dietrich in a publicity still for *Angel* (1937).

Jean Harlow with director George Cukor on the set of *Dinner at Eight* (1933). Her skin-tight sheaths of bias-cut satin required her to use a reclining board to relax between takes.

Costume sketch by Natasha Rambova for *Forbidden Fruit* (1921). Its director, Cecil B. De Mille, insisted: "I want clothes that will make people gasp when they see them. Don't design anything that anyone could buy in a store!"

Costume sketch by Irene Sharaff for Lucille Bremer in the "Limehouse Blues" number of *Ziegfeld Follies* (1945). The exotic musicals of the 1940s offered an escape from contemporary austerity.

The Latin influence on fashion was strong throughout the 1940s. Helen Rose designed this dress for Carmen Miranda, "the Brazilian Bombshell," to be worn in *Nancy Goes to Rio* (1950). Sketch by Elaine Owens.

William Travilla costume sketch for Marilyn Monroe in *There's No Business Like Show Business* (1954). The movie, the star, and Travilla's designs epitomize the innocent carnality of the 1950s.

Other studios employed outstanding designers, though none enjoyed the opportunities of Banton and Adrian. At Warner Bros., Australian-born Orry-Kelly designed Busby Berkeley's musical spectaculars and most of Bette Davis's major pictures, before leaving in the mid-1940s to freelance. Milo Anderson designed for other Warner Bros. stars, including Olivia de Havilland and Errol Flynn, Ida Lupino and Ann Sheridan. Between them, they contributed to the no-nonsense Warner Bros. look: plenty of style but few frills — except for the rare period spectacle.

Walter Plunkett spent the first half of his career at RKO (1926–39) and the second at MGM (1947–65). A master of period style and of stunning contemporary costumes for Katharine Hepburn and Ginger Rogers, Plunkett created his masterpiece in *Gone With the Wind.* For over two years, he designed and redesigned clothes for all the principals and supervised the making of costumes for thousands of extras. He transformed Scarlett O'Hara from an ingenue in girlish frills and an heirloom wedding dress to a hardened survivor of the war, in somber colors and the celebrated "portieres" dress, made up from tasseled drapes. Later achievements included the black-and-white ball in *An American in Paris* (1951), the 1920s pastiche of *Singin' in the Rain* (1952), and the nineteenth-century elegance of *Raintree County* (1957).

Hollywood costumes were designed above all to be photographed; comfort and practicality were of little importance. Many were too tight to sit in; actresses reclined on "leaning boards" between takes. Designers pampered their favorites, adding luxurious touches the camera would never see, to make the star feel good. The neophyte Edith Head won praise from Mae West: "Ah like Edith's things because they're allurin' without bein' vulgar. Ah like gowns that are tight enough to show I'm a woman and loose enough to show I'm a lady."

Color was introduced to relieve monotony, even when most films were shot in black and white. However, these colors had to respond to the properties of the film stock: Bette Davis's "scarlet" dress in *Jezebel* (1938) was actually rust-brown.

Movie clothes play many roles. They express the spirit of an era, substituting a theatrical fiction for drab reality. Our image of the 1930s is half Dorothea

Lange's photos of down-and-outs, half Fred Astaire in white tie and Ginger Rogers in a Bernard Newman dress of white feathers. And the exaggerated femininity of the 1950s is captured in Helen Rose's dresses for Elizabeth Taylor, or Travilla's for Marilyn Monroe, all cinched waists and bouffant petticoats.

Movie clothes function as shorthand, providing an instant Identi-kit for gangsters (loud pinstripe suits, dark shirts, and light ties), hookers (slit skirts and fishnet stockings), and Canadian Mounties (scarlet tunics). They accommodate historical fashions to contemporary tastes. From Theda Bara on, every screen Cleopatra has had the same hairstyle: a page-boy bob and bangs. In fact, Egyptian ladies of the period shaved their heads and wore wigs that were stiffly molded with fat and glue.

Studio-era Hollywood gave the mass of American women a taste of high fashion that was formerly reserved for a privileged few. Many of the costumes were too luxurious to provoke more than envious gasps, but a surprising number were copied, and fashion was used to sell movies and stars to the largely female readership of the fan magazines. Television and magazines have usurped the movies' function as fashion parade.

Anthea Sylbert — designer of *Rosemary's Baby* (1968), *Chinatown* (1975), and *Julia* (1977), and now turned producer — offers a contemporary point of view:

"A costume designer really is an extension of the writer, the director, and the actor. If you do your job correctly and if you have done your thinking correctly, you have helped them; if not, you have sabotaged them. You start with a screenplay. You read it, and it gives you the settings; it gives you a year; it gives you the characters. Now, there are all sorts of decisions that have to be made about the characters if the information is not in the screenplay. What economic bracket are they in? What is their background? If they are rich, were they always rich? These are things that have to be decided with a director and, finally, an actor. To think that a costume designer just puts clothes on people is a mistake.

"Let's take Shampoo. It is about a very specific place at a very specific time historically — Beverly Hills, California, on the day, night, and morning after the 1968 presidential election. It is almost more difficult when it is that close to you, because you start wanting to deny certain things that you did: 'I didn't wear my skirts that short. I never could have done such a terrible thing.' Then you start

117

Period style: Theadora Van Runkle's sketch
for one of a series of stylish changes worn by
Liza Minnelli in *New York, New York* (1977),
directed by Martin Scorsese.

Getting away from glamor: Anthea Sylbert's
sketch for Vanessa Redgrave in *Julia* (1977), a
powerful adaptation of Lillian Hellman's story,
directed by Fred Zinnemann.

In *Prizzi's Honor* (1985), Anjelica Huston outrages her Brooklyn Mafia family by attending a wedding in this dramatic dress. Donfeld designed the costumes, John Huston directed.

Bonnie and Clyde (1967): costume sketch by Theadora Van Runkle for Faye Dunaway, whose clothes launched a 1930s revival.

Gone With the Wind (1939): Walter Plunkett's sketch of a dress to be worn by Vivien Leigh as Scarlett. His designs chart the progress of the character, from ingenue to tough survivor.

looking at photographs, and there it is: men did in fact open their shirts down to the navel and hang seven thousand things around their necks, started to become the peacocks, started in a funny way to become the sex object. Warren Beatty in that movie is the sex object. None of the women is. So you say, OK, if I'm going to put him in a leather jacket, I don't want a heavy leather jacket, I want it to be the softest leather jacket; when you touch it, it should almost be a sexual experience.

"When I first did the sketch I made a mistake: I put zippers on the jacket. We started to make it, and I started to think that zippers are not really sexy, because they have something rigid about them and they are keeping me from seeing his body as well as I want to see it. We started from scratch again and we laced the jacket, had fringes hanging, so there was movement when he wore it. Even the jeans — we started off by just buying jeans; after all, jeans are jeans. Well, you couldn't see his body well enough, so we custom-made the jeans. His shirts were silk. Everything he wore had some kind of sexuality to it.

"Now we have three females: we have a young girl, Goldie Hawn; we have a slightly older person, Julie Christie; then we have Lee Grant. Goldie Hawn is the epitome of the late '60s. It was one of the times when youth was revered and age was not. And whether you are going to custom-make her clothes or not, they must look like they cost $39.95 tops, because those girls had millions of clothes that fell apart in one day. Julie Christie, the Beverly Hills mistress, wears one of those silk blouses cut rather low, with a push-up bra, stuffed from underneath. This child [Goldie Hawn] wears no bra at all. There is only one scene where you see underwear in the movie, and that is where Lee Grant puts on a bra in the first sequence and Beatty says, 'Take that off.' Why would I concern myself with their underwear at all? Because it helps the actor to feel a certain thing, and whatever an actor is feeling should finally affect the audience. You give Julie Christie an uplifted bra with pads underneath and it makes her a whole other person; this lady probably buys her underwear at places like Frederick's of Hollywood. Not big on taste. She has a brain but she knows what it is she's using that brain for: it is to make herself most appealing to the men who are going to keep her.

"Lee Grant has already gotten married. Who knows what she was before? We have to make certain decisions about her. I decided she probably was on the fringes of show business, probably had aspirations as an actress. Along came Jack

120

Edith Head's sketch for Grace Kelly's "fairy princess" ballgown in *To Catch a Thief* (1955), directed by Alfred Hitchcock.

My Fair Lady (1964): Cecil Beaton sketch for Audrey Hepburn as the cockney flower-seller.

Warden about twenty years ago; she married him before her budding career had blossomed, and there she is, this bored Beverly Hills housewife. She has nothing to do all day long but have her hair fixed and go shopping. And occasionally she has lunch with her girlfriends, and they all talk about their lovers. She does what they tell her to do in Harper's Bazaar. She has no style of her own. All she has is money. At that time one of the outfits Harper's Bazaar was pushing was a short skirt with thigh-high boots and a long fur coat. She's one of the few women in the film who wears fur during the day. It has nothing to do with the weather: she's getting dressed for something else.

"In other words, for a character like Lee Grant you have to take all the magazines from that time period, which then start to remind you of certain women you know. You start to think about what she did that was individual and peculiar in her choice of jewelry and accessories, little things that the audience may not see but will affect the performance. In her bag is every charge plate it is possible to possess; real live money hasn't a lot to do with her life. She probably has a few $100 bills that she uses only on rare occasions and some singles that are for parking boys.

"Those kinds of things are also part of a costume designer's obligation to that actress. Your obligation is to help the director and the actor create an atmosphere and an attitude, and your obligation does not end with what you can physically see: it has to do with giving the actor underwear, keys, stuffing pockets, having the actor wear the clothes, get used to them. If it can be afforded it is a good thing to give a woman like that real jewelry — not that it photographs any differently, but it makes her feel different. . . .

"One must never design with the thought of impressing the fashion world. I think it's the worst thing you can do, because then the movie becomes about the costumes. It must never be about the costumes; it must always be about the characters. You must not leave a movie whistling the clothes."[7]

Quotations

1. Edith Head, seminar at The American Film Institute; reprinted in *American Film,* May 1978.

2. Polly Platt, in *Filmmakers on Filmmaking, Volume 1,* edited by Joseph McBride for The American Film Institute (Los Angeles: J. P. Tarcher, 1983), page 135.

3. Edith Head, in *Filmmaking: The Collaborative Art,* edited by Donald Chase (Boston: Little, Brown, 1975), page 208.

4. Edith Head, in *Filmmaking.*

5. Hal Wallis, quoted in Rudy Behlmer, *Inside Warner Bros.* (New York: Viking, 1985), page 24.

6. Irene Sharaff, *Broadway and Hollywood: Costumes Designed by Irene Sharaff* (New York: Van Nostrand Reinhold, 1976), page 60.

7. Anthea Sylbert, quoted in *Filmmakers on Filmmaking, Volume 1,* pages 153–155.

Other sources

David Chierechetti, *Hollywood Costume Design* (New York: Crown, 1976).

Claudia Kidwell and Margaret Christman, *Suiting Everyone: The Democratization of Clothing in America* (Washington, D.C.: Smithsonian Institution Press, 1974).

Elizabeth Leese, *Costume Design in the Movies* (New York: Frederick Ungar, 1977).

Lee Grant, Goldie Hawn, and Warren Beatty
in *Shampoo* (1975), directed by Hal Ashby.
Costumes by Anthea Sylbert.

Billy Bitzer: detail from *Way Down East*, 1979,
a construction by Red Grooms.

"First thing, turn out all the lights in the room. Go sit in front of the mirror. Take a flashlight. Hold it at heart level. Aim it straight up, toward your face. Switch it on. What movie are you in?

"Frankenstein, right. Or Bride of Frankenstein.

"Now take your flashlight and hold it directly over your head, aimed down. What movie are you in?

"The Godfather. Very good.

"Light a cigarette, blow a lot of smoke around. Hold the flashlight behind your head, aimed forward. (This is kind of a stretch; you may need an assistant.) What movie are you in now?

"Casablanca, or Close Encounters of the Third Kind. Excellent.

"Hold the flashlight at arm's length, aim at your eyes. Don't blink.

"You got it. The evening news. Or 'Dallas.'"[1]

This practical exercise from cinematographer Tom McDonough explains why the alternate term for director of photography or cinematographer is "lighting cameraman." The finest cameramen paint with light; regrettably, most of these paintings are seen in faded prints or, worse, on television. Happily, archival restoration and the renaissance in cinematography make it easier than ever before to enjoy the full spectrum of achievement, from Billy Bitzer's work for Griffith to the luminous images of Nestor Almendros for *Sophie's Choice*. In his recent autobiography, Almendros (a Cuban-born master, who shot many of the finest French films of the 1960s and 1970s before beginning to work in America) responds to the question: "What is a director of photography? What does he do?"

"The answer is: almost everything and hardly anything. His function differs so much from one film to another that it is hard to define it exactly. My work may be simply to press the button on the camera, and sometimes not even that. There are films where the camera operator actually handles the camera while I sit nearby in a folding chair with my name on the back. In this case I am there to supervise the image, give advice, and . . . have my name on the credits. In the extreme case of the huge super-productions, with all their special effects, one hardly knows who is responsible for the photography, for it ends up absorbing everything and everybody.

"In a low-budget movie, however, a director of photography collaborating with a director who is inexperienced or just beginning can not only choose the lens but decide on the framing of the shots, the movements of the camera, the choreography of the actors in relation to the shot, and, of course, the lighting — the visual atmosphere of each scene. I even get involved in the choice of colors, materials, and shapes of the sets and wardrobe. And whenever I can, I like to operate the camera myself.

"The director of photography must always intervene when the director's technical knowledge does not allow him to express his artistic desires in material and practical terms. He must remind him of the laws of optics when they are being disregarded. But first and foremost, he must never forget he is there to help the director. Though the cinematographer may pride himself on having his own style, he mustn't try to impose it. He must do his best to understand the director's style, see as many of the director's films as possible (if there are any), and immerse himself in the director's 'manner.' It is not 'our' film but 'his' film.

"Though it is generally the director who suggests each shot, I always like to talk an idea over with him first and develop it, sometimes suggesting my own modifications; for example, what lens to use, or how much to move the camera toward or away from an actor. I like to discuss the scene, to propose photogenic ideas, even for the set. Of course, all this depends on the director. Some of them don't want any dialogue with their collaborators. Throughout my career I have noticed that the most arrogant directors are not necessarily the best."[2]

Roles were more sharply defined in the silent era. The image reigned supreme; words were of little importance. The director of photography generally operated the first camera himself, and supervised the others. (A second cameraman usually stood by his side, filming a duplicate negative that would be sent to Europe to make foreign release prints.) Pioneers were constantly developing the language of cinematography, and handled all the optical effects — like fades, dissolves, and double exposures — in the camera (tasks that would later be given to specialists).

D. W. Griffith directing an early movie with pioneer cinematographer Billy Bitzer and his Pathé camera. Behind them (left to right), actors Blanche Sweet, Dorothy Gish, and Howard Gaye, and assistant cinematographer Karl Brown.

The sturdy inventiveness of early cameramen emerges from the memoirs of Billy Bitzer, D. W. Griffith's closest associate, who shot almost all the master's pictures from the first Biograph shorts of 1908 to *Orphans of the Storm* in 1922. Neither invented the grammar of pictures, as is so often claimed. Other moviemakers of the 1910s employed close-ups and iris shots and soft focus, but none with such artistry and imagination. Bitzer recalls their first trip West—prompted by Griffith's hatred of New York winters:

"In January, 1910, the Biograph Company set foot in Hollywood [actually downtown Los Angeles] for the first time. Our studio was a vacant lot with a loft nearby to store properties. On the lot we constructed a large wooden platform and covered this area with white cotton sheets on pulleys, so that we could adjust the amount of sunlight needed for the camera. As I recall, there were no dressing rooms for the players, though I believe we set up temporary tents while there. We all stayed at the Alexandria hotel, but there were a lot of sidetrips, too. We went to the San Gabriel Mission to make The Thread of Destiny, *and to Santa Monica to photograph* The Unchanging Sea. . . . *We made dozens of films in California between January and April, after which we returned to New York."*[3]

In 1912, Griffith and Bitzer moved to a permanent site in Hollywood. They quit Biograph and, as independents, shot *The Birth of a Nation* (1914–15) and *Intolerance* (1915–16). Bitzer recalls the scale of the Babylonian set in *Intolerance* and the problems he had to solve:

"Huck Wortman, who had charge of the construction of the big sets in Intolerance, *was a rough sort of down-to-earth fellow who chewed tobacco incessantly and spat out of the corner of his mouth. In the original laying out of these sets, working without a scenario (there were no paper plans), Mr. Griffith, Huck, and myself would go over on the adjoining field and stake out where D.W. thought he would like to have them, my end being their relation to the sun—lights and shadows.*

"These sets kept growing larger and higher than the original staked-out areas, as Mr. Griffith kept asking Huck, 'Could we put another wing on here or increase the height there?' Huck generally agreed, and many a night before bedtime when Huck or I would hear a Santa Ana windstorm getting strong, we would jump into our cars and, with a couple of men Huck always had ready, go to the Intolerance

Lost Horizon (1937): cinematographer Joseph Walker and assistants shooting Shangri-La on the Columbia Ranch in Burbank. Photo by Alfred S. Keller.

lot and add a cable here and there, and tighten up the others. Huck would kind of look at Mr. Griffith when another twenty-foot-or-so higher part was suggested, but he never rebelled.

"One morning Huck stood in a sort of menacing way as I was coming toward him (at times I carried additional overnight instructions from Mr. Griffith), and it occurred to me to kid him a little. As I came up, he said, 'What's it now?' I said, 'Oh, on those side battle walls, would it be much trouble to put runways and have platforms for horses and chariots?' With a 'Well, I'll be — ! What will he want next?' he just stood there. A little later, when Mr. Griffith arrived, Huck asked him, 'How many horses and so on do you figure putting on them walls?' Mr. Griffith thought a moment and said, 'Say, Billy, that would be a good idea. Would there be too much vibration for your camera?' The horses and chariots are up there in the picture.

"Huck would say to later stupendous construction suggestions, such as the 150-foot-high moving camera dolly, 'This ain't a-going to be another horses-and-chariot gag, is it?'

"One of Huck's great designs was the big, heavy gates of Babylon, which were opened by slaves pushing big iron wheels on either side of the gates. That set with the walls is the most sumptuous affair we ever attempted. It was 150 feet high, not 500 feet, as given out in publicity.

"The reason we had to have the camera dolly was that the balloon, which we tried first, did not work. I had to get the entire set in full view — a real bird's-eye view — from the air, then zoom downward gradually to the dancing Virgins of the Sacred Fires on the steps, then zoom into the big banquet hall, for many yards, and finally pinpoint a little toy chariot, drawn by two white turtledoves, as it moved across the floor with a love letter from Belshazzar (Alfred Paget) to the Princess Beloved (Seena Owen). Now remember that the whole set was about three-eighths of a mile long and that I had to start suspended in the air 150 feet high. When we tried it first in the balloon, the trouble was that the basket rocked, the horizon kept changing, and I began to get seasick. I thought that if my camera did not fall out, I would. But Huck Wortman worked it all out fine with his next construction. The dolly was 150 feet high, about six feet square at the top and sixty feet wide at the bottom. It was mounted on six sets of four-wheeled railroad-car trucks and had an

Filming David O. Selznick's production of *The Garden of Allah* (1936) on location in Arizona. Director Richard Boleslawski is seated beneath the camera; cinematographer W. Howard Greene is lining up a shot of Charles Boyer and Marlene Dietrich.

elevator in the center. This dolly ran on tracks starting way back and taking in the entire set, on which five thousand extras were assembled, including lines of standees across the top frame of the set.

"This great dolly was moved backward and forward by manpower; twenty-five workers pushed it smoothly along the rails. Another staff operated the elevator, which had to descend at a regular rhythm as the railroad car moved forward. The whole scene had to be filmed in one continuous shot, in focus at every level. It wasn't easy to do. We rehearsed it over and over.

"It was shot with only one hand-cranked Pathé camera. Karl Brown [Bitzer's assistant], seated underneath the Pathé, did the cranking through a flexible shaft. I handled the tilt and pan cranks, looking directly through the Pathé eyepiece focusing glass in the back door of the Pathé onto the film, with a special eyepiece of rubber, which fitted around my eye, to keep the light from fogging the film. It was a brilliant sunny day, and the whole thing came out fine and clear."[4]

Bitzer kept a special lens with which to photograph Lillian Gish, Griffith's favorite actress, and she brought in photographer Hendrick Sartov, who achieved miracles of gauzy lighting on *Broken Blossoms* (1919). From that time on, and especially after the replacement of orthochromatic film by the more sensitive panchromatic film in the mid-1920s, a major role of the cameraman was to play Svengali to the leading actress. Mary Pickford insisted that Charles Rosher photograph all her movies. One of the greatest cinematographers, William Daniels, who won fame with von Stroheim in the early 1920s and stayed at the top for fifty years, was best known as "Garbo's cameraman."

"I didn't create a 'Garbo face.' I just did portraits of her I would have done for any star. My lighting of her was determined by the requirements of a scene. I didn't, as some say I did, keep one side of the face light and the other dark. But I did always try to make the camera peer into the eyes, to see what was there. Garbo had natural long eyelashes and in certain moods I could throw the light down from quite high, and show the shadows of the eyelashes come down on the cheeks: it became a sort of trade mark with her. Her eyelashes were real; after I did that many stars got false ones and had their cameramen do the same lighting for them, but it wasn't quite the same thing.

Cinematographer James Wong Howe at Paramount with the new VistaVision camera, 1955. Photo by Allan Grant for *Life*.

"I suppose the most notable moment in Queen Christina *was when Garbo strokes the bedroom. All the light in the room came from the fire — or seemed to; of course we had to cheat a little by using special small spotlights that illuminated the bedposts, the furniture, in such a way that they seemed to be the kind of light flickering flames would make. A problem was that the scene had to be done in a very subdued, natural light and still be practical for theatre display. I think I learned the realism in this scene, the way of achieving it, from von Stroheim.*

"Reflection was a very valuable tool, I liked reflections. Many of the cameramen used to spray everything with oil to make it shiny, to avoid reflections, they thought they were a nuisance. Television today has to avoid reflections, because you get light flares on the screen if you shoot into a mirroring surface, and you get a black image as a result. I was determined to have reflections because of what von Stroheim had taught me, and I had them, though they did create difficulties. You see, we try to tell the story with light as the director tries to tell it with his action.

"I'd give each director what he wanted. But of course I could improvise. And the directors always left the lighting to you. For instance, in Flesh and the Devil . . . *for the arbor love scene I just wanted a faint glow to illuminate Garbo and Gilbert's faces. So I gave Jack Gilbert two tiny little pencil carbons to hold. When they kissed the carbons lit up. His hands shielded the mechanism from the lens.*

"And then again, I was able to do something interesting in Mata Hari. *Novarro and Garbo are in a little secluded niche in a restaurant or inn. She is seducing him, and it's very romantic. I wanted to illuminate the whole scene with just the glow from his cigarette alone. I put a special window over their heads so that the smoke would drift up past it and be fully visible. Then I had another idea. I'd been to a doctor and he'd put this tiny tube up my nostrils, with a brilliant little bulb in it. Now I had a dummy cigarette made with one of those medical bulbs in it, and I stuck the ashes on with glue. I mounted another cigarette under it to cause the smoke. I had a little rheostat by the camera and each time he raised the cigarette to his lips I'd bring the bulb up bright. And the smoke would go up. All you'd see was just one gleam. . . ."*[5]

Chinese-born James Wong Howe's career ran from the 1923 *Trail of the Lonesome Pine* to *Funny Lady* in 1975. Unfailingly inventive — he shot a boxing match with a hand-held camera, following the fighters on roller skates —

Howe loved to improvise. He recalled shooting *Air Force* (1943) for Howard Hawks:

"He had a shot in which nine B-17s were coming in to land. They were supposed to be in Pearl Harbor, but we were making it in Florida. It was just after sunset, so I had to line up all my lights. About two hours before we had to make a shot, the electrician said, 'Jimmy, we're having problems. The generator doesn't work.' I told Howard. He said, 'That's not my problem; that's your problem.' So I went to the special-effects man and said, 'Look, do we have any three-minute flares?' He said, 'I got a flock of them.' What I did was to take the reflectors off the back of the lights and hang them on stands. Then I stuck these flares in front of the reflectors and had the electrician wire them up.

"So here come these planes (if I ever prayed to Buddha!) and I told him to hit the switch. All these flares came on and they flickered, and it was wonderful because the landing field was supposed to be on fire. The smoke from the flares drifted across, and these planes coming down with the landing lamps going through the smoke and the propellors swirling this smoke, it created a lot of drama. Hawks knew how it looked without even seeing the rushes. 'Wonderful effect,' he said. 'Send the generator home — we're shooting all this with the flares.'"[6]

A few cameramen formed as close an association with certain directors as with actresses. Lee Garmes (*Morocco, Shanghai Express*) and Bert Glennon (*Blonde Venus, Scarlet Empress*) shared with Josef von Sternberg the credit for the shadowy eroticism of early 1930s Marlene Dietrich movies. Robert Burks shot all of Hitchcock's major pictures, from *Strangers on a Train* (1950) to *The Birds* (1963), disciplining himself to execute the intentions of that calculating and meticulous director. The falloff in visual quality in Hitchcock's last movies demonstrates how much Burks contributed.

Gregg Toland put his signature on the pictures he shot, as he later recounted:

"Wuthering Heights [1939] was a soft picture, diffused with soft-candle-lighting effects. I tried to make the love scenes beautiful in a romantic way. It was a love story, a story of escape and fantasy. So I tried to keep it that way photographically, and let the audience dream through a whirl of beautiful close-ups.

"On the other hand, The Grapes of Wrath [1940] had to be a sharp picture. It was a story of unhappy people, people of the earth, who had real problems and

who suffered. So we made it very sharp. There wasn't any makeup used. The picture had some extreme effects in low key but they were, I think, real. As I remember the camera moved only once — a long travel shot through the sordid streets of a Hooverville. It was what the occupants of the car, after the long drive to a promised haven, were examining. Photography such as we had in Wuthering Heights could ruin a picture like Grapes of Wrath completely.*

"Long Voyage Home [1940] was a mood picture. Storywise it was a series of compositions of the mood of the men aboard the ship. It was a story of what men felt rather than what they did. The camera never moved in that picture. . . .

"The Best Years of Our Lives [1946] was another experiment. But in a different way. [Wyler and I] . . . talked at length about the story and decided it demanded simple, unaffected realism. Willy had been thinking a lot, too, during the war. He had seen a lot of candid photography and lots of scenes without a camera dolly or boom. He used to go overboard on movement, but he came back with, I think, a better perspective on what was and wasn't important. Anyway, Willy left me pretty much alone. While he rehearsed, I would try to find a method of shooting it. Usually he liked it. When he didn't, he was the boss and we did it his way. However, at this point we understand each other pretty well and Willy knows that I will sacrifice photography any time if it means a better scene."[7]

"[Orson] Welles's use of the cinematographer as a real aid to him in telling the story, and his appreciation of the camera's story-telling potentialities helped me immeasurably. He was willing — and this is very rare in Hollywood — that I take weeks to achieve a desired photographic effect.

"The photographic approach to Citizen Kane was planned and considered long before the first camera turned. That is also unconventional in Hollywood, where most cinematographers learn of their next assignments only a few days before the scheduled shooting starts. Altogether I was on the job for half a year, including preparation and actual shooting. . . .

"The Citizen Kane sets have ceilings because we wanted reality, and we felt that it would be easier to believe a room was a room if its ceiling could be seen in the picture. Furthermore, lighting effects in unceilinged rooms generally are not realistic because the illumination comes from unnatural angles. . . .

Orson Welles and cinematographer Gregg Toland set up a scene in *Citizen Kane* (1941). Their collaboration gave the film its expressive richness.

"There were other violations of Hollywood tradition in the photographic details of Citizen Kane. One of them resulted from Welles's insistence that scenes should flow together smoothly and imperceptibly. Accordingly, before actual shooting began, everything had been planned with full realization of what the camera could bring to the audience. We arranged our action so as to avoid direct cuts, to permit panning or dollying from one angle to another whenever that type of camera action fitted the continuity. By way of example, scenes which conventionally would require a shift from close-up to full shot were planned so that the action would take place simultaneously in extreme foreground and extreme background."[8]

Toland brought to *Citizen Kane* a rich and fluent vocabulary, realizing the vision of the inexperienced young director. Stanley Cortez, cameraman on Welles's second feature, *The Magnificent Ambersons*, had a similar influence on another neophyte director, Charles Laughton, when they collaborated on *The Night of the Hunter* (1955). The venture also involved screenwriter James Agee and production designer Hilyard Brown. (Robert Mitchum, Lillian Gish, and Shelley Winters star in this nightmarish tale of a murderous preacher pursuing a country widow and her small children to seize their inheritance.) Cortez recalled how they worked together:

"Every day the marvellous team that made that picture would meet and discuss the next day's work. It was designed from day to day in fullest detail, so that the details seemed fresh, fresher than if we had done the whole thing in advance. I used to go to Charles's house every Sunday for six weeks before we started and explain my camera equipment to him piece by piece. I wanted to show him through the camera what these lenses would and would not do. But soon the instructor became the student. Not in terms of knowing about the camera but in terms of what he had to say, his ideas for the camera. He was very much influenced by Griffith; we ran all the films Griffith made.

"We had a scene with a little boy in bed. We showed shadows on the wall. Charles wanted to dolly in on the child, to discover him. I suggested we start with a close-up of the child and then pull back to show the mysterious quality of the room gradually. He agreed at once.

"Perhaps the most extraordinary thing we did was the shot of a drowned girl in a car under water, her hair streaming. We used a wax dummy for Shelley Winters. I

Some Like It Hot (1958): director Billy Wilder (in glasses) and cinematographer Charles Lang, Jr., (right of camera) prepare to film a scene with Tony Curtis and Marilyn Monroe.

tested the tank at the Fox Studio, but it just wouldn't do, because the paint kept coming off the sides. Finally we used the tank at Republic. I hauled in a huge crane from which I suspended a platform, and powerful arcs that would penetrate the water to create that ethereal death-like something you had in the water. We used two cameras, one actually in the water, the other shooting through glass. We engaged Maurice Siederman, who did Kane and Ambersons, to do the hair and makeup on the Winters dummy. We had to create a current in the water to make the hair stream out, without your seeing the current at all. We used wind machines. The underwater cameraman was dressed in a scuba diving outfit, and he had an effect in which the camera is on a hook under water and it tips up and follows a thread, up to the boat. Do you know what it means to do a shot like that? We had another cameraman under water with the first man and he kicked him in the fanny and up he went along the line to the bottom of the boat! I painted the thread white so it would pick up the contrast.

"The death scene with Bob Mitchum and Shelley Winters was something I was very proud of. Shelley Winters is lying in the foreground and Bob Mitchum is in the background, and without a sound he goes through a series of strange positions in relation to her before killing her. We had an A-shaped composition formed by roof-beams, and I lit the whole thing with just five lights. Charles must have seen something on my face, something strange, because he looked at me very hard and said, 'What in hell are you thinking of right now?' I said, 'None of your God-damned business,' in the nicest way. But he insisted. And I told him — music is my hobby — I was thinking about a certain piece of music. He said, in his own typical way, 'Pray may I ask what was that music?' I told him it was Sibelius's 'Valse Triste.' . . . 'My God,' he said, 'how right you are. This whole sequence needs a waltz tempo.'

"He sent for the composer, the late Walter Schumann, and I told the composer what I was doing visually so that he could interpret it musically. I often will revert to music as a key for a photographic effect.

"People to this day ask me where we did the scene of the chase along the river. We used a tank on Stage Fifteen — and when I tell them that, their faces turn white; because it looked like a real river. In the scene when the two children are on top of the haystack and in the distance you see the mother by the light of the moon, we used some very elaborate tricks. But better still was the scene of the

133

Al Martino and Marlon Brando in *The Godfather* (1972). The mythic stature of the Corleone family was enhanced by the "Rembrandt lighting" of cinematographer Gordon Willis.

In Warren Beatty's *Reds* (1981), Vittorio Storaro's cinematography expressed the frenzy of revolution in the 1910s. Hand-colored photo by Dan Weaks.

child in the loft, looking down and seeing the preacher in the distance; we built the whole set in perspective, between the hayloft and the fence, which was about 500 feet away. The figure moving against the horizon wasn't Mitchum at all. It was a midget on a little pony. The lighting gave the illusion I needed; the feeling of mystery, of strange shadows. And I even used an iris: on the boy at the window. Charles wanted to crane in on him, but I used the iris instead."[9]

The great studio-era cameramen formed a tight-knit fraternity, and the American Society of Cinematographers discouraged younger applicants. The average age of its members rose and it became increasingly conservative in the 1950s and 1960s. The vitality and inventiveness that had characterized the industry in its heyday were lost, as older cameramen retired without passing on their skills and experience. The old guard actively resisted change, but a new breed of cinematographer — and immigrants of a quality unmatched since the 1920s — launched a renaissance outside Hollywood.

The movies shot by New York–based Gordon Willis display a mastery of art and craft (the Rembrandt lighting of *The Godfather I* and *II*; the rich textures of Woody Allen's black-and-white films; the surreal brightness of *All the President's Men*; the hard-edged glitter of *The Parallax View*), yet his work has received little acclaim from his West Coast peers. The union insisted that the great Italian Vittorio Storaro be accompanied by an American cameraman during the shooting of Francis Coppola's *One From the Heart* (1982). Sven Nyqvist, Ingmar Bergman's closest associate, had to struggle for acceptance in America.

Nestor Almendros has reflected on the technical changes that have accompanied this struggle:

"The film industry is said to have made great technological progress. I would contest this claim. From the 1930s on, when sound was added and the first color films appeared, progress has really been minimal. One has only to think of the degree of perfection achieved by John Ford in Drums Along the Mohawk *(1939) and by David O. Selznick, who produced the much better known* Gone With the Wind *(1939). The mechanism of cameras has not undergone any fundamental change in the last forty years. The most notable developments are that they have become smaller, lighter, and therefore more transportable, and now have gadgets like the reflex system, which eliminates parallax and allows direct focusing through the*

Peter MacNicol, Meryl Streep, and Kevin Kline in *Sophie's Choice* (1983). Cinematographer Nestor Almendros achieved the quality of light that was described by novelist William Styron. Photo by Douglas Kirkland.

lens. Raw stock film has become more sensitive, the lens can register images at lower light readings, but ultimately all these advances only mean that film equipment has become simpler and cheaper and is now available to all countries and budgets. There has been a generalization of what once was the Hollywood exception. Only the new ultraluminous lenses and ultrasensitive film have contributed to a significant progress from the point of aesthetics.

"Wide-aperture lenses and emulsions able to capture extremes of light have only recently appeared on the market. This has indeed been a revolution, one that is still happening and has much further to go. I like to compare this revolution in cinematography with the revolution of the Impressionists in painting. With the invention of tubes of oil paint, the artist could leave his studio carrying only a case of these tubes, go anywhere — Rouen's cathedral, for example, like Monet — and capture fleeting moments of light on the cathedral façade on different canvases. Earlier painters had been obliged to prepare and mix the colors themselves in their workshops. Nowadays, those of us who work in color film can also capture instantly difficult and extreme moments of light even at low exposures. . . ."[10]

Among the products of this revolution are Almendros's interiors in *Sophie's Choice*; Vilmos Zsigmond's *McCabe and Mrs. Miller* (1971; directed by Robert Altman); Haskell Wexler's *The Conversation* (1975; directed by Francis Coppola); Richard Kline's *Body Heat* (1981; directed by Lawrence Kasdan); and John Cronenweth's *Blade Runner* (1982; directed by Ridley Scott), to name a few.

Almendros has remarked, in *Man With a Camera*, that "cinema [is] a generous art form. . . . Everything seems more interesting on film than in life . . . the camera heightens reality." Andrew Sarris takes a more critical position:

"Movies have never looked better, and never before have they made less sense. . . . Within the last twenty years, cinematographers have been let loose on the world in a frenzied exploration of the 'reality' the old studios were content to simulate and imitate. A tension has developed between fresh images and stale plots.

"One could make the point that cinematography has always seemed to be more advanced and more assured than the cinema it ostensibly served. To put it another way, pictures have always seemed to promise more than all but a very few scenarios could deliver."[11]

Woody Allen and Diane Keaton silhouetted in the Museum of Modern Art sculpture garden in *Manhattan* (1979); photo by Brian Hamill. Gordon Willis's black-and-white cinematography revived the lost glories of the studio era.

Quotations

1. Tom McDonough, "Tender Is the Light," *American Film,* April 1984.

2. Nestor Almendros, *A Man With a Camera* (New York: Farrar, Straus & Giroux, 1984), pages 3–4.

3. G. W. Bitzer, *Billy Bitzer — His Story* (New York: Farrar, Straus & Giroux, 1973), page 77.

4. G. W. Bitzer, pages 133–135.

5. William Daniels, quoted in Charles Higham, *Hollywood Cameramen* (Bloomington, Ind.: Indiana University Press, 1970), page 70.

6. James Wong Howe, in *Filmmakers on Film-making, Volume 1,* edited by Joseph McBride for The American Film Institute (Los Angeles: J. P. Tarcher, 1983), pages 106–107.

7. Gregg Toland, interviewed for *The Screen Writer,* 1949; reprinted in *The Voices of Film Experience,* edited by Jay Leyda (New York: Macmillan, 1977), pages 461–462.

8. Gregg Toland, quoted in *Popular Photography,* June 1941; reprinted in *Focus on Citizen Kane* (Englewood Cliffs, N.J.: Prentice-Hall, 1971), pages 73–75.

9. Stanley Cortez, quoted in *Hollywood Cameramen,* pages 112–115.

10. Nestor Almendros, pages 16–17.

11. Andrew Sarris, "The Cinematographer as Superstar," *American Film,* April 1981.

Other sources

Todd McCarthy, "Hollywood Style, '84," *Film Comment,* March–April 1984. Credits and comment on eight contemporary cinematographers.

Leonard Maltin, *The Art of the Cinematographer* (New York: Dover, 1978).

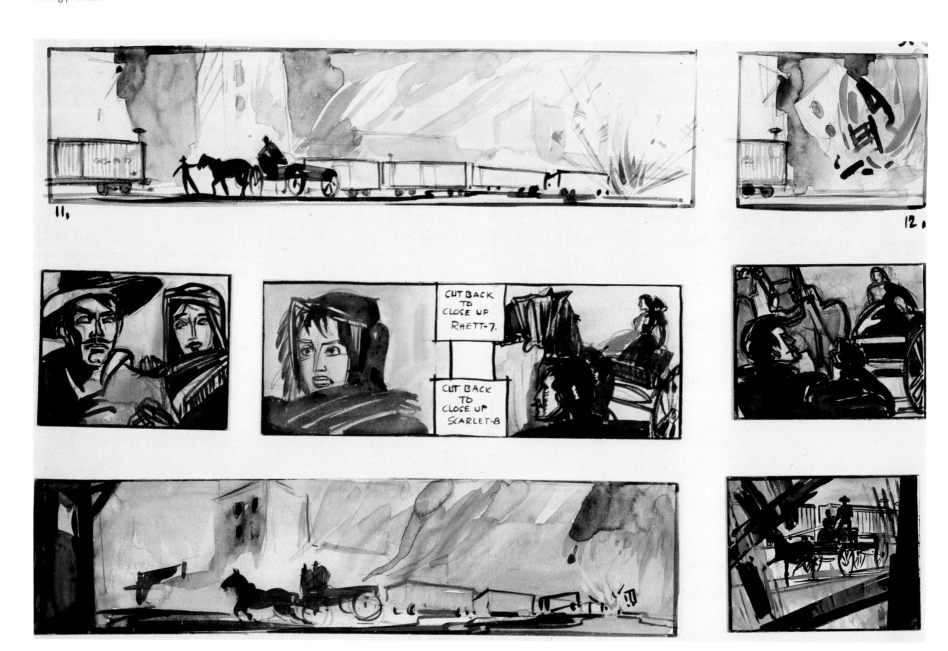

Gone With the Wind (1939): storyboard showing Scarlett and Rhett's flight from Atlanta. Such sketches serve as a blueprint for the cinematographer and offer an analogy to the editing process.

★ 9 EDITING

A typical feature film will generate twenty to forty hours of footage, from which the editor — working with the director and/or producer, and the assistants who physically cut the film — will produce a two-hour release print. In the best available account of the craft, *When the Shooting Stops . . . the Cutting Begins*, Ralph Rosenblum and Robert Karen describe how the editor finds the film hidden in this mass of material, much as a sculptor discovers the statue within a block of marble. They define cutting as the process of making meaningful juxtapositions — action, reaction — as unobtrusively as possible.

Rosenblum recalled his experience of editing Woody Allen's *Interiors* (1978):

"Anguished moans and angry cries burst out of the cutting room and fill the entire apartment as pieces of the uncut film are run through the editing machines over and over again. Four people are working in the darkened space. My two assistants, Sandy Morse and Sonya Polonsky, are winding my selections and rejections from the great mass of film onto small, carefully coded spools. These spools of film, each about the diameter of a salad plate and the thickness of a ten-dollar novel, are sitting in piles of twos and threes on surfaces all around the room.

"I sit in a corner at one of the Moviolas piecing together a sequence that was shot from five different perspectives. I work quickly, long lengths of film flying through my white-gloved right hand. I stop, mark the film with a grease pencil, fly on, make another mark, cut, splice together the desired portions, and hang up the trims, pieces of deleted film.

"Off to my right, at the large rented Steenbeck editing machine — whose TV-sized screen offers a better view of the raw film than does the traditional Moviola — Woody Allen is viewing and reviewing a tiny piece of action from an early scene. 'Scene Seventeen, take two,' cries an anonymous voice for the nth time. A prop man races across the twelve-inch screen just before Diane Keaton and Marybeth Hurt appear and begin arguing again. After their short altercation, Woody stops the film. 'The second take,' he says at last, and, without looking up, Sandy stops winding film and marks his choice in her fat script book.

"Several times in the course of the day, Woody and I confer on the editing of a troublesome scene. Once we go down the hall to the bedroom for a more serious discussion. Woody is worried about the episode in which Sam Waterston breaks down. I assure him the whole sequence can be cut out without leaving too glaring a gap.

"Five film barrels crowd the cutting room, with long trims hanging into them from an overhead rod. There's a lot of film on the floor — not rejected film, as the cliché has it, but film that's in the process of being viewed or edited or wound. The blast of voices running backward over tape heads repeatedly shatters the air. From my machine a man screams, 'So far I have nothing but compassion for you!' Then a Swedish sounding 'Bhaw-ooo-ai-ya,' as I rewind looking for the right place to make the cut. 'Compassion for you!' No one pays attention to the sounds emanating from my corner or to the voice of Sam Waterston on Woody's machine as he cries that he is able to care for people only en masse, not as individuals (a sentence that will never make it to the theaters). 'Clip! Clop!' as I make the cut and apply the tape in two quick gestures. After four months of this, the film is edited and ready to go to the sound studio and the lab for the finishing touches. . . .

"Why so long? Why such painstaking devotion? Because as an editor you are constantly faced with choices that subtly influence the character of the film. Imagine a man who has just bolted upright in bed from the midst of a deep sleep. You are provided with coverage of the next moments from two perspectives. You have a choice. You can cut from the just-awakened protagonist clutching the blankets to his chest to a stranger standing in the shadows at the foot of the bed, pointing a gun and talking in a menacing fashion. Or you can cut from the startled sleeper sitting up in bed to a tight close-up of his face, which reveals the terror in his eyes as the menacing voice of a gunman, unseen by the audience, is heard on the sound track.

"Your decision will be based on many factors: the degree of tension you want to generate, whether you want the terror to be muted or to reach climax proportions, your concern about repetitive images and moods, your desire to avoid clichés. Once you decide which way to go, you will have to make other choices — first regarding the selection of the strongest performance (or 'take'), then the best camera angle, and finally the exact frame (and there are twenty-four frames in a second) where you will cut each shot and make the transition. The cumulative impact of these little decisions may make the difference between a classic and just plain good entertainment — or between good entertainment and a flop. For

Mount Rushmore at J. C. Backings on the
MGM lot. This was one of the backdrops for
Alfred Hitchcock's *North by Northwest* (1959).
Photo by Michael Webb.

Storyboard by Mentor Huebner for art director Robert Boyle, showing set-ups from the climactic scene on Mount Rushmore in *North by Northwest* (1959). As in so many of Alfred Hitchcock's thrillers, rapid cutting encouraged the audience to suspend disbelief.

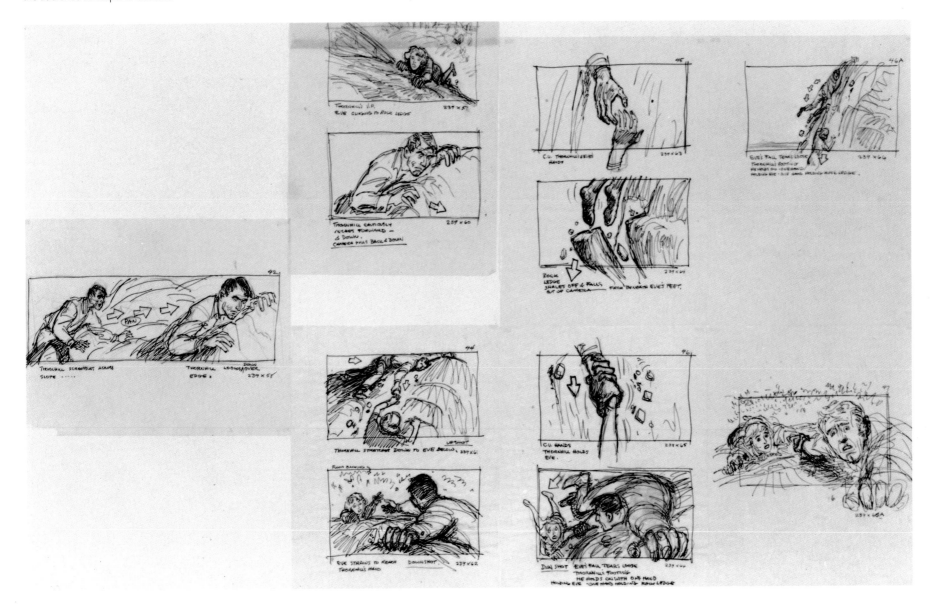

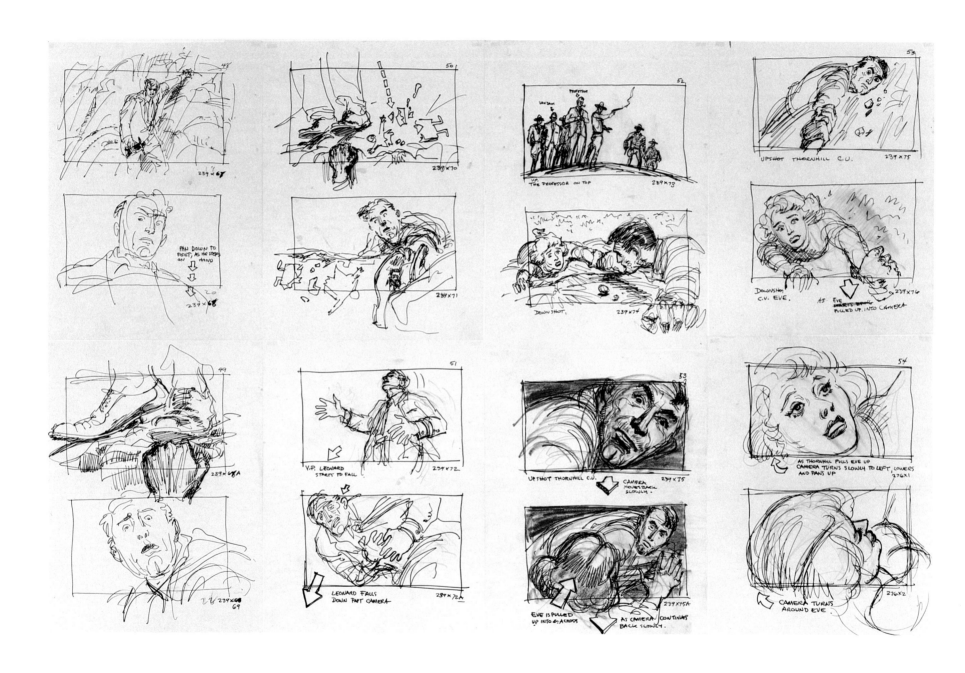

142

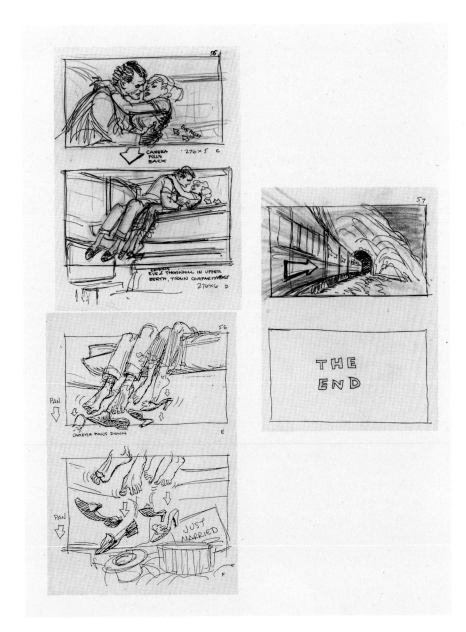

although audiences are unaware of editing, they are as affected by it as they are by a writer's style.

"No matter how you cut it, really dead material can never be brought to life, but if the raw footage has quality, it faces almost infinite possibilities during the months it passes through an editor's hands. But because an editor's prerogatives depend so much on his relationship with the director, it is impossible to say what his contribution is to any given film. A director may demand absolute control of his picture and give the editor little room to offer creative solutions; or he may walk away, leaving no more than a handful of instructions and an occasional word of encouragement.

"Under the old Hollywood system editors were often considered strictly mechanics and not expected to offer ideas. But during certain periods, like the heyday of the silent film, the era of the great producer-tycoons, and throughout much of TV's history, certain editors have achieved immense authority and power. In recent years, as the studio system has crumbled and as filmmakers have become more and more inclined to break out of the confines of the script, the editing profession as a whole has begun to come into its own. But even today the situation varies dramatically — from a picture like Apocalypse Now that spends years in the cutting and goes through several generations of editors to a less complicated picture like Slow Dancing in the Big City, which director John Avildsen virtually edited himself.

"Because so much goes on in the cutting room, because it is a major center of film creation, an inevitable tension infects the director-editor relationship. Directors never give special mention to their editors when they lope up to receive their Oscar — lest an overeager critic surmise that the film had been in trouble and was saved by heavy editorial doctoring. And editors, understanding the explosive ego issues involved, wisely stay true to the bent for anonymity that led them to their chosen profession."[1]

Classic films have been rescued in this way, but only insiders know of the unique contribution that Rosenblum made on *The Night They Raided Minsky's* (1968), Elmo Williams on *High Noon* (1952), and Frank Keller on *Bullitt* (1968).

Things were simpler in the earliest years of Hollywood, as pioneer director Allan Dwan recalls:

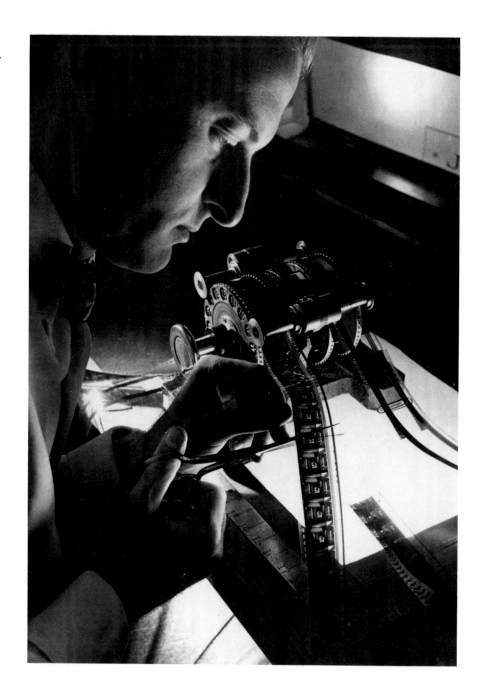

Watson Webb cutting *The Razor's Edge* (1946). The technique of editing has changed little in the six decades since the coming of sound. Photo by Ralph Crane for *Life*.

"We would work, say, Monday, Tuesday, and Wednesday shooting and make 2 pictures. Then on Thursday and Friday I'd develop and cut them and take Saturday and Sunday off. . . .

"And we developed our own negatives. I rented a couple of stores. One was for offices, the other was for the development process, the lab. Our cameraman had to be able to develop film in those days.

"I cut the negative — never saw a print . . . we didn't have cutters. And we didn't have any instruments or machines — we did it by hand. I would take the reels and run them through in front of a light. I could read the negative. Wherever I wanted to end a scene, I'd just cut it with a pair of scissors and that'd be a scene. Then I'd get the next scene I wanted and we'd glue it together. When I'd have 1,000 feet — one reel — I'd roll it up and send it to Chicago. . . . They'd simply print it that way when it got to Chicago, and that's the way it stayed. . . ."[2]

In 1937, David O. Selznick reminisced on the changes that sound had wrought:

"In the silent days the cutter had a much more important post than he has today. A good cutter could ruin a picture in the silent days or he could help it enormously, because you were able to take your film and juggle it around any way you saw fit. Scenes that were intended for reel four could be put in reel one; maybe the middle of the scene was taken out and a close-up from some other scene inserted, and even though the lips moved, the film could be matched with no one being aware of the change.

"But in talking pictures you are limited by dialogue. Cutting today hasn't nearly the range of possibilities in the changing of the film that it had in the silent days . . . and that means you have to be much more right with your script. In the silent days you could save a bad film simply with cutting and clever title writing. Those days are gone. You can improve a picture, to be sure, by cutting out slow spots, trimming out dull lines, which is done after previews. But if the tempo is slow in the playing, it is going to be slow in the finished picture . . . and only retakes can save you."[3]

Many of the finest editors have been women. June Mathis was a screenwriter who discovered Valentino, and who was trusted with the final cut of von Stroheim's *Greed* (1925). Margaret Booth was a top editor for fifty years, at

MGM and later as an independent. Sandra Morse took over from Rosenblum as Woody Allen's favorite editor. None has achieved greater celebrity and won more professional friends than Verna Fields, who became known in the 1970s as "Mother Cutter" to such innovative young directors as Peter Bogdanovich, George Lucas, and Steven Spielberg. Her mastery was best demonstrated on *Jaws* (1975), a roller coaster of a movie, whose shock effects depended on split-second timing and a precise selection of available takes. She described her methods:

"Every editor works a little differently, so I can only speak for myself: I work very closely with the director. I'll climb inside the director's head if he'll let me. I think it's just a fiasco when the editor is not near production; I see no way at all for the editor to know what the director is trying to do. Hopefully, the director has in mind how he wants the picture cut; he's visualizing the picture together, not just little shots. I don't like to cut a picture twice; . . . I want to cut it his way. If I have different ideas, though, I want to argue with him. I'm terribly stubborn; I fight.

"You usually get the dailies in the morning; an assistant will synch them up [match sound with picture]; I like to look at them then, assuming that I have not been on the set the day before, so that when I finally do see the director, who may have very little time, I will have studied it in advance. Possibly the producers will see it at noon or maybe the company breaks at noon and sees it and the director doesn't see it until the end of the day. In any event, a list is made up with the scene numbers, and when I have enough material to fill out a whole scene I will start cutting it.

"Probably the next day I will try to snag the director and talk to him about the sequence I cut. I'll say, 'It went together magnificently, just the way you shot it' or 'I had a bit of trouble with such-and-such. Do you want to see it?' There are times when a director will say to me, 'Please don't cut that sequence until we have the time to look at it closely. I have some really crazy ideas that you couldn't know by the way I shot it, but I realized afterward that I wanted to do something different.' So I'll leave it intact and that's the way it goes. Pretty soon a sequence becomes a reel and a reel becomes half a film and eventually a whole film.

". . . There's a feeling of movement in telling a story and there is a flow. A cut that is off-rhythm will be disturbing and you will feel it, unless you want it to be like that. On Jaws, each time I wanted to cut I didn't, so that it would have an anticipa-

tory feeling — and it worked. A perfect example is the early beach scene; I broke the pace for the anticipation. You see a dog go into the water; you see a woman go into the water; you see someone else go into the water; and so forth. And the second time you see them you've now gotten the feeling that you expect a cut, and then all of a sudden I don't cut. I just hold it for about eight frames, in one case twelve frames, after I normally would have cut.

"When you see Taxi Driver [directed by Martin Scorsese, edited by Sidney Levin], you're going to see a very good example of what can be done with editing. It is not cut in an ordinary smooth-flowing fashion; you are aware of cuts, and some are jarring, and they work incredibly well. That's the way the film is: it's shot rough. I don't mean jiggly — it's New York at its worst, it's grungy and it's a paranoid picture and it's irritating, and the editing helps create the feeling.

"Cutting a film is really a matter of feeling. As far as I'm concerned, there are no rules except the film: the emotion or the impact of whatever you're trying to get. If it's a laugh you're trying to get or tears or a smile or a good feeling — whatever it is, if it works, do it."[4]

As a final example of what a good editor can bring to a picture, here is Ralph Rosenblum's account of how he worked with Woody Allen to create an effective ending for *Annie Hall* (1977):

"As usual, Woody was in a terrible quandary about how to end the film. On three separate outings in October, November, and December of 1976 he shot additional material for the last segment, much of it an attempt to show the process by which Alvy comes to miss Annie. He shot scenes in which he's calling Annie on the West Coast over and over again, scenes in which he's doing public-service commercials for educational TV, scenes with a new girl friend with whom he seems to be living while still unable to overcome his longing for Annie. He would audition this material for me in the cutting room and we would try to insert it in the movie. But finally I urged him to forget all of these dramatic transitions and have Alvy say 'I miss Annie — I made a terrible mistake,' on a flat cut from the scene in which Annie and Alvy are sorting out their things in his apartment — which is finally how the last segment gets underway.

"The final moments gave Woody the biggest problems. Several conclusions were shot. One of them, true to Woody's inclinations, was a real downer. He meets

Annie, repatriated in New York, dragging her new boy friend to see The Sorrow and the Pity. *The former lovers achieve 'maximum awkwardness,' and then, the awkwardness serving as the tear-jerker, they say good-bye. As I had done on* Take the Money and Run *and* Bananas, *I suggested he return to the beginning of the film for a clue about how to end.*

"In the opening monologue he attempts to summarize his attitudes toward life and toward women. He relates an old Groucho Marx joke — 'I would never wanna belong to any club that would have someone like me for a member' — and says, 'That's the key joke of my adult life in terms of my relationships with women.'

"Woody agreed that returning to this material in some way was his best option. He had hardly given it any thought before we were in a cab heading down to the studio, Woody scribbling notes on a piece of scrap paper on the way. The reading (which I do not remember and of which there is no record) came close to providing the finale we wanted, but it wasn't close enough. The following day he said he wanted to try something else, so again we jumped into a cab and Woody jotted down some new ideas as we rode. 'It was no big planned thing,' he recalls. 'I mean we were sitting grousing all day, looking at footage, cutting, recutting, dealing with other problems. I remember sitting with Ralph in the cutting room at five o'clock preparing for a seven o'clock screening that night and saying, let's go down to the sound studio and I'll put a jump at the end of the picture and wing the joke about the eggs. At five-thirty that night we got into the recording booth, ran back uptown and stuck that joke in, and it stayed forever.'

"The joke about the eggs was a tired old vaudeville gag that Woody adapted to his context. 'It was great seeing Annie again . . .' Woody narrates, as Annie and Alvy shake hands and part after a reminiscing lunch near Lincoln Center. 'I realized what a terrific person she was, and how much fun it was just knowing her. And I thought of that old joke: You know, this, this, this guy goes to a psychiatrist and says, "Doc, uh, my brother's crazy. He thinks he's a chicken." And, uh, the doctor says, "Well, why don't you turn him in?" And the guy says, "I would but I need the eggs." Well, I guess that is pretty much how I feel about relationships. You know, they're totally irrational and crazy and absurd and, but, uh, I guess we keep going through it because, uh, most of us need the eggs.'

"I suggested that Woody read the lines against the picture — that is, read them while simultaneously viewing the image of him and Keaton on the screen saying good-bye, something he rarely cares to do. When he was finished, he said, 'What do you think?' I knew his inclination would be to do a dozen more readings, each with slightly different accents and pauses and carefully timed stammers. I said, 'Leave it alone. Let's just walk away from it.' And later that night when I saw that ending with an audience, I knew my instinct was right. They were grabbed, the picture wrapped up, and the ending gave everything that came before it a new coloring: this was not just an hour and a half of light humor, but something more poignant.

"At one point during the editing of those last few minutes, after it was decided to have Alvy and Annie meet for the Lincoln Center lunch, Woody said something to me like, 'What about memory — shouldn't we have them discuss old times?' It was an incident I had forgotten about until, during the writing of this book, I asked my assistant, Sandy Morse, what had struck her most about the cutting of that pic-

ture. *As soon as the subject of memory arose, I knew what we needed to do. Sandy, who was relatively new to the cutting room then (she has since edited Woody's* Manhattan), *was startled by what followed. I rattled off descriptions of pieces of film I wanted her to get for me — a shot of Annie and Alvy driving uptown from the tennis courts, a shot of Woody squeamishly putting a wild lobster in the pot, a shot of them at the beach, a shot of them in bed (Annie reading and Alvy reaching over to kiss her), shots of Annie arriving at Alvy's apartment with her luggage, Annie holding up the porno negligée Alvy bought her for her birthday, and perhaps a dozen others — many more than we finally used.*

"Sandy quickly fetched me the reels, and I held them up to the light, showing her which frames I wanted — twenty feet of this, three feet of that, eight feet of this . . . make this number one, this number two, and so on. She spliced them all together on a single reel, and I edited them down to a reprise of Keaton singing her nightclub number, 'Seems Like Old Times' (all the memory moments are silent). One of my favorite cuts in that montage was Woody and Diane on a pier. He points, and we cut to what they 'see,' which turns out to be another memory cut of them kissing. That little transition helped augment the power of the reprise, although I put it together so intuitively I was hardly aware of its existence until Woody and I screened the film some time later."[5]

Quotations

1. Ralph Rosenblum and Robert Karen, *When the Shooting Stops . . . the Cutting Begins* (New York: Viking, 1979), pages 6–8.

2. Peter Bogdanovich, *Allan Dwan — The Last Pioneer* (New York: Praeger, 1971), page 120.

3. David O. Selznick, lecture at Columbia University, November 1937; reprinted in *Memo from David O. Selznick,* selected and edited by Rudy Behlmer (New York: Viking, 1972), page 475.

4. Verna Fields, quoted in *Filmmakers on Film-making, Volume 1,* edited by Joseph McBride for The American Film Institute (Los Angeles: J. P. Tarcher, 1983), pages 139–140.

5. Ralph Rosenblum and Robert Karen, pages 286–288.

"You must remember this": the original piano, newly restored, from Rick's Café that Dooley Wilson played in *Casablanca* (1943).

Music is the inseparable companion of movies. Certain songs or themes trigger our memories: the zither music from *The Third Man*, the ballad in *High Noon*, "As Time Goes By" in *Casablanca*, Scott Joplin's rags in *The Sting*, David Raksin's haunting theme from *Laura*, John Williams's from *Jaws*. Movies have enlarged the audience for the classics: Liszt's "Les Preludes" conjures up the *Flash Gordon* serials; Richard Strauss's "Thus Spake Zarathustra," the apes in *2001: A Space Odyssey*. *Amadeus* brought Mozart to the millions.

Even in the so-called silent era, the smallest theater had a pianist. The grander the showcase (and the first 5,000-seat movie palace was constructed as early as 1913), the more elaborate the musical accompaniment. Gaylord Carter, who recently celebrated his sixtieth anniversary as a theater organist, recalls his early years at the keyboard:

"I was earning a stupendous fifteen dollars a week [in 1922], and my hero was Jesse Crawford, probably the most famous theater organist who ever lived. He played all the great theaters in Los Angeles and Chicago and finally went to the Paramount in New York, where he earned twenty-five hundred a week, more than most movie stars — then and now.

"What the organ did was punctuate, underscore, bridge, follow the action musically in order to add a dimension to the picture that wouldn't be there otherwise. Believe me, without the organ accompaniment in silents most of the picture would have been as dull as succotash.

"People forget that silent pictures were never silent. Even when they were shooting these emotional scenes at the studio, say, John Barrymore making love to Mary Astor in Don Juan, there would be a violinist or a string quartet on the set. The music put the actors in the right mood. So in presenting organ music in the theater you were just amplifying what they were working to when the picture was being photographed.

"There was a different movie every night at the Sunshine. I never saw the picture till I got there. They would have what they called thematic cue sheets which would give the title of the picture and the musical cues all the way through. That was supplied by the studio. Each picture had a cue sheet which was delivered to the theater with the print of the film. Sometimes the cue sheets didn't help. I could

always tell when the projectionist had a heavy date — he'd speed up the tempo of the film, and I had to do some very fast improvising.

"After playing at the Sunshine, this little neighborhood house, for about two years, I got a job at the Seville Theater in Inglewood. Now this was a little better house. I had a nice pipe organ, a little larger than the one I'd been playing.

"I'd played for Arbuckle, Chaplin, Mary Pickford and Douglas Fairbanks pictures, but the biggest attraction was Harold Lloyd. . . . Harold and I got to be very, very dear friends. He was responsible for the biggest leap in my career. One day his representative apparently went to Lloyd and said something like, 'There's a kid in that theater, and he's just kicking the heck out of the score. He's really making the picture do something.' That particular picture, I recall, was The Freshman. Then Lloyd himself came down to see what I was doing. I guess he was satisfied. Years later, during one of my visits to his estate in Beverly Hills, he told me that he had mentioned me to the manager of the Million Dollar Theater in downtown Los Angeles. 'There is a kid out in the sticks you ought to get in your theater.'

"Let me tell you about my first show at the Million Dollar. Here I was, really a kid from the sticks, flung into a crème de la crème atmosphere. The picture was The Temptress, with Greta Garbo and Antonio Moreno. The pit orchestra had thirty-five pieces. On the stage there was an atmospheric prologue with live performers and Paul Whiteman and his concert orchestra. That night Whiteman played George Gershwin's 'Rhapsody in Blue.' It was the first time I'd heard it.

"The Million Dollar was a presentation house, where many of the pictures would run six months. A presentation house was something. The program would open with me playing a solo. Then the pit orchestra would appear to play the overture, and I accompanied them. This was followed by a newsreel and a comedy short, which I played. After that came the atmospheric prologue preceding the picture. The orchestra would play the first four or five minutes of the picture, and I'd be at the console for the rest of it. Then an attraction like Paul Whiteman. All this for thirty-five cents if you got in before four o'clock in the afternoon. Incredible!

"Our biggest premiere at the Million Dollar was the original Ben Hur in 1925, which played six months and could have played six years. In those days a premiere was as big an event as a Broadway opening. Outside there were klieg lights and

limousines and crowds, a bubble of excitement, of enchantment. Everybody would dress for the occasion, the men in black ties and tails, the women in stunning gowns. The stars of Ben Hur, Ramon Novarro and Francis X. Bushman, were there for the first night. So was the director, Fred Niblo. And Mary Pickford and Douglas Fairbanks.

"When the doors opened, I was playing. Before I went on, . . . the general manager . . . came to me and said, 'Gaylord, the people have to listen to you for a long time so just perfume the air with music.'"[1]

Max Steiner was one of the first and most prolific composers for sound pictures. A child prodigy in his native Vienna, and a professional conductor at age sixteen, he came to Hollywood by way of Broadway. Said Steiner: "Mahler predicted that I would become one of the greatest composers of all time.' Little did he know that I would end up at Warner Bros.!" His 300-film career began at RKO, establishing his reputation with *King Kong* (1933) and *The Informer* (1935). He moved to Warner Bros., where his successes included *Dark Victory* (1939), *Now Voyager* (1942), *Mildred Pierce* (1945), and *The Search-ers* (1956). But his triumph was *Gone With the Wind*, made while on loan to Selznick. He wrote:

"The way I approached writing music for films was to fit the music to what I thought the dramatic story should be and score according to the way a character impressed me, whoever he might be. He may be a bastard, she may be a wonder-ful woman, he may be a child. I write what I see. This is very difficult for anybody to understand. Especially for anybody with such bad eyesight as I have. But I see a character on the screen and that is what makes me write the way I do. That is also the reason that people enjoy what they hear because it happens to fit.

"I never write from a script. I run a mile every time I see one. If I started to write when I first saw the script, I would have been in Forest Lawn long ago because what they can do to a script is unheard of. I had one very bad experience like that. There was a picture called Pursued. It starred Robert Mitchum. So I read the script and thought it was the finest I had ever seen. I sat down and started writing themes for the picture. And I did the entire score. Then I saw the picture. It was terrible. What I had seen in the script was completely changed when the movie was released. I've never been so disappointed in a picture in my life. Since that day,

I've never looked at a script, because all the characters appear different to me in the script than in the picture.

"Strangely, in a musical, the musical director doesn't do anything. You're told what to do. They say, 'There's a number; orchestrate it.' That's all there is to it. Other-wise, there's a very technical aspect to this. That is, when you score or orchestrate for a sequence, you have to get it in proper timing with the film. There's a whole elaborate mathematics involved. You start with cue sheets. Everything is measured to a split second. I write a cue that may last for one minute and two-thirds sec-onds. It might be only a chord or some kind of musical trick. But I wait to do this until the picture is finished, unless, of course, they need some music for a song or a dance sequence while it is being shot. Otherwise, I never do until it's entirely com-pleted. Then I look at it once, maybe twice, but very rarely more than that. I have a photographic memory. I look at a picture once, and then the second time I run it with my cutter and my editor and tell them where to put the music. Then I get my timing, my cue sheets on which everything is written down. For example, there might be the line, 'Darling, I love you.' It says five seconds. Then after ten seconds he sits down, at fourteen seconds he gets up, at twenty-one seconds he punches her in the nose, at twenty-five seconds, and so forth. And then you write against that. I said in a book I once wrote years ago that to me the toughest thing for a film composer to know is where to start, where to end; that is, how to place your music. You can ruin a scene with music in the wrong place, and on the other hand, you can help it. Silence may be the most difficult problem of all.

"For me, there's no doubt about the way the character or a scene hits me. I can help a scene that may be too slow, or I can help a scene that's too fast. You might change the tempo of your music, and, if it's an uninteresting scene, the music can make it so exciting that you think they really said something."[2]

A few studio-era composers enjoy a legendary reputation. Erich Wolfgang Korngold — another child prodigy, from Czechoslovakia — had a twelve-year career with Warner Bros. In that short time, he created scores for *A Midsum-mer Night's Dream* (1935), *Anthony Adverse* (1936), and *King's Row* (1942); but his best-remembered work is for such Errol Flynn swashbucklers as *Captain Blood*, *The Adventures of Robin Hood*, and *The Sea Hawk*, in which his fanfares capture the essence of derring-do.

Gold Diggers of 1933: the Shadow Waltz number, staged by dance director Busby Berkeley, in which a hundred girls "play" neon-edged violins.

Gold Diggers of 1933: neon-edged violin used in the Shadow Waltz number. The violins were wired and lit for a spectacular finale in which an overhead camera shows all the small violins forming one giant illuminated violin, glowing in total darkness.

Promotional novelty for *Flying Down to Rio* (1933), marking the movie debut of Fred Astaire and Ginger Rogers. At its climax chorines appear to dance on the wings of a plane flying low over Rio.

Alfred Newman was a concert pianist at seven, and later, a symphony orchestra and Broadway conductor, before beginning his 200-film, forty-year triumph in Hollywood, during which he scored *Wuthering Heights* (1938), *Gunga Din* (1939), and *All About Eve* (1950), besides winning nine Oscars. German-born Franz Waxman was a master of atmosphere in such movies as *Rebecca* (1940), *Sunset Boulevard* (1950), and *A Place in the Sun* (1951).

At a time when concert hall attendance was much smaller than today, and the classics were considered intimidatingly highbrow, serious composers were able to express themselves and to include references to their favorites in movie scores. One of the most revered, Bernard Herrmann, studied at the Juilliard School and established an innovative chamber orchestra before joining CBS as composer and conductor for radio dramas. In 1936, he was assigned to Orson Welles's weekly program, "The Mercury Theater on the Air," and accompanied Welles to Hollywood. *Citizen Kane* was the movie debut for both men:

"I worked on the film [Citizen Kane, 1941], reel by reel, as it was being shot and cut. In this way I had a sense of the picture being built, and of my own music being a part of that building. Most musical scores in Hollywood are written after the film is entirely finished, and the composer must adapt his music to the scenes on the screen. In many scenes in Citizen Kane an entirely different method was used, many of the sequences being tailored to match the music.

"This was particularly true in the numerous photographic 'montages' which are used throughout the film to denote the passing of time. When I first saw the picture, I felt that it might be interesting to write complete musical numbers for these montages. In other words, instead of a mere atmospheric or rhythmic cue, a brief piece would be written. Welles agreed, and once the music was set, cut many of his sequences to match the length of the pieces.

"The most striking illustration of this method may be found in the breakfast montage between Kane and his first wife. Here, in the space of three or four minutes, Welles shows the rise and fall of affection between two married people. The setting is a breakfast table. The young couple enter, gay and very much in love. They talk for a few seconds, then the scene changes. Once more we see them at the breakfast table, but the atmosphere has changed. Discord is beginning to creep

into the conversation. Brief scene after brief scene follows, each showing the gradual breakdown of their affection, until finally they read their newspapers, opposite each other, in silence.

"For this montage, I used the old classic form of the theme and variations. A waltz in the style of Waldteufel is the theme. It is heard during the first scene. Then, as discord crops up, the variations begin. Each scene is a separate variation. Finally, the waltz theme is heard bleakly played in the high registers of the violins. . . .

"Leitmotifs are used in Citizen Kane to give unity to the score as a whole. I am not a great believer in the leitmotif as a device for motion picture music — but in this film it was practically imperative, because of the story itself and the manner in which it is unfolded.

"There are two main motifs. One — a simple four-note figure in the brass — is that of Kane's power. It is given out in the very first two bars of the film. The second motif is that of Rosebud. Heard as a solo on the vibraphone, it first appears during the death scene at the very beginning of the picture. It is heard again and again through the film under various guises, and if followed closely, is a clue to the ultimate identity of Rosebud itself.

"The motif of power is also transformed, being a vigorous piece of ragtime, a hornpipe polka, and at the end of the picture, a final commentary on Kane's life.

"In handling these motifs, I used a great deal of what might be termed 'radio scoring.' The movies frequently overlook opportunities for musical clues which last only a few seconds — that is, from five to fifteen seconds at the most — the reason being that the eye usually covers the transition. On the other hand, in radio dramas, every scene must be bridged by some sort of sound device, so that even five seconds of music becomes a vital instrument in telling the ear that the scene is shifting. I felt that in this film, where the photographic contrasts were often so sharp and sudden, a brief cue — even two or three chords — might heighten the effect immeasurably.

"In orchestrating the picture I avoided, as much as possible, the realistic sound of a large symphony orchestra. The motion picture sound track is an exquisitely sensitive medium, and with skillful engineering a simple bass flute solo, the pulsing of a bass drum, or the sound of muted horns can often be far more effective than half

Robert Usher's sketch for the movie version
of the Gershwin revue *Putting On the Ritz*
(1929), a stylized view of Manhattan.

Production sketch by Patrizia von Branden-
stein for *A Chorus Line* (1985), the ultimate
backstage musical, which was directed by
Richard Attenborough in an empty Broadway
theater.

Sammy Davis, Jr., leads the chorus of "It Ain't Necessarily So" in Sam Goldwyn's production of George Gershwin's opera *Porgy and Bess* (1959).

a hundred musicians playing away. Save for the opera sequence, some of the ballet montages, and a portion of the final scene, most of the cues were orchestrated for unorthodox instrumental combinations."[3]

Herrmann went on to score *The Magnificent Ambersons* for Welles (1942); *Vertigo* (1958), *North by Northwest* (1959), and *Psycho* (1960) for Hitchcock; and *Taxi Driver* (1976) for Martin Scorsese. Each score is counted among the finest of its kind.

Another giant of the studio era was Miklos Rozsa. A child violinist, Rozsa wrote his first movie compositions for 1930s classics produced in England by fellow Hungarian Alexander Korda. His forty-year career in Hollywood ranged from psychological drama *(Spellbound, A Double Life)* to historical epics *(Ben Hur, El Cid)*. Herrmann's experience on *Citizen Kane* was exceptional— no other director enjoyed the privileges Welles secured for his first outing. Rozsa had to struggle to get his way:

"In Double Indemnity *(1944) I introduced certain asperities of rhythm and harmony which wouldn't have caused anyone familiar with the 'serious' musical scene to bat an eyelid, but which did cause consternation in certain musical quarters in Hollywood. The musical director of Paramount—a former café violinist—couldn't stand the score from the beginning, and told me so. Did I really have to have a G sharp in the second fiddles clashing with a G natural in the violas an octave below? In his opinion the place for such eccentricities was Carnegie Hall, not a movie studio. I thanked him for the compliment, and he assured me it wasn't meant as such and that the score would be thrown out lock, stock, and barrel after the sneak preview. In fact, everybody liked what I'd done and the score was used, but the story gives you some idea of how difficult it was to maintain any decent level of musical integrity in the Hollywood of those days. People with a 'serious' musical upbringing such as myself, Herrmann and Korngold were the exception rather than the rule.*

"If a song such as 'Yes, We Have No Bananas' is used in a picture about the twenties, painstaking research ascertains the date of publication, but no one seems to care much if early Christians in the first century sing 'Onward, Christian Soldiers' by Sir Arthur Sullivan, composed a mere nine hundred years later! Of course compromise is involved, since what is stylistically accurate isn't necessarily dramatically practicable, and I've made a point of taking each picture on its own terms. In

Plymouth Adventure *(1952), the story of the Pilgrim Fathers, I used as the main theme a melody from the one book with music the Pilgrim Fathers had on board when they sailed: Henry Ainsworth's Psalter. Elsewhere I imitated the manner of the 17th-century English lutenists. In this way I could get a convincing sense of period atmosphere and at the same time make the music do what dramatically it had to do.*

"In Quo Vadis *(1951) I used fragments from contemporary Greek and early Christian sources, but in* Julius Caesar *(1953), where the focal point is the Shakespearean drama, not the setting, I made no such attempt. I simply wrote interpretative incidental music in my own idiom, as for a modern stage production. I don't think I have the reputation of being difficult to work with, although I did have to put my foot down over* Ben Hur *(1959) when I was expected to use 'O Come All Ye Faithful' for the Nativity scene, 'because it was the first Christmas.' They also wanted me to use my theremin for Christ, but I opted for something much less arty — soft organ chords and high strings — and I have a feeling it worked."*[4]

Today's composers suffer from the paradox that movie music, formerly denigrated, has become almost too popular. Producers are interested more in a hit sound-track album than a well-matched score. Title songs and anthologies of rock numbers can generate millions. John Williams has achieved unprecedented wealth and celebrity: his music for *Jaws,* the *Star Wars* trilogy, *Superman, E.T.,* and the Indiana Jones pictures has outsold the sum of every other movie score, and allows him the luxury of returning to the concert stage.

But other important contemporaries are underemployed. Elmer Bernstein (*The Magnificent Seven, To Kill a Mockingbird,* and *Thoroughly Modern Millie*) and Alex North (*A Streetcar Named Desire, Who's Afraid of Virginia Woolf?,* and *Under the Volcano*) deserve greater exposure. Leonard Rosenman has been more fortunate. A professor of music and an innovative composer/conductor who studied under Arnold Schoenberg, he continues the tradition of Korngold, Herrmann, and Rozsa in combining serious endeavor with popular success. He won Oscars for *Barry Lyndon* (1975) and *Bound for Glory* (1976) and Emmys for television movies. He offers outspoken opinions on his craft:

"There's too much music in movies. When I first started to work in films I worked at Warner Brothers, and they had wall-to-wall music. If the film was an hour and a half long the score was an hour and a half long. At that time the last of the filmic Mesozoic giants, Jack Warner, was the head of the studio; he had been indoctrinated very strongly by his own experience in silent films. The function of music in the silent films was to add sound effects and also to cover up all kinds of realistic sounds — popcorn, the toilet flushing, the projection machine — to remove the idea of reality so that the audience would be able to suspend disbelief. The minute you suspend disbelief you are in films. Like most of the early pioneers in films, Jack evidently felt that music had a magical mystery power, a subliminal power. So they began to use it indiscriminately. It was like an enema in the Jewish family tradition. 'It can't hurt you' was the idea.

"They did not realize that diminishing returns set in — that if you had music from frame alpha to frame omega, you had come back to the original idea of the silents: after a while you didn't hear the music anymore. If you happen to see an old Warner Brothers movie like Anthony Adverse *[1937], those films with wall-to-wall music, after a while you feel like saying, 'Stop the music!' Music couldn't possibly do for the audience what Jack and the other old filmmakers felt music could do. Because if you don't hear it, why use it?*

"Alex North and I are credited with bringing film music into the twentieth century. When I came on the scene in 1954 to do East of Eden, *I was an ex–college professor and had made some kind of a reputation in the concert field as an avant-garde composer, concert pianist, and conductor. James Dean [the star of* East of Eden*] was a piano student of mine, and took Elia Kazan [the director of the film] to a concert I gave at the Museum of Modern Art in New York. Kazan asked me if I would score a film. I knew nothing about movies except that I liked them. When I came on the scene, the big composers in this town were Max Steiner, Dimitri Tiomkin, Bernard Herrmann, and Erich Wolfgang Korngold, who was already dying but was still there.*

"The kind of music these composers wrote basically had its roots in the nineteenth century with the romantic music of Rachmaninoff, Strauss, Tchaikovsky, Schumann, and Brahms. If, for example, there was a single line in a film, that line was not played by an oboe or a flute; that line was played by all the violins, all the trumpets, all the flutes, all the oboes, and all the clarinets. No one ever took any chances. If you hear a lot of the old scores extracted from the films — which you

can today because the sound-track records are coming back — the music has an incredible thickness to it. It's not a thickness of luster, it's a thickness of turgidity, a lack of profile, a lack of inner voices moving, a lack of counterpoint. It just sounds elephantine.

"I remember the first time they recorded *Eden*. I had a solo flute play something and he stopped in the middle and looked around; I said, 'What's the problem?' He said, 'There isn't anyone playing with me.' I said, 'No, I'm afraid you have to count.' So it became an entirely new development, having a large orchestra but using small chamber ensembles within that orchestra, and using very few entire orchestra sections. You had a curiously different sound in film music. You had much more of a clear focus of the drama, a potentially much greater palette of color in the score. Jack Warner felt rather strange about that because he saw all the orchestra doing nothing, and he didn't like the idea of not having them playing at the same time.

"Ideally speaking, the composer should make you see something in that film that you couldn't have seen without the music. The music enters the plot directly.

"For example, you have an opening shot, which you've seen many times, I'm sure — a helicopter shot of New York. This helicopter goes down into the canyons of New York, and you see people rushing around, cars; it goes smack into the so-called concrete jungle. You have several options with the sound track. You have the option of having it silent, which would create a certain kind of mood. You have the option of the sound effects of the city, which would be a kind of realism, a documentary style. You have the option of writing the kind of big-city music you used to hear in the old films, a lot of xylophones, à la Gershwin, musical sound effects which don't really add to anything you've seen on the screen except reinforce it to some degree.

"Then you might have another idea. Suppose the filmmaker says, 'Is there any way for the music to say that the city, for all its tremendous crowds, is a very lonely place?' If the composer took a lonely saxophone line with a lot of echo and played a long, slow, plaintive tune against this terrific mélange, you would get an idea of the city you couldn't have gotten without that sound track. In other words, the sound track would tell you something about the scene that the image itself couldn't tell you. This, in my estimation, is the role of music in movies.

"It has to do with the communication between the filmmaker and the composer. The composer has to be interested enough to get into the film at the very beginning, before the script has even jelled. Generally film composers are not that interested; it takes too much time and they don't make enough money. Step two, if the scriptwriter knows enough about music to understand its nature and its relationship to the drama he's creating, if he can say, 'I think the music can take the place of the written word in this scene' — if he can do that, a real collaboration begins. It would seem to me that the only way to communicate between a filmmaker and a composer is verbally, and that is extremely imprecise. The only advice I can offer to all potential filmmakers in regard to working with a composer — and I have to resort to the language of the young — is that the vibes have to be very good. There has to be a sense of trust. There has to be a mutual understanding of what the music is trying to say in the film. That's the most important consideration."[5]

Quotations

1. Gaylord Carter, interviewed on music for silents in *You Must Remember This*, edited by Walter Wagner (New York: G. P. Putnam, 1975), pages 68–70.

2. Max Steiner, interviewed in *The Real Tinsel*, edited by Bernard Rosenberg and Harry Silverstein (New York: Macmillan, 1970), pages 392–393.

3. Bernard Herrmann, interviewed in the *New York Times*, May 25, 1941; reprinted in *The Voices of Film Experience*, edited by Jay Leyda (New York: Macmillan, 1977), pages 198–199.

4. Miklos Rozsa, interviewed in *Music & Musicians*, December 1972; reprinted in *The Voices of Film Experience*, pages 409–410.

5. Leonard Rosenman, in *Filmmakers on Filmmaking, Volume 1*, edited by Joseph McBride for The American Film Institute (Los Angeles: J. P. Tarcher, 1983), pages 114–119.

Other sources

Irwin Bazelon, *Knowing the Score: Notes on Film Music* (New York: Van Nostrand Reinhold, 1975).

Miles Kreuger, *The Movie Musical — From Vitaphone to 42nd Street* (New York: Dover, 1975).

James Limbacher, *Film Music: From Violins to Video* (Metuchen, N.J.: Scarecrow Press, 1974).

Lawrence O'Toole, "Moving Music," *Film Comment*, September–October 1981.

John Springer, *All Singing, All Talking, All Dancing* (New York: Citadel Press, 1966).

King Kong (1933): concept sketch drawn by
Mario Larrinaga, Willis O'Brien, and Byron
Crabbe to help sell the project to RKO.

French poster for *King Kong* (1933), whose spectacular retelling of the fable of *Beauty and the Beast* achieved international acclaim.

"Scriptwriters have no limits on their imagination. What we do is make photographable anything they can come up with. All it takes is mechanical ability, a knowledge of hydraulics, pneumatics, electronics, engineering, construction, ballistics, explosives and no acquaintance with the word *impossible.*" — Danny Lee[1]

That catalogue of expertise covers only a part of the world of special effects. Full-scale mechanical effects — a man-made shark, an exploding bridge, or a runaway car — can be supplemented with miniatures and stop-motion puppets, optical effects and matte work. These techniques are used, singly or in combination, to conjure up places that never were or which are inaccessible (an alien planet, a dinosaur's lair, the inside of a nuclear reactor). They can be used to protect live actors or to save money. They may be employed unobtrusively or to bring the audience to the edge of its seats.

Illusions can be achieved through human imagination or electronic wizardry. Arnold Gillespie, who engineered the earthquake in *San Francisco,* the tornado in *The Wizard of Oz,* and the chariot race in both *Ben Hurs,* created the locust swarm in *The Good Earth* by filming coffee grounds settling in water, reversing the film, and combining it with footage of actors. *The Return of the Jedi* involved over 900 special-effects shots, some comprising up to twenty-eight visual elements each; a professional team of 300; computer-controlled cameras and other state-of-the-art equipment.

Actor Rod La Rocque recalled how Paramount expert Roy Pomeroy parted the Red Sea for Cecil B. De Mille's *The Ten Commandments* (1923):

"Two blocks of Jello [sic], carved with waves, were set on a huge table which was split in the center. These two blocks were held together with water rushing over them. On cue, winches turned the blocks and separated them as water came over the edge. With the screen Jello shimmering and going away, they ran the thing forward, and it closed. When [the film] was reversed, it opened. We had double exposures which were so realistic that we were hounded by the Society for the Prevention of Cruelty to Animals, who wanted to know why we had treated the horses so cruelly. Chariots, horses and riders had tumbled into the Jello. Mr. De Mille asked these people, 'Aren't you worried about the human beings at all?' When we proved that it was a trick, all was forgiven."[2]

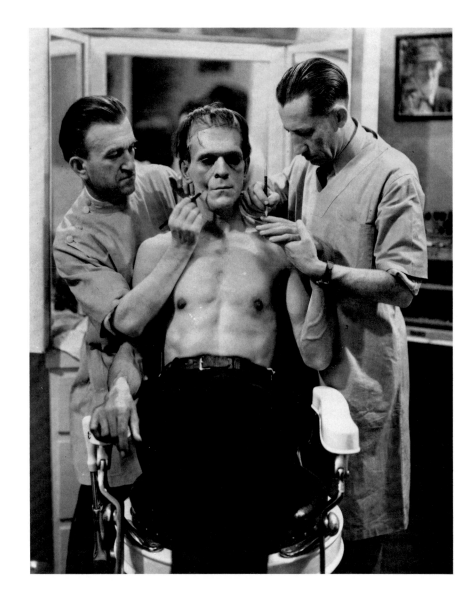

Frankenstein (1931): makeup artist Jack Pierce (left) and assistant transform Boris Karloff into the monster.

The Exorcist (1973): Dick Smith's swivel-headed mannequin of Linda Blair possessed by the devil.

Many techniques that are still in use date back to the earliest years of the movies. French pioneer Georges Méliès created striking optical effects in the camera in the 1900s. Glass paintings were introduced around that time to supplement partial sets and painted backdrops. Later, glass or "matte" paintings were used in combination with live action.

Similar effects were achieved using hanging miniatures, a process that is now rarely employed. A hanging miniature, representing the upper storeys of the cathedral in *The Hunchback of Notre Dame* (1923), was suspended in a position that appeared to the camera as though it matched the life-size set of the lower storeys. In the 1925 *Ben Hur,* a hanging miniature that was used in conjunction with the set of the Roman circus contained rows of miniature figures that could be moved up and down in response to the actions of the live actors on the bleachers.

Miniatures were used from the beginning. In 1898, showman E. H. Amet presented what he claimed was a newsreel of the U.S. naval victory over the Spanish fleet in Santiago harbor — shot from six miles away, using "a supersensitive moonlight film." What he had done was construct a scale model of the harbor and use several toy boats to recreate the battle according to the press accounts.

Willis O'Brien developed puppet animation for the first successful dinosaur picture, *The Ghost of Slumber Mountain* (1919), and refined it in *The Lost World* (1925) and *King Kong* (1933). The Kong that climbs a model Empire State Building was an eighteen-inch-high jointed metal skeleton, covered in fur, that was filmed in stop-motion, one frame (i.e., one twenty-fourth of a second) at a time. Countless monster pictures — as well as *Star Wars* — have used similar techniques in the years since.

Linwood Dunn helped invent the optical printer and used it for *King Kong* and later films at RKO (including *Flying Down to Rio* — in which chorus girls appear to dance on the wings of a plane in flight — and *Citizen Kane*). The device, which Dunn perfected in the 1940s, is the workhorse of trick photography. In essence it is a camera that rephotographs reels of film, adding fades and dissolves, double exposures and composite scenes, and a variety of special effects.

Miniature ship used in the filming of *Mutiny on the Bounty* (1935) at MGM Studios. The opening scenes of the movie were staged with miniatures, each of which was fastidiously crafted.

Farciot Edwards developed rear projection at Paramount in the 1930s. As the term suggests, film (typically of a street as seen from a moving car) is projected as a backdrop to live action, on a screen behind the actors. It became a cliché in the films of the studio era and has largely been replaced by front projection, which allows a brighter, more credible image.

Arnold Gillespie at MGM was unfailingly inventive. In 1945, he budgeted the re-creation of an atomic bomb explosion at $10,000. No film had yet been released on the tests or of the attacks on Hiroshima and Nagasaki. Gillespie filmed dye in water — inspired by an old Tarzan movie — and the footage was so convincing that it was incorporated into a USAF training film. On *The Wizard of Oz* (1939), he created an anthology of special effects. The tornado was a thirty-five-foot-long muslin wind sock, suspended from a steel gantry and stiffened with wire so that it would hold its shape as it snaked around. An air hose blew dust through the muslin to soften the outline. A three-foot model house was dropped onto the stage; when the film was reversed the house appeared to be flying into the sky. The wizard's disembodied head was projected on a cloud of steam. In the scene where the Wicked Witch melts away, Margaret Hamilton stood on an elevator; her costume, pinned to the floor, flattened as she descended.

Hitchcock's pictures were always a challenge. Production designer Robert Boyle recalls the making of the Mount Rushmore sequence in *North by Northwest*. The original plan was to shoot on location in South Dakota. But the working title of the movie, "The Man in Lincoln's Nose," and some tactless remarks by Hitchcock persuaded the National Park Service to refuse permission. Boyle was lowered over the edge in a rusty bosun's chair (originally used by the sculptor) to take stereoscopic photos of the heads. These served as models for a painted backdrop, matte paintings, and constructed sections, all of which were shot on stage at MGM and optically combined.

Alfred Hitchcock described his experience on a later film:

"The Birds posed so many problems that I didn't even bother bringing them up before we started the picture. I did not say, 'Can you do this? Can you do that?' The scenes were written in and we had to discover how to do it afterwards. We trained 3,200 birds all told: gulls, crows, ravens, individual ones, groups. The whole thing was a matter of double-printing.

"The shower of birds down the chimney was real. We rented so many finches. The trouble was that we had to keep them flying by the use of air hoses (of course we had the Society for the Prevention of Cruelty to Animals on the set) because by nature they want to perch, they wouldn't fly around, they were domestic birds. Then we printed them. Then we put a lot in a glass cage and let them fly around against a plain background and printed it on top of the real ones. So we had a double lot of birds: those in the room around the people and those in the glass cage.

"The final scene of the birds' going out was done with about sixteen exposures on one piece of film. One little tiny section was shot down a road with five hundred ducks painted grey. Foreground birds were printed over. That was a tremendously complicated job. It's done by optical printer; a man from Disney was in charge of it. It's quadruple-treble printing. It's by far the most difficult single shot I've ever done, but nobody will ever know.

"Nor does anyone apparently wonder about the 'bird's eye view' shot over the gasoline station, asking, 'Where was that shot from? A balloon?' The seaside was up at Bodega Bay. The other side of the road was on the studio back-lot, because there were only meadows opposite at Bodega Bay. We created the town on a matte. We did it by putting the camera on a high hill shooting down to a new parking-lot they were building. We put in the blazing car, etc., and all the rest was left blank. Then the matte artist painted in the whole scene and we fitted the two pieces together. In other words, on his painting the live parts looking down are black. On our side you can see the live part, but all the rest, all his part, is painted black. Then you put the two together.

"Now the travelling matte system is a means of printing one thing over another without ghosting. In order to do that you must have a silhouette. Let me describe how it was done in the old days. Say I wanted to do two men talking on the corner of Fifth Avenue. Normally we'd do that in Hollywood with a back projection: Fifth Avenue on the screen and the two men in front. But supposing we are making this film in the summer and we want snow on Fifth Avenue. We aren't going to release it until January. In those circumstances we photograph the two men against a white backing (I'm talking about a black-and-white film). We put that film aside and wait until about November or December when the first snows fall and then we photograph the background independently.

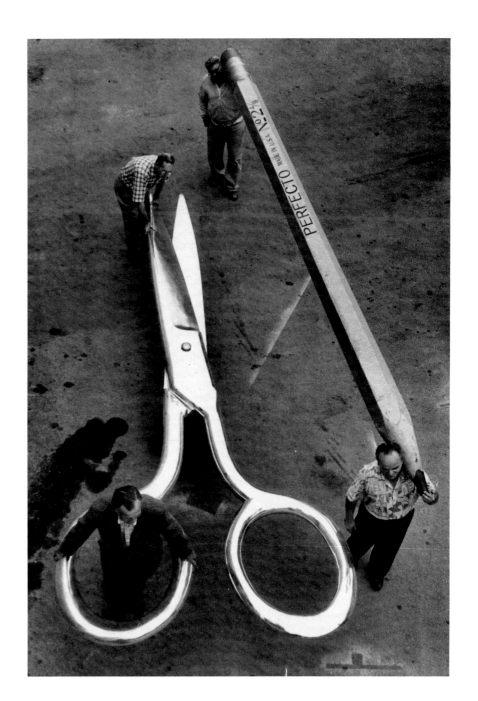

Los Angeles in ruins: Albert Whitlock's matte painting for the climactic scene of *Earthquake* (1974). Film of live actors was superimposed on the blacked-out area of this background.

"What do we have now? We have a background of Fifth Avenue with snow and two men shot last July against a white backing. You have to superimpose one over the other without ghosting. In other words, if we printed the two together you'd see through the men, as happened in the old days when you could take two snaps on the same film. So we take the positive, the print of the two men against the white, and overdevelop it to such a degree that the two men become silhouettes. That is called a travelling matte. Then we put raw, unexposed film in the printing-machine. Against that we put the negative of Fifth Avenue and against that the silhouette of the two men. Now you print that.

"As the printing light goes through, it's printing Fifth Avenue blocked off by the two men. If we were to print that at that moment, we'd have two white figures, two white silhouettes against Fifth Avenue. But you don't print it. You rewind your first film, the raw film, take away the negative of Fifth Avenue — you've finished with that — and take away the black silhouettes of the two men. Now you put in the negative of the two men which was shot against a white background. On the negative it's now black, and you can see through the two men. So you put it through again so that the unexposed portion — the two men — is now printed in its proper place.

"That's how we made The Birds, *except that we made our silhouette at the same time we made our color shot. Our color shot is done against a yellow background, and in the camera is a prism. The prism will take the straight color negative and at right angles it will take a second image on black-and-white film through a red filter, turning that image into a silhouette. The red filter, the prism, is what we call a split beam: it takes the thing twice, once straight through and once at right angles. The right-angled one is on ordinary black-and-white film, not on color film. The reason the background's yellow is the same as fog light's yellow: it's the lowest band in the spectrum of color and comes out black. It's the one color that won't photograph, this yellow light, called sodium light.*

"So in that shot I described before — the one from above — I wanted the gulls to descend. We went out here to a high cliff, put some food behind the camera and gulls came immediately. Then we took the food and threw it down to a beach below the cliff, whereupon the gulls went down for the food, away from the camera and down to the beach.

Alfred Hitchcock's *The Birds* (1963): sketch by Albert Whitlock for a composite shot that combined live action, a matte painting by Whitlock, and other special effects. Production designer: Robert Boyle.

"When the film was brought back to the studio we had gulls going down towards a beach against surf, sand, and the side of a cliff. It took two women three months to copy each gull on to a plain board and a silhouette on another board, frame by frame. They had a method whereby they transferred the thing almost like a lantern slide on to a card, and they merely had to paint over the actual birds themselves. Then they would take that and make a silhouette as well. When they made their film, we had live gulls against a plain background, each one drawn separately, and that was printed over the other matte shot. And people thought we shot it from a balloon or a helicopter!

"Similarly, in the birds' attack on the children, we shot the children in a real place running down the street, and then in the studio, against a plain background, we shot the birds flying from one perch to another, about thirty feet apart. We made a silhouette of that against a yellow background and printed it over the shot of the children, and then the real birds over that.

"The bird pecking 'Tippi' Hedren's head was done by the same method. We let a bird dive against a plain background, and double-printed it over a shot of 'Tippi' against the sea to coincide with the moment when we sent a squirt of air through a tube placed in her hair, which shot up as if the bird had actually pecked her."[3]

The success of *The Birds* depended, in part, upon the artistry of Albert Whitlock, one of the great matte painters. His association with Hitchcock began in England in the 1930s. Whitlock's Hollywood credits include *Earthquake* (1974) and *The Hindenburg* (1975) — both of which won Oscars; *The Man Who Would Be King* (1975), and *Greystoke* (1984). He uses an impressionistic technique, in which the brush strokes and the vibration of the colors create an illusion of reality when lit for the camera. In *Bound for Glory* (1976), he simulated a prairie dust storm so convincingly, it was used for a report on drought in the CBS Evening News. To create the effect:

"The Sacramento delta town of Isleton was photographed from high atop a water tower. Later, back in the studio, this image was projected and traced onto a large pane of glass. Al Whitlock then painted directly on the glass, adding some buildings, changing the landscape and covering all evidence of the [past] four decades. The finished painting, perfectly matching the color and tone of the original photography, became its own matte, the camera acting as an optical printer, with the glass lit from behind and Whitlock's painting masking out unwanted parts. The film was then rewound and, on a second camera pass, the painting was relit — this time from the front — and a finished piece of film was created: a prairie town in the thirties.

"So much for the background. To achieve the actual dust-storm effect, Whitlock photographed three revolving discs (roughly the size of buffer attachments you might add to your electric drill to wax your car) on which he had glued cotton and that he had spray-painted dusty brown and gray. In a separate series of three shootings, he photographed the buffers — two revolving clockwise, the other counterclockwise — which he then superimposed as a collage over the painting of the town. By overexposing the top half and angling the buffers away from the camera to get a sense of depth, Whitlock was able to create the perfect effect...."[4]

Still active, Whitlock is a link to a past era of personal craftsmanship; of individuals creating effects unaided and with the simplest of tools. It was a tradition that almost died with the decline of the studios. The 1950s were alive with aliens and monsters; Hollywood landed its first man on the moon as early as 1950. But, by the 1960s, fantasy had lost ground to reality; the movies had nothing to put up against NASA.

The watershed between old and new was *2001: A Space Odyssey* (1968). Director Stanley Kubrick hired the young Douglas Trumbull, who had created the short film *Universe* for the Canadian National Film Board. Made under tight security in London, *2001* had an electrifying impact on the young, while bewildering older critics with its elliptical narrative and emphasis on the poetry of the unknown. Trumbull's effects were like nothing ever seen before: they launched his career as a technical wizard and attracted scores of young recruits to a moribund profession. These whiz kids — often artists doubling as technicians — move from one special-effects house to another, from one movie to the next (like medieval stonemasons), creating ever more complex and sophisticated illusions.

Largest of these companies is Industrial Light and Magic, established in 1975 by George Lucas to create special effects for *Star Wars* — and the movies that he and others have produced since then. A fluctuating staff of up to 300 enjoys

Sketch of a space station in Stanley Kubrick's
2001: A Space Odyssey (1968). Its success made
a star of special effects and attracted a host of
talented newcomers.

Ghostbusters (1984): Mark Stetson with the miniature "Gozer Temple," whose construction he supervised. It was combined on film with paintings, optical effects, and location footage to suggest a real building on Central Park West in New York. Photo by Virgil Mirano.

resources and a status that remind some of Walt Disney Productions in the heyday of animation. ILM was formerly headed by John Dykstra, who now has his own company, Apogee, and Richard Edlund, who won four Oscars for his work with Lucas and then took over Trumbull's Entertainment Effects Group (now Boss Film Corporation) and created the effects for *Blade Runner* and *Ghostbusters*.

Each company has its own style and area of expertise, but all use similar tools. Most important of these, and the key to the *Star Wars* generation of special effects, is the high-speed, 65mm computer-controlled camera. Used in conjunction with such well-established tools as matte paintings, miniatures, and blue screen, this camera can be used to generate multiple high-resolution images, which are layered together like a collage. Typically, the camera might move across a tabletop model, to which master shot will be added tiny projections of moving lights; miniature space vehicles, filmed one at a time, to simulate movement; and finally, film of figures that appear to be moving within these craft. The high speed of the camera (four or five times normal) will create the illusion of scale, in just the same way as a camera was rigged to capture the fall of the model King Kong from the model Empire State Building in 1933.

This comparison suggests that very little in the movies is new: the latest equipment may have greater capability, but the results depend less on tools than the quality of the story and the artist's eye. At his best, Steven Spielberg is able to rise above effects to achieve a timeless magic. His account of how he and his designers conceived the *Close Encounters* mother ship and extraterrestrials is instructive:

"My first concept of the mother ship was terrible. It was a black, pie-shaped wedge, with a little tip on the end; a phantom shape that blotted out the stars. All you knew was that something darker than the sky was moving out from behind the mountain. For me, that was going to be very terrifying, to see something so huge that it just blacked out the sky. No bulkhead, no rivets, nothing! Then, at the last minute, it would turn on its lights and land. That was the concept and the wedge was built. Then I said to myself, 'What am I leading up to, a Sara Lee pie tin in the third act of my movie? After all that's gone before, a black wedge is going to offer cosmic bliss?'

Producer George Lucas with space hardware created by Industrial Light and Magic for *The Return of the Jedi* (1982). Photo by Terry Chostner.

Concept sketch by Ron Cobb for one of the Cantina creatures in *Star Wars* (1977).

HIGH TUNDRA
(MAMMAL LIKE)
HERBIVORE.
EXCELENT MECHANIC.
VERY GRUMPY - SMELL BAD.

RON COBB
2403 A
34TH ST. SANTA MONICA
90405.....

Miniature of the *Millennium Falcon* used in the production of *Star Wars* (1977) at Industrial Light and Magic. Each of the important miniatures in the trilogy was constructed in different sizes to be used for long and close shots. Photo by Terry Chostner.

Mother Ship from *Close Encounters of the Third Kind* (1977), in which Steven Spielberg invested the extraterrestrial with a childlike sense of wonder. The alien craft was inspired by the night view of a Bombay oil refinery.

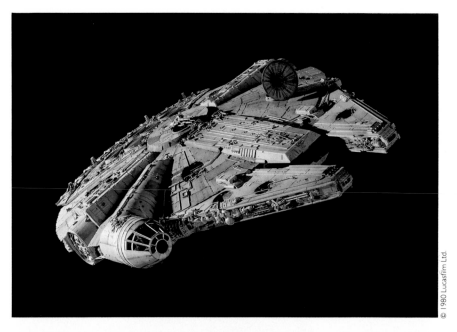

"The catharsis came in Bombay, India. On the way to and from the Bombay location, I passed a huge oil refinery with about ten thousand lights inside pipes and tubes. It was amazing to see at night. I made a sketch of it. When I came back to Los Angeles, I was up on Mulholland Drive, and I said, 'Wouldn't it be neat to take the lights of the San Fernando Valley and invert them beneath the oil refinery concept from Bombay.' I had George Jensen draw it up, then Ralph McQuarrie took it further, and that's how the mother ship came into being. It's a distillation of both of those thoughts. The mother ship was the last four weeks of effects photography. Otherwise you would have seen a frozen-food tray landing at Devils Tower.

"There were things that I wanted to get on the screen that I didn't get. There was a sequence I committed to film in which fifty extraterrestrials mass themselves around three or four technicians and touch and stroke and fondle them. It was a beautiful idea, but it just didn't work on film. It looked like a violation of the Morals Act.

"It was always my original intention to go all the way and show the extraterrestrials. I never had any doubts that I would not show the extraterrestrials until I began seeing the dailies. Then I said, 'Stanley Kubrick's right. He withheld his information for a reason. He made the same test I made.' But I decided to just hold my breath, accept the criticism, and show them.

"They were always going to be humanoid, because that's what people report. I was walking a fine line between my own imagination and what people report when they see a UFO and its occupants. They report small, spindly creatures. They don't report blobs on skateboards. It's really a human shape. I wanted to stay true to the extraterrestrial hypothesis here on earth. But I tried different faces; I tried different kinds of bodies. At one point, I said, 'Hey, I don't want these extraterrestrials to walk; they don't use their legs.' We built some roller skates, set up the cameras with heavy backlight, then sent kids in leotard costumes over the ramp on the roller skates. It was amazing. Forty extraterrestrials falling and picking themselves up, sliding down backward, trying to crawl up on all fours. Complete disaster! A full day wasted. Another problem arose when they began walking down the ramp. The ramp was too slippery, so they began sliding on their rear ends. It was as if Chuck Jones had written the scenario for the last part of Close Encounters. We couldn't get anything right.

Teddy bears triumph over technology: concept painting by Ralph McQuarrie of Ewoks attacking Walkers in *The Return of the Jedi* (1982).

Three-stage preparatory sketch for E.T. by Carlo Rambaldi. Right to left : model covered with skinlike foam rubber; schematic anatomical structure; actual mechanical structure.

Painting by production designer Anthony Masters for *Dune* (1984), a richly textured adaptation of Frank Herbert's visionary novel.

© 1983 Lucasfilm Ltd.

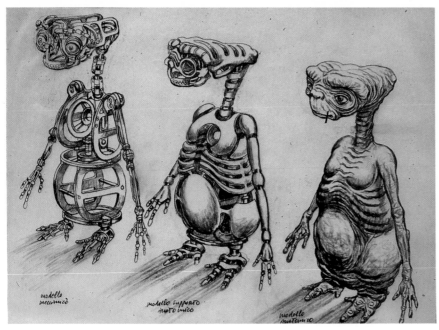

Ridley Scott's *Blade Runner* (1982) offered a
nightmare view of twenty-first-century urban
life. The "Hades" scenes were created from
multiple camera passes over the miniature
and enhanced by a layering of optical effects.
Photo by Virgil Mirano.

Shooting a table-top model of the "Hades" industrial zone for *Blade Runner* (1982) at Boss Film Corporation, using a computer-controlled, high-speed 65mm camera. Photo by Virgil Mirano.

© 1982 The Blade Runner Partnership

"There were three kinds of extraterrestrials. The first, the kids in leotards, were mostly little black girls. Boys are tough and stand stiffly, but girls are much more poised and graceful. So all summer long we had about fifty little girls running around. The second, which comes out and raises its arms in greeting, was a marionette developed by Bob Baker. The third was a Carlo Rambaldi invention controlled off-camera with levers and wires. It had musculature operating under a pliable substance that's like baby skin. I kissed it on the cheek, and it was like kissing an infant. We had to study the facial reactions of a child smiling and then pull the right levers in the right sequence to allow the extraterrestrial to smile in a posthuman way. That took a week."[5]

The star appeal of special effects is cyclical, and it is sure to wane. Like production numbers, special effects can advance the action or stop it dead. Remarked one critic: "Effects that aren't novel don't dazzle, and for audiences used to oversize sharks, cute robots and world-class explosions, familiarity breeds contempt. When you've seen one spaceship as big as Manhattan drift gracefully over your shoulder into deep screen space, you've seen them all. . . ."[6]

The future is sure to yield still more spectacular hardware and light shows; today's moviegoers are very young and, as Disney has discovered, there's a new wave of fans every seven years. But the man who started the present cycle, Douglas Trumbull, has moved in a new direction. His current concern is to spread the word on Showscan, a projection system of such high resolution that the images achieve a visceral impact. It draws on the same technology used in special-effects cameras. And ILM's thrust is toward computer simulation of real environments — electronic sets that will dramatically cut the costs of conventional productions.

Quotations

1. Danny Lee, in *American Cinematographer*, March 1965.

2. Rod La Rocque, interviewed in *The Real Tinsel*, edited by Bernard Rosenberg and Harry Silverstein (New York: Macmillan, 1970), page 245.

3. Alfred Hitchcock, interviewed in *The Celluloid Muse: Hollywood Directors Speak*, edited by Charles Higham and Joel Greenberg (Chicago: Henry Regnery, 1969), pages 99–100.

4. Pennfield Johnson, "So That's How They Do It!," *Playboy*, January 1978; © 1977, Playboy.

5. Steven Spielberg, seminar at The American Film Institute, quoted in *American Film*, September 1978.

6. Donald Chase, "War of the Wizards," *American Film*, June 1982.

Other sources

The ASC Treasury of Visual Effects, conceived by Linwood G. Dunn, edited by George E. Turner (Hollywood: American Society of Cinematographers, 1983).

John Brosnan, *Movie Magic* (New York: New American Library, 1976).

John Culhane, *Special Effects in the Movies* (New York: Ballantine, 1981).

Christopher Finch, *Special Effects: Creating Movie Magic* (New York: Abbeville Press, 1984).

Orville Goldner and George E. Turner, *The Making of King Kong* (New York: Ballantine, 1976).

Clark Gable chatting to an extra between takes on *San Francisco* (1936). Photo by Alfred Eisenstaedt.

Jules Feiffer recalls his first heroes:

"Not for a moment did I believe that I was meant to live in the Bronx. I was not meant to be poor. A terrible mistake had been made. At four and a half, I learned that only movies could correct it.

"Shirley Temple was my age exactly, and there she was up there on the great screen, my size, surrounded not by Depression-ridden adults but by men in dinner jackets, women in gowns, Negro butlers, long white marble stairways.

"I lived three flights up. It was a bore, at four and a half, to climb up and down three flights. But to dance with my black butler on Shirley Temple's stairway, steeper than ten Bronx flights, would have fixed my life. To be surrounded just once by rich, doting, tap-dancing, dinner-jacketed adults would have made up for gym, math, music, and art appreciation classes.

"Little Freddie Bartholomew was my kind: both of us small, delicate, adorable. Freddie lived in a slum; I lived in a neighborhood a step or two above a slum. We both had rough times on our respective streets. One look at us was proof enough that we belonged in another place. We seemed different. Then, fifteen minutes into Little Lord Fauntleroy, word came that Freddie was different. He was the long-lost son of an English Lord. In the blink of a frame, Freddie was whisked off to an English country estate. I sat in the murk of the Ward Theater on Westchester Avenue, the elevated train outside rattling me inside, convinced at last that my suspicions were correct: I was not the son of Dave and Rhoda Feiffer, I was kidnapped. I was not Jewish, I was of another religion: English.

"When Snow White sang 'Some Day My Prince Will Come,' she was speaking for my generation: someday my future will come, my money will come, my job will come, my sweetheart will come, my house in the country, my dance with Ginger Rogers. I will be delivered from this place which is the wrong place, for I am not of the poor class, or the working class, or the peasant class, or the Jewish class. I am of royal blood.

"Immigrant Jewish producers and first-generation Irish Catholic directors taught me that I was High Episcopalian. The secret of the melting pot was to melt into a goyishe prince. . . .

"Later, there **was** Gary Cooper and Jimmy Stewart. To take them on as heroes meant a move away from anglophilia. I was nine or ten, ready to give up childish things, prepared to approach the prairie where men walked slow and tall and threw long silhouettes. Coop and Jimmy and Hank Fonda, too, were plain-spoken. 'Ma' came out as 'Maw,' which made motherhood Lincolnesque. 'Maw' spoke soft and warm and made sense. 'Maw' was larger than life but not as threatening. And, most important, when 'Maw' had sons, they were Tom Joad or Tom Destry or Bill Hickok, proof that it was okay to be born an American, not a Duke or a Lord or anything fancy; that it was okay to rise from poverty, with the people all holding hands in grand and glorious union. . . .

"It was left to John Garfield to let the word out that it was acceptable to be Jewish and still be a movie star. Not fixed by quota to the outer edge of the screen, not limited to the role of best friend, schlepper, tailor, a loupe in one's eye, owner of the corner candy store. Garfield stood in privileged isolation, on a tenement roof, not on a prairie, shaking his fist at the Manhattan skyline, its penthouses above, its women in gowns, its men in dinner jackets. 'I'll lick you yet,' he cried, meaning, 'I'll join you yet. I'll have my own penthouse, just as good as yours. I'll have my own woman in a gown, and when she and I fight, I mean spat, I, no less than you, will taxi off to my men's club for the night.'

"What a lesson this Garfield taught: that I could remain Jewish and not be relegated to the supporting cast. I didn't have to be Protestant to be a hero! Social Darwinism was also for Jews. What a surprise! . . ."[1]

Down in Brooklyn, Woody Allen also had his role models: "The first Humphrey Bogart movie I saw was The Maltese Falcon. I was ten years old and I identified immediately with Peter Lorre. The impulse to be a snivelling, effeminate, greasy little weasel appealed to me enormously. . . ."[2]

Director Jose Luis Borau grew up in a small Spanish town in the 1940s — the bleak aftermath of the Civil War. "My best friends at that time were Mickey Rooney, Freddie Bartholomew and Deanna Durbin. Some of the things we saw in those films were clearly impossible! Mickey invites Judy Garland home for dinner . . . and she accepts! Dinner was at ten thirty. My father wouldn't have allowed it — and the girl's father certainly wouldn't. America was too much of everything . . . the country was rich and beautiful; the girls accessible and always smiling."

Former Secretary of State Henry Kissinger told Italian journalist Oriana Fallaci: "I've always acted alone. Americans admire the cowboy leading the caravan alone, the cowboy entering a village alone on his horse . . . a Wild West tale, if you like."

The star system was an integral part of the old Hollywood, its most valuable asset, the gold from which it cast idols for public adoration. Early producers sought to fabricate stars, studios to breed them; many more were plucked from obscurity by popular acclaim. Success has always depended on the collective vote of the moviegoer — and every picture is a new election. Talent and good looks are not enough. Said director Howard Hawks:

"I have a theory that the camera likes some people. Other people the camera does not like. And the people it likes can't do any wrong. Almost everything they think comes out when you photograph it. I met probably the most beautiful girl I ever saw, marvelous personality and everything — one look at her on the camera and I told her she might as well give up. She had no chance. But people like Bogart, who was not a good-looking man — everything he did, you seemed to know why he was doing it. Gary Cooper — things would happen that wouldn't [be visible] to the eye. Gable — all of the people who are great personalities. They're not actors as much as they are personalities. The camera likes them."[3]

The public compelled studios to identify favorite screen personalities — at a time when producers and actors favored anonymity. The producers correctly anticipated that celebrity would boost salaries; the actors regarded the "flickers" as demeaning work, well paid but allowing little opportunity for creative expression. Before 1910, only John Bunny — unmistakably huge and familiar from the stage — and actor-producer "Bronco Billy" Anderson were known by name. In that year, producer Carl Laemmle identified Florence Lawrence — formerly known as "the Biograph Girl" — and launched her as the first movie star with a press interview and public appearance in St. Louis.

Early stars tailored their personalities to different needs and tastes within what was then a more homogeneous audience than in later years. Most played types, with little change from one week's part to the next and a consistency in all their public appearances — on and off the screen. Mack Sennett's stock company — Chester Conklin, Mack Swain, Mabel Normand, and Fatty

180

Arbuckle among them — improvised their comic routines within the frame-work of characters that were as sharply defined as those of the commedia dell'arte. Chaplin developed his "Little Tramp" character at Sennett by canni-balizing clothes from his fellow comics.

Observed film historian David Thompson: "Chaplin and Fairbanks were per-fect symbols of aspiring immigrant America — the one succeeding by luck and dash, the other surviving by pluck and pathos." Chaplin was acclaimed "the sensation of the year" by a trade magazine after the thirty-five short movies he made for Sennett in 1914. Subsequent contracts gave him the freedom to deepen and refine his comedy, but the Tramp's pathos always remained. The Douglas Fairbanks of the early social satires (before he embarked on his cos-tume epics of the 1920s) seemed to dance on air and poke good-natured fun at affectation. A 1919 title, *His Majesty, the American,* expressed his buoyant optimism and the affection he engendered. Mary Pickford was already an accomplished stage actress when she joined Biograph in 1909 at age sixteen; she soon achieved independence and a unique fame as "America's Sweet-heart," the embodiment of small-town virtue and spunk.

These three were among the first modern celebrities. As early as 1914, crowds lined the track and jammed Grand Central Terminal when Chaplin took a train to New York. All three drew vast crowds to War Bond rallies. Their fame was global. By 1917, each was earning around a million dollars a year, largely free of tax, at a time when the dollar was worth ten times what it is today.

Stars were paid huge sums, then as now, because they were bankable com-modities. They identified and sold movies; producers could raise money and sell an entire season's output on the strength of their names. A few stars achieved legendary status, embodying the spirit of an era for contemporaries and later generations. Colleen Moore was the first on-screen flapper and claims to have set the fashion for bobbed hair, but it is Clara Bow who is best remembered as the "It" girl who expressed the cheerful hedonism of the 1920s. Rudolph Valentino, adored and slandered in his six years as a Latin lover, has survived such rivals as Ramon Novarro and Antonio Moreno to become an icon of the cinema and a symbol as universally recognizable as the Little Tramp.

Douglas Fairbanks, Mary Pickford, and Charlie Chaplin, in 1917. Each offered an inspiring role model for the mass audience; each was earning about a million dollars a year.

As Hawks suggested, and Mae West reiterated, "Goodness had nothing to do with it." Acting ability and good looks seldom hurt a screen career, but they were far from indispensable. Clark Gable played an extra in the mid-1920s. Hulking, gap-toothed, and big-eared, he had little chance of competing against the poetic, intense young men of current fashion. "Definitely, there was no future for me in Hollywood," he recalled. "I was no Valentino or Gilbert. I was somewhat of a roughneck." By the early years of the Depression, tastes had changed. The audience acclaimed Gable's tough-guy, working-stiff portrayals, and made him the biggest star of the 1930s; a shoo-in for the role of Rhett Butler in *Gone With the Wind*.

A few stars serve as instant time capsules. Humphrey Bogart personifies 1940s film noir: the laconic private eye chronicled by Hammett and Chandler, Hemingway's existential hero. James Dean and Marilyn Monroe are 1950s icons; but they are also an abstraction of stardom, like Garbo and Fred Astaire — timeless and universal.

Will Rogers consoled America in the Great Depression. Cowboy, humorist, and homespun philosopher, he was, for a few years before his death in 1935, the best-paid and most popular male star. His appeal was to middle America: a shrewd provincial outwitting city slickers; a rustic Rip Van Winkle who, in the words of historian Peter Rollins, "preserved the values and humor of the past . . . confronted and subdued the anxieties of the public, which surrendered to the nostalgia of his films."[4]

When John Wayne fought on-screen, the level of enlistments rose. But stars can express our fears as well as our fantasies. Clint Eastwood's popularity as a vigilante has deep roots:

"What Dirty Harry did in the 1970s was to outrun an American political phenomenon by close to a decade. In the series involving the rebellious detective, Eastwood caught a mood of blue-collar discontent with a country portrayed in the films as being run by bureaucrats, sociologists, appeasers and incompetents. American society's deepest incapacity, the Dirty Harry films said, was in failing to protect the lives of its normal people, and its most galling trait was rationalizing crime and the intolerable with guidance-counsellor jargon. In the films, the country is reduced to the scale of San Francisco, and Dirty Harry roams the city, defying the bureaucracy and restoring order."[5]

Audrey Hepburn and Grace Kelly in 1956.
Photo by Allan Grant for *Life*.

Joan Crawford without conventional makeup:
a photo taken by George Hurrell in 1930 to
reveal Crawford's dramatic potential at a time
when she was typecast as a flapper.

During their years of fame, stars serve as role models. Their phrases, from
Theda Bara's "Kiss me, my fool!" to Eastwood's "Make my day!," by way of
Peter Finch's "I'm mad as hell, and I'm not going to take it any more!," are now
a part of the culture. Molly Haskell chronicles the importance of the actress:

*"Women in the movies had a mystical, quasi-religious connection with the public.
Theirs was a potency made irresistible by the twin authority of cinematic illusion
and flesh-and-blood reality, of fable and photography, of art and sociology. . . .*

*"And women, in the early and middle ages of film, dominated. It is only recently
that men have come to monopolize the popularity polls, the credits, and the
romantic spotlight by allocating to themselves not just the traditional male warrior
and adventure roles, but those of the sex object and glamor queen as well. Back in
the twenties and thirties, and to a lesser extent the forties, women were at the
center. . . .*

*"Far more than men, women were the vessels of men's and women's fantasies and
the barometers of changing fashion. Like two-way mirrors linking the immediate
past with the immediate future, women in the movies reflected, perpetuated, and
in some respects offered innovations on the roles of women in society. Shopgirls
copied them, housewives escaped through them. Through the documentary
authenticity (new hair styles, fashions in dress, and even fads in physical beauty)
that actresses brought to their roles and the familiar, simplified tales in which they
played, movie heroines were viscerally immediate and accountable to audiences in
a way that the heroines of literature, highbrow or popular, were not. Movie stars,
as well as the women they played — Stella Dallas, Mrs. Miniver, Mildred Pierce,
Jezebel — were not like the women in print or on canvas. They belonged to us and
spoke to us personally from what, until the sixties and seventies, was the heart and
emotional center of film itself."[6]*

No star had a greater influence on how women dressed than Joan Crawford.
As a flaming youth in such late-1920s movies as *Our Dancing Daughters* and
Our Modern Maidens, she popularized the flapper look. Macy's sold 50,000
copies of Adrian's ruffled-shoulder dress that she wore in *Letty Lynton* (1932).
As a fan magazine chattered: "Paris may decree this and Paris may decree
that, but when that Crawford girl pops up in puffed sleeves, then it's puffed
sleeves for us before tea-time."

Joan Crawford in *Letty Lynton* (1932). Portrait by George Hurrell, whose theatrical lighting immortalized Crawford and other stars of the past fifty years.

From the mid-1930s on, Crawford's impact was inescapable, as Irene Sharaff confirms:

"Adrian told me how he had arrived at using shoulder pads, a feature that became like his signature on clothes he designed. It seems that Joan Crawford insisted on feeling absolutely free in her dresses and suits. At fittings she would rotate her shoulders vigorously, with arms outstretched, to test the stretch of the garment across her shoulder blades. As this feeling of unhampered freedom in clothes is possible only in loose jersey or a sweater, all other fabrics Adrian used for her clothes had to be let out across the back to such an extent that padding was necessary on the shoulders to take up the slack. The result accentuated her own broad and angular shoulders. With each outfit Adrian designed for her, the shoulders became increasingly exaggerated. As Crawford was one of the leading stars and of glamorous repute, her silhouette became a pattern, soon copied, and for ten years, shoulder pads were the outstanding item manufactured in the fashion industry." [7]

MGM was a factory of style, which gave Adrian the opportunity to exploit the distinctive personalities of a dozen stars at once. Garbo was another chameleon. Women eagerly copied the pillbox she wore in *As You Desire Me,* the turban in *The Painted Veil,* the cloche in *The Kiss, Mata Hari*'s skullcap, and the tilted Eugenie hat in *Romance.* Remarked an appreciative Adrian, "I have noticed that Garbo's hats usually become fashion Fords." Garbo also helped popularize the beret and trenchcoat, her favorite wear off the set.

Marlene Dietrich started a vogue for slacks, Carole Lombard for lounging pajamas. Mothers dressed their little girls like Shirley Temple, adopted Ginger Rogers's dress from *Kitty Foyle* as an office uniform, and slipped into long draped dresses and snoods inspired by Barbara Stanwyck in *The Lady Eve.* Lana Turner made sweaters big business. Asked *Silver Screen:* "Have you the secret wish to become a beautiful island enchantress? Well, lovely Dorothy Lamour's slinky native sarongs will soon be available to every plain Jane."

The influence went beyond clothes. Declared *Vogue* in 1937, "The way you make up your lips, apply your rouge . . . ten to one it came from Hollywood and was designed for some famous star." Women bleached their hair platinum blond in response to Jean Harlow, and dyed it to match Hedy Lamarr.

Marlene Dietrich in *The Devil Is a Woman* (1935): portrait by William Walling, Jr. Josef von Sternberg, the director who had played Svengali to Dietrich since *The Blue Angel* (1930), supervised this sitting.

German poster for *Blonde Venus* (1932). In the darkest hour of the Depression, moral restraints were loosened — in Hollywood as well as in Europe.

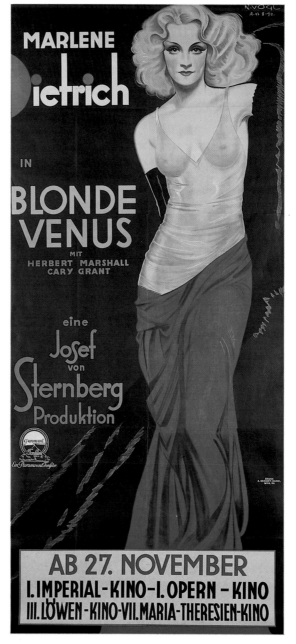

Austrian poster for *The Painted Veil* (1934). Garbo's films enjoyed their greatest popularity in Europe, and Hollywood's loss of this market in the Second World War put an end to her career.

Carole Lombard, a 1932 portrait by Eugene Robert Richee, that out-Dietrichs Dietrich. Two years later, Lombard developed her own style as a breezy comedienne.

Columnist Hedda Hopper interviews Gene Tierney in the Twentieth Century Fox commissary, beneath the watchful gaze of studio chief Darryl F. Zanuck. Photo by Ralph Crane for *Life*, 1946.

Claudette Colbert inspired a short cut, Veronica Lake a peekaboo — until Lake warned women on the swing shift that long hair could get tangled in the lathe. Carmen Miranda spearheaded the Latin invasion, boosting bright colors and tutti-frutti accessories.

On occasion, men succumbed to movie dress codes. When Clark Gable revealed a naked torso in *It Happened One Night* (1934), the sale of under-shirts dropped 50 percent. John Wayne and Gary Cooper were among the first to boost (nondesigner) jeans; later, Dean and Brando made them a uni-form for the counterculture. When John Travolta appeared in *Urban Cowboy* (1981) wearing city-slicker rodeo regalia, U.S. jeans sales surged to 600 million pairs. And high-fashion Italian menswear of the 1980s has shown the influence of the casual, draped suits that Cary Grant and Gary Cooper wore in the 1930s, and the spirit of what Nino Cerruti called the "happy, successful hero," as seen in Hollywood revivals on European television.

The impact of movies on fashion has slipped sharply. In the 1950s, Audrey Hepburn was a role model for young women and an inspiration to such designers as Edith Head (*Roman Holiday, Sabrina*), Givenchy (*Funny Face, Breakfast at Tiffany's*), and Cecil Beaton (*My Fair Lady*). The strapless white tulle dress by Edith Head that Elizabeth Taylor wore in *A Place in the Sun* (1951) inspired countless copies, as did Helen Rose's white chiffon dress for Taylor in *Cat on a Hot Tin Roof* (1958) and her lightweight swimsuits for Esther Williams's water ballets. Among the few examples from the last twenty years are Theodora Van Runkle's modified 1930s look for Faye Dunaway in *Bonnie and Clyde*, Diane Keaton's *Annie Hall* look, and Jennifer Beals's torn sweatshirt in *Flashdance*. Rock musicians and street fashion have usurped the movies as sources of inspiration.

Much of the star's influence was the product of studio expertise. The transfor-mation of Spangler Arlington Brough, of Filley, Nebraska, into MGM luminary Robert Taylor, is instructive:

"You can't imagine how the studios cosseted us in those days. They had to. If we weren't looked after and guarded the fans would tear us to pieces.

"When they finally decided I was going to make it as a star, Louis B. Mayer called me into his office and said: 'How's your wardrobe, son?' I told him I'd got a couple

George Hurrell's portrait of Tyrone Power
and Loretta Young, 1935.

Eugene Robert Richee's portrait of Louise
Brooks, 1928.

Gloria Swanson mourns the 1960 destruction of New York's Roxy, largest and grandest of movie palaces, which she had helped inaugurate in 1927. Photo by Eliot Elisofon for *Life*.

of $10 suits and he said that wasn't good enough. So he sent me down to his own tailor — the best in Hollywood, of course — and ordered me four new ones, together with some evening kit. And he had me in his office to inspect them.

"He was entitled to that — after all, he was paying for them! Everything in those days was aimed at glamor. There was no such thing as an unflattering still — the studio wouldn't release it. And I used to wear pounds of make-up — yes, even lipstick — when I was filming. On top of that they always photographed me softly to enhance the glamor.

"It was the same with the women. Their dresses were always approved by the studio. I tell you, when women like Joan Crawford and Norma Shearer went out, you knew you were looking at stars."[8]

"I don't care what scheme of lighting you use: my stars have to be beautiful," Irving Thalberg told an MGM portrait photographer. Each major studio had one or more star photographers who, with their staff, would create thousands of images a year for distribution to the press and the publicity department. The best were superb artists, masters of lighting and composition, who played as important a role in the creation and development of a star as any cinematographer. But all were obliged to improve on reality; to achieve, through retouching, an ideal vision of beauty.

Louise Brooks, herself the subject of memorable portraits by George Hommel and Eugene Richee, declared: "What people remember of those stars is not from films, but *one* essential photograph. . . . And when I think of Garbo I do not see her moving in any particular film. I see her staring mysteriously into a camera. She is a still picture — unchangeable."[9]

Top studio photographers included Clarence Sinclair Bull and Laszlo Willinger at MGM; Eugene Robert Richee and William Walling, Jr., at Paramount; Ernest Bachrach at RKO; Elmer Fryer, Bert Six, and Scotty Welbourne at Warner Bros.; Frank Powolny at Twentieth Century Fox. Independent photographers, including George Hurrell, Edward Steichen, George Hoyningen-Huene, Cecil Beaton, and Alfred Eisenstaedt, freelanced or executed commissions for *Vogue* and *Vanity Fair*, *Esquire*, and *Life*.

Occasionally, stars would take the initiative:

"There is a famous series of photographs by George Hurrell of Joan Crawford in 1930, when she was tired of being a dancing daughter and wanted to convince the studio that she could play the kind of dramatic role usually assigned to Norma Shearer. Hurrell's answer was to strip off the painted doll makeup to show her natural freckles, to blow the hair off the face in loose waves, and to persuade her to show some sort of emotion before the camera instead of having the impassive mask which was de rigueur for glamor photography at the time. The photographs made her point, and she moved on, not as it happened to more 'human' roles but into her 'mature' period in which she became more masklike than ever — all commemorated in the stunning series Hurrell did of her at MGM in the thirties."[10]

In 1927, Gloria Swanson married a French aristocrat and cabled Paramount: "Am arriving with Marquis tomorrow stop Please arrange ovation." Barbra Streisand recalled her stint at Loew's Kings in Brooklyn: "I hid my face when I directed people to their seats because I knew I'd be famous one day and I didn't want the embarrassment of having them say later: 'Oh, yeah, the big star. She used to be an usherette at the local theater.'"

Streisand aside, the mythic tradition may have ended with Marilyn Monroe and James Dean. The currency has been devalued. Today, almost anyone with a speaking role is called a star; a couple of hits make you a superstar. Many of today's leading performers reject the trappings of stardom. They think of themselves as actors, rather than glamorous pawns. They are likely to live far from Hollywood, and to divide their time between the stage, movies, and other pursuits. They use their freedom to change character from one movie to the next, terrified at the thought of being typecast. They ration their appearances; strive to be unobtrusive. Many have formed corporations to produce their own pictures or to advance favorite causes. A Robert Redford or a Jane Fonda can secure the green light for a doubtful project — or speak out on controversial issues — something the studio-era stars would never have risked.

A last comment from one of the most versatile and thoughtful of contemporary actors, Dustin Hoffman:

"There are probably a lot of uncredited occasions where actors have pushed directors into areas that they haven't gone into before, and I think there have been

more than a few occasions where a picture is better because of the actor who is in it. They will say, 'The actor is subjective — only cares about his own part.' Not so. An actor is as capable of considering 'the whole' as the director, and often does. Sure we care about our own parts, but we have a responsibility to the entire film also, and I don't think many of us ignore that responsibility. And, believe me, I know some very subjective directors, who focus mostly on covering their ass. Yet actors generally are thought of as somehow less intelligent or responsible or aware of what filmmaking is about than the director or the producer.

"I think Brando once said it — we're housewives, we're these emotional creatures. They say, 'We're going to make you look good, just don't argue. Don't try to make the big decisions. Leave that to us. Leave that to the daddies, the husbands.' It doesn't have to be that way. I think there should be a real partnership, not the classically imagined situation where a supposedly 'solid, objective' director simply 'handles' a 'neurotic, subjective' actor.

"Picasso said a painter walks around for months with a movie of images in his mind and he winds up with one image on canvas — imagine the tension, because he's got fifty million images he's rejecting. Every new stroke destroys the painting before. That's exactly the way a movie is, because we can work on a screenplay, we can work on a structure, we can work until we're blue in the face, then look at the first day of rushes and it's different. It's either worse or it's better, but it's not what it was on the page. You've got to be led by what's on the screen, and yet you work with people sometimes who are not led by that — it's like they're blind. It's not translating from the page, yet they want to stick with it anyway, and you go crazy because you see how little it takes to hurt a film. Another painter once said, 'I'm so afraid when I'm painting, because the slightest little thing, the slightest little move, one stroke, collapses the tension of the canvas.'

"Sometimes, I don't think film is set up to get the best work out of anybody. In a sense, it's set up for you to fail, by virtue of the fact that you're told what amount to create every day. And implicitly it's stated that you can't go home again — you're usually not going to get another chance to do retakes, which are very expensive.

"Woody Allen told me that he has written in his contract that he can come back during postproduction to shoot maybe twenty, thirty percent of the film, and in

195

Marilyn, 1962, décollage by Mimmi Rotella.

that way do what a writer or a sculptor does — you go back and you keep working on it till it's right. Most movies aren't that way. They always say, 'Don't worry about the sets; they'll be there.' And then they're not there. Studios are funny that way. They don't want you to go back again. Woody Allen told me, 'I never shoot sets. That's why I shoot Rockefeller Center, because I know it's going to be there.'"[11]

Quotations

1. Jules Feiffer, "Someday My Star Will Come," *The Movies*, July 1983. Copyright © Jules Feiffer.

2. Woody Allen, quoted in *Life*, March 2, 1969.

3. Howard Hawks, in *The Men Who Made the Movies*, edited by Richard Schickel (New York: Atheneum, 1975), page 102.

4. Peter Rollins, "Will Rogers and the Relevance of Nostalgia," in *American History, American Film*, edited by John E. O'Connor and Martin A. Jackson (New York: Frederick Ungar, 1979), page 79.

5. John Vinocur, "Clint Eastwood, Seriously," *New York Times Magazine*, February 24, 1985.

6. Molly Haskell, *From Reverence to Rape* (New York: Holt, Rinehart & Winston, 1973), pages 11–12.

7. Irene Sharaff, *Broadway and Hollywood: Costumes by Irene Sharaff* (New York: Van Nostrand, Reinhold, 1976), page 59.

8. Robert Taylor, interview in *Sunday Express*, London, August 12, 1962; reprinted in *The Voices of Film Experience*, edited by Jay Leyda (New York: Macmillan, 1977), page 455.

9. John Kobal, *The Art of the Great Hollywood Portrait Photographers* (New York: Alfred A. Knopf, 1980), page 122.

10. John Russell Taylor, "The Image Makers," *American Film*, July–August 1976.

11. Dustin Hoffman, seminar at The American Film Institute, quoted in *American Film*, April 1983.

Other sources

Paul Trent and Richard Lawton, *The Imagemakers* (New York: Harmony Books, 1982).

Alexander Walker, *Joan Crawford: The Ultimate Star* (New York: Harper & Row, 1983).

———, *Stardom — The Hollywood Phenomenon* (New York: Stein & Day, 1970).

Paris acclaims Clint Eastwood. American action stars enjoy even greater esteem abroad than at home. Photo by Jacques Prayer.

Miriam, 1983, painting by Dan McCleary inspired by the image of the girl who is murdered at the carnival in Alfred Hitchcock's *Strangers on a Train* (1950).

EPILOGUE

by Carl H. Scheele

Set within the complex cultural framework of twentieth-century America, Hollywood and its movies emerged to permeate the nation's vision on an unprecedented scale, far outpacing rival forms of art and artifice. The movies reached millions of people across the land and provided unforgettable images that helped to shape the perceptions of Americans at every level of society. The appearance of this dynamic and new popular art form coincided with the emergence of the United States as a leading power in the world. And American movies, like American economic and political influence, spread over the globe, providing people everywhere with the special brand of American images and visions fashioned in Hollywood. The movies, as if responding to the shifting moods of a nation composed of peoples whose diverse cultural origins often set them at odds with each other, reflected the alternating tensions, exuberance, tentativeness, belligerence, and change inherent in the American social stew.

Although a number of scholars have begun to appraise the cultural implications of American movies, the critical investigative process is unfinished. It is a worthy scholarly pursuit in that movies provide not only a better understanding of popular entertainment as a potent social force but, as well, a better understanding of the society itself in which the movies were created and functioned. As a special form of the visual and dramatic arts, movies contributed greatly to the ongoing dialogue about life in this country. Filmmakers participated energetically in the American practice of discussing events and issues, indulging in social introspection as much as commentators working in newspapers, novels, or (after 1920) radio. This self-centered preoccupation with life in America was, for a very long time, a distinguishing characteristic of American movies.

Social issues as central themes are readily identifiable in their various guises: Westerns, war films, romances, comedies, swashbucklers, musicals, crime films, etc. A subtle form of social commentary also appeared through prejudicial and attitudinal conventions that divulged a great deal of information about America's self-image at any given moment. A few examples illustrate the point. Evidence of prejudice against American Indians in hundreds of films is ample. Until recent times, in many of these films — mostly Westerns — the

Indians may have had little to do with the central plot or theme, but when they did appear they were often savage, bloodthirsty, and prone to drunkenness. If depicted as a noble friend, the stereotypical good Indian was wise in the ways of nature, physically strong, perhaps philosophical, but never worldly in the ways of the whites. Hispanics usually fared little better. Two stereotypes that frequently appeared in the pre–World War One two-reel comedy were the working person (factory hand, shop girl, waiter), sympathetically portrayed and invested with abundant virtues, and the wealthy person (man or woman with no visible job), unsympathetically represented as snobbish, insensitive, and of dubious moral character. Filmmakers depicted their view of a pre-1915 America sharply divided by class. Orientals were "inscrutable," but in the 1930s the Chinese were presented more favorably than the Japanese, a reflection of attitudes of the popular press and politicians. Italians were plentiful as criminals in film — tough but devious, cruel, and untrustworthy.

Stereotypes, of course, are an oft-met convention in the popular arts. Many had developed in vaudeville and were adopted wholesale by Hollywood. But women in general were depicted in a wide variety of roles and character types after World War One, when Hollywood captured the middle-class market. While certain types of women were in vogue for a long time — the vamps and flappers of the 1920s and the later "dumb blondes" among them — movies definitely did not cling to the image of the weak, innocent, and defenseless female presented before 1918. New stereotypes and individually modeled characters reflected Hollywood's preference for the "enlightened" or "advanced" woman. Women in pictures often smoked, wore the newest or most daring fashions, drank liquor, drove cars, danced, worked professionally, got divorced on occasion, and led generally independent lives. At times on the screen, women themselves often decided when to act seductively and when, as well, to deflect the advances of men. The changed status of women in society remained a concern of considerable importance to the middle class — and to Hollywood — from the earliest years of the century, when women campaigned for and eventually won the right to vote, when they fought for social reforms, and when they questioned sexist and marriage-oriented attitudes of an older, male-dominated world.

Hollywood's movies directly challenged the outside-the-home entertainment market when feature-length photoplays appeared with more frequency after 1918. Within ten years, Hollywood's audience base included most of the middle class in its broadest definition. To capture the middle class as regular moviegoers, Hollywood identified and developed popular themes, with Hollywood points of view. Without some "angle," the films would have lacked punch and interest; a certain social tension was artistically desired. And like the middle class, Hollywood could hold several views on the same issue.

If the social status of women was a middle-class concern, so was the problem of crime. Crime as a popular topic in literature dated from the eighteenth century and before. Prior to World War One, many crime films dealt with the problem of "white slavery," a topic much in vogue with the popular press. With the coming of Prohibition, however, Hollywood's treatment of crime broadened and became more sophisticated. The themes of the real world were adopted: political and legal-system corruption; bootlegging and gang wars; and crime in relation to the larger issues of delinquent youth and the struggle between the poor and rich — outsiders vs. insiders. These issues persist in films today, even though details have changed — for example, racketeering in drugs instead of booze. In the process, Hollywood dealt with certain fundamental issues of everyday life: the effects of environment on personalities and slums on crime; police and court corruption; the free press as the people's ultimate weapon against wrongdoing or injustice. In this way society's problems were aired under the guise of entertainment.

Along with gender and crime, of course, a myriad of other themes were presented both overtly and unself-consciously. The catalogue includes authority, democracy, work, social mobility, moral choice, psychological problems, the natural environment, city life, and many more. Each issue was not necessarily met head on or with consistent viewpoints, and at least two major problems of American society were avoided or shabbily dealt with until the post–World War Two years: the Great Depression and the issue of race.

Despite some cleverly crafted films that nibbled at the edges of the economic collapse, the superficial aspects of the Depression came into Hollywood's main focus. Early musicals often depicted out-of-work troupers and starving singers who persevered for eighty minutes until success arrived in the last reel.

The message was false. It was the crime films that came closest to Depression issues. Once again, however, despite sidelong glances at poor domestic interiors or unkempt city streets, Hollywood's message was simply that jobless young people must not fall into a life of crime, but keep faith in the work ethic. Hollywood gave no real clues as to where factory and office workers might find employment or why there were practically no jobs to be had. Not until Franklin D. Roosevelt was elected president did Hollywood take up the issue of the Depression. By then, the country's mood and that of Hollywood had shifted to a more optimistic footing.

The term "escapist" is often applied to a considerable body of films — especially musicals — produced during the Depression, suggesting that Hollywood sensed a need for audiences to take leave of their troubles. There is some truth in this, of course, but the idea seems often overstated. The early musicals appear to have had two phases. The first group, sometimes hastily patched together to exploit the first sound capabilities, often lacked good audio fidelity and suffered from poorly written scripts. The second cycle blossomed to exploit newly improved sound technologies. Talented principals had fully incubated and matured — Busby Berkeley, for one, who by 1933 used the screen as a canvas on which to deftly paint exquisite patterns and movement to complement the improved sound. By the mid-1930s, too, Broadway composers fully realized that the screen was not necessarily inferior to the conventional stage. Indeed, as technology and artistry rapidly developed, while Broadway struggled with the Depression, there was a near-wholesale migration of musical talent from New York to Hollywood. As for escapism, Hollywood musicals and lightweight comedies must not be viewed in isolation, but rather in the context of art forms well established onstage long before the onset of the Crash of 1929.

Via Hollywood, the white, American middle class encountered American blacks, who were often featured in musical spots and, on occasion, in all-black musical productions. Blacks were confined to a "place" in every genre and forced to accept a racist set of stereotypes that removed the true spectrum of human dynamics from their representations. This had not always been the case. The earliest one- or two-reelers often enough depicted blacks in a straightforward fashion. With the effort to capture the largest potential audience, photoplays became more complex and more biased in socially oriented points of view. The most successful and forceful, of course, was D. W. Griffith's *The Birth of a Nation* (1915), a film about the Civil War and Reconstruction. While the film was rich in photographic and editorial innovation, Griffith's personal biases concerning blacks were offensive and devastating to Afro-American dignity. Images of blacks ranged from simpleminded, loyal, and shiftless slaves to vindictive and viciously cruel freedmen. The "Clan" (the Ku Klux Klan) was depicted as the savior of decent (white) society. When the film was released, the NAACP raised vigorous objections, blacks in New York and Boston attempted to get the film banned, and riots broke out in Boston. Griffith — and the industry — was taken aback, surprised to realize that this personal interpretation of history and society was not universally shared.

As a consequence, notwithstanding a few exceptional films, Hollywood thereafter simply avoided the presentation of blacks in films as much as possible. When blacks did appear, they assumed the roles of domestic servants, porters, doormen, musicians, dancers, and singers. If invested with personalities, they were further stereotyped as subservient, loyal to the whites, shuffling, and often clownish.

Similar conditions prevailed in other fields. Blacks were excluded from professional baseball, for example, and formed their own version of the major leagues during the same period. Not surprisingly, blacks began to produce their own films with limited circulation. In the years following World War Two, these conditions began to change and, under the administration of President Truman, blacks were integrated into the armed forces. Hollywood's attitude began to change about that time as well, although the first films with a different perspective were stilted and often sensational. *Pinky* (1949) and *Lost Boundaries* (1949) dealt with "passing" (hardly a major issue); *Intruder in the Dust* (1949) was about lynching (important, but certainly sensational). On the other hand, as the civil rights movement strengthened, Hollywood's new stereotype of the Afro-American presented images of blacks that were incredibly "perfect." Representations since Sidney Poitier's heyday have become more balanced.

To Hollywood's credit, most of its offerings since the arrival of television have become more searching. Pictures now are usually targeted for specific seg-ments of the audience. The nullification of the old Production Code has further enabled Hollywood to compete more ably with home television. The rise of the independent film producers and the virtual disappearance of the monopolistic studios — or their absorption by conglomerates — have resulted in more audacious and biting social commentary. While *All Quiet on the Western Front* (1930) could only have been released midway between two world wars, it became possible to produce *Paths of Glory* (1957) and *M*A*S*H* (1970) when America had become heavily militarized and bellicose.

If the movies have lost their first position in terms of competing entertainments and recreational activities, they have become less encumbered by conventions that so often degenerated into stereotypes. Modifications within the star system now enable players to assume a greater variety of roles, providing more freedom to develop and individualize characters on screen. The motion picture's capability to manipulate time and direct the viewers' attention to precisely what the camera selects creates an illusion that is as powerful today as it was in the beginning.

Yet despite these assets, it is remarkable that the movies of Hollywood have become as socially effective as they have after enduring the denial of First Amendment rights by the Supreme Court in 1915, at least three self-censorship production codes, and two onslaughts by the House Un-American Activities Committee. After midcentury it became clear that motion pictures could again become a powerful force in shaping American social and political attitudes. It is a tribute to the enterprising spirit of Hollywood artists that, in the twenty-five years following such assaults, a philosophical recovery could restore their critical outlook. After nine decades of filmmaking, the motion pictures survive as a valid principal commentator on American society as well as on human concerns universally held.

Vargas-designed poster for *Moon Over Miami* (1940). Two years later, with the outbreak of war, Betty Grable's legs became a symbol of the decade, ornamenting bombers, battleships, and GIs' lockers.

Cartoon by Carl Rose, published August 24, 1935, in the *New Yorker*, satirizing Busby Berkeley's grandiose production numbers.

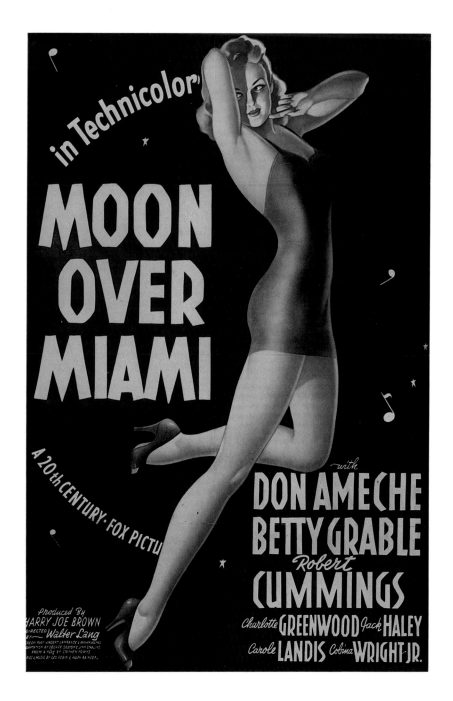

"Now in this scene, Franz Schubert, the composer, falls asleep and dreams his melody while the girls dance it out on the piano keys. Get it?"

ACKNOWLEDGMENTS

Hollywood — "the Dream Factory" — has been an essential part of American life for more than seventy-five years. We have lived our fantasies and escaped our sometimes difficult realities, we have tested our heroes and triumphed over our villains, through the magic of the silver screen. Yet for all our love and even addiction to the cinema, we have never accorded it a place of very great honor in our society.

But if a quick perusal of the corner newsstand and Southern California's tourism figures are any indication, people from across the United States and all over the world are fascinated by Hollywood and the world it portrays. Books and magazines entrance readers with gossip from the film industry, the major studios offer extremely popular tours, and one can even gain entry to a sound stage on rare occasions — but still, so much of the mystery remains. How do they do it?

When I came to the Smithsonian Institution Traveling Exhibition Service five years ago, it seemed to me there was no better subject for a major traveling exhibition than Hollywood — not only in its larger-than-life extravagance, but in its seldom-seen reality. What could be a more proper undertaking for America's national museum than a study of (with all due respect to baseball fans) America's national pastime, the movies? If this seems almost self-evident, it must be remembered that the museum community has traditionally ignored Hollywood's efforts as anything resembling serious art. If such a project were to have any chance of success, it would be essential that the treatment be serious and scholarly without sacrificing any of the fantasy that is at the heart of our love of Hollywood. The exhibition would only succeed, I felt, if we could capture both sides — the legend and the reality.

As the idea took shape, it became clear we would need a curator with unusual credentials, someone recognized as an authority on film and familiar with museum exhibitions. I had known Michael Webb for many years because of his affiliation with the American Film Institute, and received from him an enthusiastic response to the exhibition's concept. Born and educated in England, Michael was regional program manager for the British Film Institute before coming to the United States in 1969 to take charge of national film programming for the AFI. He established the AFI Theater at the John F. Kennedy Center in Washington, D.C., and created a series of programs of new and classic American films for exhibition nationwide, working closely with leading art museums and advising them on innovative special events. Since leaving the AFI in 1980, Michael has written and produced a television special on Hollywood; scripted a Smithsonian Institution film on movie palaces; and published a book and organized a SITES exhibition on neon. He worked with us to develop the concept of the exhibition and, in 1983, became its curator. It is his knowledge and passion for the subject that made this show possible.

All of us working on this project quickly learned that assembling an exhibition is not unlike making a motion picture — what one sees as the finished product is the result of the work of many hands and creative intellects, much time, and a considerable amount of money, with audience success and critical acclaim in mind.

We were particularly gratified to have our enthusiasm for "Hollywood: Legend and Reality" shared early on by the organization that became our sponsor, Time Inc. Following several previously successful commitments to cultural exchange, most notably "The Search for Alexander," Time Inc. found this Hollywood exhibition an opportunity to draw on its own vast resources in communications to assist with the many challenges posed by such an undertaking. Our special thanks go to Henry A. Grunwald, Editor-in-Chief, who supported the exhibition practically from its inception and opened Time Inc.'s editorial resources to the curator and to the staff of SITES. We are also grateful to Philip Kunhardt, the former Managing Editor of Life magazine, whose counsel on editorial content and photographs was invaluable. I would also like to make special mention of the contributions of Zachary Morfogen, Director of Corporate Cultural Affairs and my first contact at Time Inc., for his dedication and generosity with his time and expertise; he saw the potential for "Hollywood: Legend and Reality" and immediately helped make this a collaborative project in every sense. To Harry Harding, Consultant to the Office of Corporate Cultural Affairs, Time Inc., I extend warm and personal thanks for his numerous contributions, especially those in the area of design and public relations. Further thanks go to Richard B. Holcomb, Vice-President of Corporate and Community Affairs, and Cheryl Barnes, Manager of Special Projects at American Television and Communications Corporation, and to

Mal Albaum, Neil Pennella, and Sheila Shayon of Home Box Office, Inc., for their advice and contribution to the video aspects of the exhibition.

With funding in hand and the curator selecting artifacts, negotiating loans, and developing the script, our challenge was to juggle the budget, space considerations, exhibition dates and locations, and deadlines. The coordination of these myriad responsibilities was masterfully handled by SITES Exhibition Coordinator Betty Teller, ably assisted by Mary Bet Dobson and Ann Scully. Betty literally developed SITES' first computer program for collections management to cope with the complexity and sheer volume of objects and information involved with the show. An experienced exhibition coordinator, she admirably balanced curatorial issues with those of design, budget, and available space.

The responsibility for gathering artifacts from 130 lenders from all parts of the United States and several foreign countries was ably assumed by SITES Head Registrar, Mary Jane Clark, with Fredric Williams and Gwen Hill. These registrars made shipping, insurance, and conservation arrangements. For their assistance and advice on costume display and handling, we are grateful to Claudia Kidwell and Karyn Harris from the National Museum of American History; to Mary Ballard at the Smithsonian's Conservation Analytical Laboratory; and to Susan Wallace, Office of Exhibits Central.

We are particularly grateful to our colleagues at the Smithsonian's Office of Exhibits Central for their technical and editorial expertise, especially James A. Mahoney, Jr., Director, and Karen Fort, who edited the exhibition script. Walter Sorrell, Ken Clevinger, and the staffs of the model and fabrication shops lent their technical skills to preparing the models for exhibit and travel.

The task of designing an exciting environment for a collection of images and artifacts on the topic of Hollywood was a challenging one. Not only did we at SITES require that the exhibit elements break down to fit into trucks for transport, but we also needed a design flexible enough to suit the variety of museum gallery spaces provided by our host institutions, from the 1901 Carnegie Mansion, which houses the Cooper-Hewitt Museum, to the newly constructed Center for the Fine Arts in Miami. Our admiration and appreciation go to Stuart Silver and to Michael Donovan and Susan Berman of Donovan and Green for their indefatigable efforts. These experienced designers, well known for putting a little of "Hollywood" into museum exhibitions, finally turned their attention to the subject itself, and have creatively and successfully juxtaposed the legend with the reality.

SITES Publications Director Andrea Stevens was responsible for coordinating all aspects of producing this book, from book proposals and contract negotiations to photography, design review, and press inspections. Nancy Eickel, SITES Editor, handled rights and permissions. We are particularly grateful to the staff of New York Graphic Society Books/Little, Brown, especially Betty Childs, Senior Editor, and Nancy Robins, Production Manager, for their cool management of design and production under very tight deadlines. At Little, Brown and Company, Ray Roberts, Senior Editor, and Peggy Freudenthal, Senior Copyeditor, gave valuable editorial support. The handsome design of the book was provided by Carl Zahn, assisted by Mary Reilly.

Marjorie Share, SITES' Director of Education, was responsible for developing the interpretive materials and coordinating the public programs for the exhibition. Marjorie also became our resident expert in audiovisual technology, helping us to realize the "moving image" component that became an integral part of the overall exhibition presentation. We are most appreciative, also, to Gregory Peck for agreeing to narrate our educational audio tour and for sharing the tradition and spirit of Hollywood.

No salute to Hollywood would be complete without moving images. Major studios and independent distributors generously supplied the excerpts selected by the curator, and went to great trouble to provide the best materials available. A special thank-you to ABC Video Enterprises, the American Film Institute, Stanley Caidin, Columbia Pictures, Walt Disney Productions, the Harold Lloyd Estate, Lucasfilm, MGM/UA Entertainment, Paramount Pictures, RKO Pictures, Raymond Rohauer, Twentieth Century Fox, UCLA Film and Television Archives, Universal Pictures, and Warner Bros.

For the moving image component of the exhibition, our deep appreciation goes to Eastman Kodak for support toward the production, printing, and editing of the film sequences shown in seven viewing locations throughout the exhibition. Additional support and technical assistance were provided by

Toshiba America, Inc., for the video monitors, and by Pioneer Electronics, for laser-disc manufacturing and disc players.

Two Los Angeles companies made generous contributions to the creation of these sequences. Tom Ellington of Consolidated Film Industries in Hollywood offered laboratory services. Compact Video Services in Burbank kindly provided editing expertise and post-production facilities. Our appreciation is also extended to Roy Huggins and Gary Winter at Stephen J. Cannell Productions. Nazaret Cherkezian, Director of the Smithsonian's Office of Telecommunications, offered valuable advice and support, and Karen Loveland, Director of Special Projects, served as coproducer of the video units.

Getting the word out about this exhibition was a task shared by a number of organizations and individuals. At SITES, the public affairs responsibilities were assumed by Ronald Geatz and Liz Hill. Arts and Communications Counselors handled liaison work with Time Inc., and much of the national coverage. We are particularly grateful to the efforts of Nina Wright, Philippa Polskin, Karen Hughes, and Pamela Sweeney.

Many others devoted their talents and expertise to "Hollywood: Legend and Reality." At Time Inc., we would like to acknowledge Corporate Manufacturing and Distribution: Ruth Ann Pouliot, Production Director, Michael J. Clayton, Operations Manager; Corporate Cultural Affairs: Vivi Duffy, Arlene Lemanski, Anne Ruthven; *Life* magazine: James Watters, Senior Editor, Marthe Smith, Manager, Life Picture Service; Magazine Group: Harry M. Johnston III, General Counsel, Robin Bierstedt, Associate Counsel; Photo Lab: Peter D. Christopoulos, Chief, Hanns Kohl, Deputy Chief, John Downey, and Thomas Stone; Picture Collection: Beth B. Zarcone, Chief, Kathleen Doak and Joseph E. Schilling, Deputy Chiefs; Time-Life Books, Inc.: Miriam Hsia, Bureau Chief; Christina Lieberman and Carolyn Chubet, Researchers; Washington Office: Janet Olson.

At SITES, Antonio Diez, Associate Director for Administration, managed administrative details, ably assisted by Allegra Wright and Marie-Claire Jean. We are especially grateful for the talents and efforts of Associate Director for Communications Claire Fronville, who was instrumental at many levels, from contracts to matters of education and publications to public affairs. Martha Cappelletti provided valuable technical exhibition advice. Very deep thanks go to my assistant, Irene Spector, who helped all of us with a vast array of organizational details, as well as following up on schedules and contracts with participating museums on the tour.

To those museum directors and colleagues who have embraced the subject of Hollywood, giving it a temporary home within their hallowed halls, I express my thanks. They include Roger G. Kennedy, Director, National Museum of American History; Lisa M. Taylor, Director, Cooper-Hewitt Museum, New York; former Director, Jan van der Marck, and current Director, Robert Frankel, Center for the Fine Arts, Miami; Millard F. Rogers, Jr., Director, Cincinnati Art Museum; Richard S. Teitz, Director, Denver Art Museum; and Craig C. Black, Director, Natural History Museum of Los Angeles County. Specifically, at the Smithsonian's Museum of American History, thanks go to Ellen Hughes, the museum's Project Director for "Hollywood" from the Division of Community Life, and Carl Scheele, Curator, Division of Community Life. Carl agreed early on to serve as curatorial adviser, and his comments throughout were most helpful.

Other Smithsonian Institution staff who contributed to the successful completion of this major undertaking include John Cobert, Deputy Director, Office of Supply Services; Robert A. Dierker, Associate General Counsel; Samuel J. Greenberg and his staff, Museum Shops; Ann Leven, Treasurer; Sir Valentine Abdy, Bt., European Representative; Janet Solinger, Director, Resident Associate Program. I would also like to acknowledge that the Smithsonian's Special Exhibition Fund helped to make possible the showings at the National Museum of American History and the Cooper-Hewitt Museum. In the early stages of the project, the Smithsonian Women's Committee provided a seed grant that enabled us to start working.

All of those mentioned above join me in thanking those who have generously made their collections available for the tour, provided photographs, and given us their special brand of Hollywood expertise. While the lenders are noted in the exhibition checklist, the following deserve special mention:

The Academy of Motion Picture Arts and Sciences: Linda Mehr and the staff of the Margaret Herrick Library, Robert Cushman, Sam Gill, and Gene Allen,

Past President; and the American Film Institute: Anne G. Schlosser and Howard H. Prouty of the Louis B. Mayer Library.

Donfeld, through the support of Giorgio Inc., shared his special insights and contacts in the field of costume design. Patrick Downing generously contributed the fruits of his research into production design. And Ronald Haver, Head of the Film Department at the Los Angeles County Museum of Art, offered sage advice on the script and the film excerpts.

Our grateful appreciation is due ABC Video Enterprises: Thomas Emma and Archie Purvis; Amblin Entertainment: Steven Spielberg, Julie Moscowitz; American Museum of the Moving Image: Rochelle Slovin, Eleanor Mish; La Belle Epoque: Kenneth Taylor; Bermans and Nathans: Monty Berman; Black Star: Howard Chapnick; Boss Film Corporation: Richard Edlund, Mark Stetson, Laura Buff, Claire Wilson; British Film Institute: Michelle Snapes; Burbank Studios: Gary Paster, Connie Baggetta, Catena Passalacqua, Ronald Stein; Camera 5: Ken Reagan; Jean-Louis Capitaine; Cincinnati Historical Society: Laura L. Chace; Cinémathèque Française: Marianne de Fleury, Noelle Giret; Columbia Pictures: Guy McElwaine, Ivelisse M. Orta. Kathy Orloff, Michael C. Gross, Deborha Neiditch; Walt Disney Productions: Jim Garber, David Smith, Sherry Warner, John M. Mansbridge, T. J. Baptie, Lee Bertram; De Mille Estate: Mrs. Randall Presley, Helen Cohen; Edwards-Lowell Luxury Furs: Merrill and Grace Lowell; Charles Fries Productions: Charles W. Fries; Gamma-Liaison: Jennifer Coley; Gemini G.E.L.: Debra Burchett; Giorgio Inc.: Fred and Gayle Hayman; Samuel Goldwyn Company: Samuel Goldwyn, Jr., Tom Bodley; Lee Gross: Carolyn Arnold; Hollywood Sound: Les Harrison; John Kobal Collection: Simon Crocker; Los Angeles County Museum of Art: Earl A. Powell III, Edward Maeder; Los Angeles County Museum of Natural History: Peter Keller, Janet R. Fireman; Library of Congress: Elena Millie, Jerry Maddox, Donna Elliott; Lucasfilm Ltd.: George Lucas, Sidney Ganis, Roberta Cairney, Deborah Fine, David Craig, Kathy Wippert, Nancy Jencks; Matthews Studio Equipment: Edward Phillips; MCA/Universal City Studios: Michele Reese, Frank Wright, Frank Rodriguez, Albert Whitlock, Bill Taylor; MGM/UA Entertainment Co.: Roger L. Mayer, Steven Newman, Herbert S. Nusbaum, Jerry Solowitz, Alan Gavoni; Museum of Modern Art: Mary Lea Bandy, Mary Corliss, Eileen Bowser, Cora Rosevear, Susan Kismaric; National Air and Space Museum: Walter J. Boyne, Linda N. Ezell, Lynda Hartigan; National Museum of American Art: Elizabeth Broun, Bob Johnston; National Museum of American History: Roger White, Doug Evelyn, Gary Kulik; National Portrait Gallery: Alan Fern, Beverly Cox, Linda Best; Northern Kentucky University: Lyle A. Gray, Howard Storm, Rose Stauss; Orion Pictures Corporation: Fred Skidmore; Paramount Pictures Corporation: John Bloechle, Jon Gould, Walter Hoffman, Eileen Cox, Bill Kenley, Michael Berman, Steven Kotlowitz; Carlo Rambaldi Enterprises: Peter Georgianni; Harry Ransom Humanities Research Center, University of Texas at Austin: Decherd Turner, Raymond Daum, Devon Susholtz, Paul Bailey; RKO Pictures: Steven Ellis, John Hall, David Chierechetti, Joseph E. Ondrick; Mr. and Mrs. George Sidney; Lee Strasberg Institute: Anna Strasberg, Victoria Crane; Swedish Film Institute: Elisabet Helge; Sygma, New York: Eliane Laffont; Sygma, Los Angeles: Françoise Kirkland; Tri-Star Pictures: Ellen Pasternack; Twentieth Century Fox Film Corporation: Elizabeth A. Colloty, Betty Einbinder; UCLA Microfilm: Sharon Huling; UCLA Special Collections: David S. Zeidberg; UCLA Theater Arts Library: Audree Malkin; University of Southern California Special Collections: Robert Knutson, Leith Adams, Edward Comstock; Variety Arts Center: Milt Larsen, Carl Fleming; Visages: Marysa Maslansky; Warner Bros.: Rob Friedman, Judith Singer, Jess Garcia; Wesleyan University, Frank Capra Archives: David Rivel.

In closing, I would like to express warm appreciation to Smithsonian Secretary Robert McC. Adams for his support of the concept and organization of "Hollywood: Legend and Reality," for his enthusiasm for the national tour, and for his contribution in the form of a Foreword to this book. The Smithsonian is a home for many wonders, and now we are able to add "Hollywood" to the list.

PEGGY A. LOAR
Director, SITES

PICTURE SOURCES

Academy of Motion Picture Arts and Sciences (AMPAS): pp. 6 (bottom left), 9, 26, 64, 71, 113 (left), 146, 154, 180; AMPAS, courtesy Twentieth Century Fox: pp. 80, 109 (left); AMPAS, courtesy Columbia Pictures: p. 81 (left); AMPAS, courtesy Paramount Pictures Corporation. All rights reserved.: pp. 81 (right, © 1932), 103 (© 1949), 109 (right, © 1919); AMPAS, courtesy MGM/UA Entertainment: pp. 76 (© 1925 by Metro-Goldwyn Pictures Corporation, renewed 1952 by Loew's Incorporated), 113 (right, © 1933 by Metro-Goldwyn-Mayer Corporation, renewed 1960 by Metro-Goldwyn-Mayer Incorporated), 129 (© 1927 by Metro-Goldwyn-Mayer Corporation, renewed 1954 by Loew's Incorporated); AMPAS, courtesy RKO General: p. 155.

Bison Archives: pp. 4, 5 (top and bottom), 6 (right), 7, 11, 191.

Kobal Collection: pp. 8, 117 (© 1941, courtesy Paramount Pictures Corporation. All rights reserved.), 187.

Prints and Photographs Division, Library of Congress: pp. 16, 28, 40, 42, 45.

Life Picture Service: photographs by J. R. Eyerman: pp. 12, 13; Francis Miller: p. 30 (left); Leonard McCombe: p. 30 (right); Ralph Crane, courtesy Black Star: pp. 52, 53, 79, 95, 144, 150, 190; Edmund Bert Gerard: p. 55; Walter Sanders: p. 57; Allan Grant: pp. 108, 130, 167, 185; Edward Clark: p. 165; Alfred Eisenstaedt: p. 178; Eliot Elisofon: pp. 193, 195; N. R. Farbman: p. 220.

The Museum of Modern Art (MoMA), Collection: p. x; Film Stills Archive (MoMA/FSA): pp. 24 (© 1931 by Warner Bros. Pictures, Inc., renewed 1958 by Associated Artists Productions Corporation), 62, 126, 182; MoMA/FSA, courtesy Twentieth Century Fox: p. 44; MoMA/FSA, courtesy Universal Pictures: pp. 88, 164 (left); MoMA/FSA, courtesy MGM/UA Entertainment: pp. 10, 112; MoMA/FSA, courtesy RKO General: p. 132; MoMA/FSA, courtesy Paramount Pictures: p. 134 (© 1972 by Paramount Pictures Corporation. All rights reserved.).

Theater Arts Collection, Harry Ransom Humanities Research Center, University of Texas at Austin: Gloria Swanson Archives: p. 46; David O. Selznick Archives: pp. 54, 65, 66 (left), 67, 90 (bottom right), 93 (bottom), 98 (top), 138, 189 (left).

Film studios: Courtesy Universal Pictures: pp. 59, 168, 175. Courtesy Lucasfilm Ltd.: pp. 104, photo by Nancy Moran (© 1981 by Lucasfilm Ltd. All rights reserved.); 173 (left), photo by Terry Chostner (© 1983 Lucasfilm Ltd. All rights reserved.); 173 (right, © 1977 Lucasfilm Ltd. All rights reserved.); 174 (top), photo by Terry Chostner (© 1980 Lucasfilm Ltd. All rights reserved.); 175 (top left, © 1983 Lucasfilm Ltd. All rights reserved.); 175 (bottom left, © 1977 Lucasfilm Ltd. All rights reserved.). Courtesy Columbia Pictures, p. 123. Courtesy MGM/UA Entertainment: p. 133 (© 1959 by Ashton Productions, Inc.). Courtesy Warner Bros.: p. 152 (left). Courtesy Samuel Goldwyn Company: p. 158.

Photographs provided by individual photographers: David Strick, front cover, p. 218; Edward Weston, p. iv, courtesy Center for Creative Photography; David Sharpe Studios, pp. vii, 2, 20, 87, 89, 90 (top left), 92 (bottom), 94, 111 (left and right), 114 (left), 141–143, 152 (right), 153, 156, 157; Garry Winogrand, p. viii, courtesy Daniel Wolf, Inc., New York; Chris Casler, pp. 18, 31, 35, 38 (bottom), 50, 86, 90 (bottom left, top right), 92 (top), 93 (top), 96, 97, 101, 110, 114 (right), 115 (left and right), 118 (left and right), 119 (left and right), 120, 148, 162, 163, 166, 169, 171, 181, 183, 198, 211, 217; Dick Busher, p. 21, courtesy 5th Avenue Theatre; Helen Levitt, p. 25, courtesy Daniel Wolf, Inc., New York; Steve Schapiro, pp. 27, 34, 84 (bottom right), 106 (courtesy Paramount Pictures, © 1974 Newdon Company. All rights reserved.), 188 (right), 202; Nancy Moran, p. 82 (top); Michael Webb, pp. 82 (bottom), 140; Dan Weaks, pp. 83 (courtesy MGM/UA Entertainment), 135 (courtesy Paramount Pictures, © 1981 Barclays Merchantile Industrial Finance Ltd. All rights reserved.); Nancy Ellison, p. 84 (left, courtesy MGM/UA Entertainment, © 1978 by United Artists Corporation); Peter Sorel, p. 84 (top right, courtesy Sygma, MGM/UA Entertainment, and

Fantasy Films, © 1975 by N. V. Zwaluw); Alfred S. Keller, A.S.C., p. 127, courtesy Columbia Pictures; Douglas Kirkland, p. 136, courtesy Sygma and Universal Pictures; Brian Hamill, p. 137 (courtesy MGM/UA Entertainment, © 1979 by United Artists Corporation); Theo Westenberger, 159, courtesy Orion Pictures; Virgil Mirano, pp. 172 (courtesy Boss Film Corporation and Columbia Pictures), 176, 177 (courtesy Boss Film Corporation and Warner Bros.); Slim Aarons, p. 184; Bob Willoughby, p. 194; Jacques Prayer, p. 197, courtesy Gamma-Liaison.

Photographs from other sources: Northern Kentucky University: pp. ii, 75, 124; Robert S. Birchard Collection: p. 6 (top left); Marjorie and Charles Benton Collection: p. 17; Whatcom Museum of History and Art, Bellingham, WA: p. 19 (top); UCLA Theatre Arts Collection: p. 19 (bottom); Galerie Cine-Images, Paris: p. 22; UCLA Research Library: p. 23; Swedish Film Institute: p. 32; Ron Haver: pp. 36, 37, 91, 128; Ken Adam: p. 38 (top); Time Inc.: pp. 39 (© 1967 Time Inc. All rights reserved.), 48 (© 1969 Time Inc. All rights reserved.); Los Angeles County Museum of Art: p. 43; Papers of F. Scott Fitzgerald, Princeton University Library: p. 66 (right); Christopher Huss: p. 98 (bottom); Brian Shapiro: p. 99; The New Yorker Magazine, Inc.: pp. 116 (drawing by Richard Decker, © 1943, 1971, The New Yorker Magazine, Inc.), 202 (drawing by Carl Rose, © 1935, 1963, The New Yorker Magazine, Inc.); Cinémathèque Française, Paris: p. 121 (left); National Film Archive, London: p. 121 (right); Dick Smith: p. 164 (right); W. F. Clark, ARCO: p. 174 (bottom); Robert Kobal: pp. 186, 188 (left), 189 (right), 192 (right); photograph by George Hurrell, courtesy Allan Rich: p. 192 (left); Frits and Agnes Becht: p. 196; A. Alfred Taubman: p. 208; Forrest J. Ackerman, Scientifilm Museum, Hollywood: p. 215; Jim Marx: p. 216.

Silver Marlon, 1964, acrylic and silkscreen on canvas by Andy Warhol. The image is derived from *The Wild One* (1954), in which Marlon Brando plays the leader of a motorcycle gang.

EXHIBITION CHECKLIST

Page references are to illustrations.

DREAM FACTORY

Way Down East, sculpture by Red Grooms, 1977–79. Painted, cast, and fabricated aluminum, 216" × 148" × 77". (0/1) pp. ii, 75, 124
From the permanent collection of Northern Kentucky University, Highland Heights, KY

J. M. Wall 35mm motion-picture camera, Mitchell tripod and finder, and four Baltar lenses. (1/17)
Lent by Grant Loucks, Alan Gordon Enterprises, Inc., Hollywood

Stage light. (1/18)
Lent by the AMERICAN MUSEUM OF THE MOVING IMAGE

Director's chair. (1/19)
Lent by Kay Armour, D. H. Arts Society, Hollywood

Clapperboard. (1/20)
Lent by Twentieth Century Fox

Miniature sailing ship used in the production of *Mutiny on the Bounty* at MGM, 1935. (1/0) p. 166
Lent by the Variety Arts Center, Los Angeles

Aerial photograph of MGM Studios, Culver City, 1932. (1/1) p. 4
Courtesy Bison Archives

Set construction at Warner Bros., 1944. (1/3)
Photograph by Ralph Crane, courtesy Black Star and Life Picture Service

Painting backdrops at MGM for *Meet Me in St. Louis,* 1943. (1/4)
Photograph by Walter Sanders, courtesy Life Picture Service

Cutaway house set for *The Diary of Anne Frank* on a Twentieth Century Fox stage, 1959. (1/5) p. 95
Photograph by Ralph Crane, courtesy Black Star and Life Picture Service

Moving giant props for *The Incredible Shrinking Man* at Universal Studios, 1957. (1/6) p. 167
Photograph by Allan Grant, courtesy Life Picture Service

Alfred Hitchcock rehearsing the cast of *Rope* at Warner Bros., 1948. (1/7) p. 79
Photograph by Ralph Crane, courtesy Black Star and Life Picture Service

Cinematographer James Wong Howe with VistaVision camera at Paramount, 1955. (1/8) p. 130
Photograph by Allan Grant, courtesy Life Picture Service

Filming *The Razor's Edge* at Twentieth Century Fox, 1946. (1/9) p. 53
Photograph by Ralph Crane, courtesy Black Star and Life Picture Service

Joseph Walker and assistants shooting the Shangri-La set of *Lost Horizon* at the Columbia Ranch, 1937. (1/10) p. 127
Photograph by Alfred S. Keller, courtesy Columbia Pictures

Hiring extras at Paramount Studios, 1928. (1/11) p. 7
Courtesy Bison Archives

Filming *Top Hat* at RKO, 1935. (1/10.1) p. 155
Courtesy AMPAS and RKO Pictures

Studio chief Darryl F. Zanuck viewing rushes of *The Razor's Edge,* 1946. (1/13) p. 52
Photograph by Ralph Crane, courtesy Black Star and Life Picture Service

Watson Webb editing *The Razor's Edge,* 1946. (1/15) p. 144
Photograph by Ralph Crane, courtesy Black Star and Life Picture Service

Composer Alfred Newman conducting the studio orchestra during scoring of *The Razor's Edge,* 1946. (1/16) p. 150
Photograph by Ralph Crane, courtesy Black Star and Life Picture Service

GOLD RUSH 1910–18

Hollywood in 1905. (2/1) p. 5
Courtesy Bison Archives

Jesse Lasky, Adolph Zukor, Sam Goldwyn, and Cecil B. De Mille, 1916, at the formation of Famous Players–Lasky (later, Paramount Pictures). (2/2) p. 5
Courtesy Bison Archives

Filming at the Flying "A" Studio in Santa Barbara, ca. 1912. (2/3) p. 6
Courtesy Robert S. Birchard Collection

Map of Hollywood, 1915, showing the location of the movie studios. (2/4)
Courtesy Los Angeles County Museum of Natural History

Production still of the Keystone Kops, ca. 1915. (2/10)
Courtesy Museum of Modern Art/Film Stills Archive

Keystone Kops helmet. (2/11)
Lent by Los Angeles County Museum of Natural History

Nickelodeon marquee, 1917. (2/12) p. 19
Courtesy UCLA Theater Arts Library

Poster for *The Moving Picture Cowboy,* 1914. (2/5)
Lent by the Library of Congress

Hat worn by cowboy star Tom Mix. (2/7)
Lent by Los Angeles County Museum of Natural History

"Inceville," ca. 1914, producer Thomas Ince's Western town in the Santa Monica Mountains. (2/8)
Courtesy Bison Archives

Filming a Western at Universal Studios, ca. 1917. (2/9) p. 6
Courtesy AMPAS

D. W. Griffith with Blanche Sweet, Dorothy Gish, Howard Gaye, Karl Brown, and Billy Bitzer. (2/13) p. 126
Courtesy Museum of Modern Art/Film Stills Archive

Pathé camera and tripod, ca. 1910. (2/14)
Lent by the AMERICAN MUSEUM OF THE MOVING IMAGE/Lawrence Williams Collection

Poster for the 1922 reissue of *The Birth of a Nation.* (2/15) p. 34
Lent by Steve Schapiro

Babylon set for *Intolerance,* 1916. (2/16) p. 6.
Courtesy Bison Archives

Fan magazines, 1912–17. (2/17-22) p. 2
Lent by Robert S. Birchard Collection

Publicity still of Douglas Fairbanks, Mary Pickford, and Charlie Chaplin, 1917. (2/24) p. 182
Courtesy Museum of Modern Art/Film Stills Archive

Poster for *The Cold Deck,* 1917. (2/25)
Lent by Michael Shaw

Poster for *The Little American,* 1917. (2/26) p. 35
Lent by Academy of Motion Picture Arts and Sciences

Huge crowds gather on Wall Street as Douglas Fairbanks sells War Bonds, 1918. (2/27)
Courtesy Kobal Collection

BONANZA, 1919–29

Production still from *Manslaughter,* 1922. (3/1)
Courtesy AMPAS and Paramount Pictures

Production still from *The Ten Commandments,* 1923. (3/2)
Courtesy AMPAS and Paramount Pictures

Thomas Meighan and Gloria Swanson in *Male and Female,* 1919. (3/3) p. 109
Courtesy AMPAS and Paramount Pictures

Costume design by Natasha Rambova for *Forbidden Fruit,* 1921. (3/5) p. 114
Lent by John Kobal

French poster for "Fatty" Arbuckle, ca. 1920. (3/6) p. 22
Lent by Galerie Cine-Images, Paris

Headlines on the Arbuckle scandal from the *Los Angeles Examiner,* 1921. (3/7) p. 23
Courtesy UCLA Research Library

Time Magazine cover on Will Hays, 1926. (3/8)
Copyright © 1926, Time Inc. All rights reserved.

Hollywood Chamber of Commerce advertisement, 1921. (3/9)
Courtesy Bruce Torrence Historical Collection

Poster for *The Son of the Sheik,* 1926. (3/10)
Lent by Steve Schapiro

Suit of lights worn by Rudolph Valentino in *Blood and Sand,* 1922. (3/11) p. 110
Lent by Michael Shaw

Publicity still of Greta Garbo, 1925. (3/12)
Courtesy Kobal Collection

Erich von Stroheim directing *Foolish Wives,* 1922. (3/14) p. 88
Courtesy Museum of Modern Art/Film Stills Archive and Universal Pictures

Mae Murray in *The Merry Widow*, 1925. (3/15)
Courtesy AMPAS and MGM/UA Entertainment

Karl Struss, Charles Rosher, F. W. Murnau, and camera crew for *Sunrise*, 1927. (3/17) p. 80
Courtesy AMPAS and Twentieth Century Fox

Production sketch by Harold W. Grieve for *So This Is Paris*, 1926. (3/17.1) p. 90
Lent by Harold W. Grieve

Hobbyhorse (bicycle) ridden by Buster Keaton in *Our Hospitality*, 1923. (3/19)
Lent by Division of Transportation, National Museum of American History, Smithsonian Institution, presented by Buster Keaton, 1924

Harold Lloyd in *For Heaven's Sake*, 1926. (3/21)
Courtesy Kevin Brownlow

French poster for Charlie Chaplin, designed by Auguste Leymarie, ca. 1919. (3/22) p. 45
Lent by Simon Dargols Collection, Paris

Poster for *The Covered Wagon*, 1923. (3/23)
Lent by Steve Schapiro, courtesy Paramount Pictures

Production sketch by William Cameron Menzies for *The Thief of Bagdad*, 1924. (3/24) p. 86
Lent by Jean Menzies Lauesen

Hanging miniature used in *The Thief of Bagdad*, 1924. (3/25)
Lent by La Cinémathèque Française, Paris

Costume sketch by Mitchell Leisen for Douglas Fairbanks in *The Thief of Bagdad*, 1924. (3/26)
Lent by La Cinémathèque Française, Paris

Hand-painted poster by Batiste Madalena for *The Black Pirate*, 1926. (3/27) p. 87
Lent by Judith and Steven Katten

Poster for *The Phantom of the Opera*, 1925. (3/30)
Lent by Steve Schapiro

Hand-painted poster by Batiste Madalena for *Rough House Rosie*, 1927. (3/32) p. 181
Lent by Judith and Steven Katten

Joan Crawford in *Our Dancing Daughters*, 1928. (3/33)
Courtesy AMPAS and MGM/UA Entertainment

Marie Dressler and Marion Davies in *The Patsy*, 1928. (3/34)
Courtesy AMPAS and MGM/UA Entertainment

Production still from *Our Modern Maidens*, 1929. (3/35)
Courtesy AMPAS and MGM/UA Entertainment

SOUND AND FURY, 1927–33

RCA microphone, ca. 1928. (4/1)
Lent by Les Harrison

RKO Product Book for 1929–30. (4/3)
Lent by Dan Price

Sound effects device made at RKO Studios to simulate an airplane engine, ca. 1929. (4/5)
Lent by Los Angeles County Museum of Natural History

Production sketch by Charles Hall for *All Quiet on the Western Front*, 1930. (4/7)
Lent by Lura E. Hall Trust

Production sketch by Robert Usher for *Putting On the Ritz*, 1929. (4/9) p. 156
Lent by The Museum of Modern Art, Department of Film

New York premiere of *The Jazz Singer*, 1927. (4/2)
Courtesy Warner Bros. and MGM/UA Entertainment

Recording the MGM lion, 1928. (4/4) p. 8
Courtesy Kobal Collection

Production still from *Broadway*, 1929. (4/8)
Courtesy AMPAS and Universal Pictures

Rouben Mamoulian directing Jeanette MacDonald in *Love Me Tonight*, 1932 (Paramount). (4/11) p. 81
Courtesy AMPAS and Universal Pictures

Walter Huston in *American Madness*, 1932. (4/12)
Courtesy AMPAS and Columbia Pictures

Paul Muni in *I Am a Fugitive From a Chain Gang*, 1932. (4/13)
Courtesy Warner Bros. and MGM/UA Entertainment

Adolphe Menjou, Mary Brian, and Pat O'Brien in *The Front Page*, 1931. (4/14)
Courtesy AMPAS

James Cagney and Jean Harlow in *The Public Enemy*, 1931 (Warner Bros.). (4/15) p. 24
Courtesy Museum of Modern Art/Film Stills Archive and MGM/UA Entertainment

Edward G. Robinson in *Little Caesar*, 1931 (Warner Bros.). (4/16.1)
Courtesy Museum of Modern Art/Film Stills Archive and MGM/UA Entertainment

German poster for *Blonde Venus*, 1932. (4/18) p. 188
Lent by Steve Schapiro

Poster of Mae West, 1933. (4/19) p. 27
Lent by Steve Schapiro

Dinner gown of ivory crepe embroidered with silver sequins and beads, designed by Travis Banton for Mae West in *I'm No Angel*, 1933. (4/20)
Lent by Paramount Pictures

Evening gown of black silk chiffon-velvet embroidered with gold thread and pearls, designed by Travis Banton for Marlene Dietrich in *Blonde Venus*, 1932. (4/21.1)
Lent by Paramount Pictures; mink trim courtesy Edwards-Lowell Luxury Furs

Production sketch by Robert Usher for *She Done Him Wrong*, 1933. (4/22) p. 90
Lent by The Museum of Modern Art, Department of Film

Caricature of Mae West by Miguel Covarrubias. (4/20.1)
Lent by Prints and Photographs Division, Library of Congress

Publicity still of Boris Karloff in *Frankenstein*, 1931. (4/23) p. 164
Courtesy Museum of Modern Art/Film Stills Archive and Universal Pictures

Production sketch by Herman Rosse for *Frankenstein*, 1931. (4/24) p. 89
Lent by the estate of Herman Rosse

"Vulcan Traveling Arc" designed by Ken Strickfadden for *Frankenstein*, 1931. (4/25)
Lent by Ed Angell

Storyboard by Mario Larrinaga for *Creation*, ca. 1932. (4/27)
Lent by Dr. Steven Lazaro, from the collection of Orville Goldner

Concept sketch by Mario Larrinaga, Willis O'Brien, and Byron Crabbe for *King Kong*, 1933. (4/28) p. 162
Lent by Mrs. Merian C. Cooper

French poster for *King Kong*, 1933. (4/30) p. 163
Lent by La Belle Epoque, Los Angeles

Stop-motion puppet of *King Kong*, 1933. (4/29)
Lent by Los Angeles County Museum of Natural History

Bela Lugosi in *Dracula*, 1931. (4/31)
Courtesy Museum of Modern Art/Film Stills Archive and Universal Pictures.

STARS IN OUR EYES

Audrey Hepburn and Grace Kelly, 1956. (5/102) p. 185
Photograph by Allan Grant, courtesy Life Picture Service

Clark Gable, Van Heflin, Gary Cooper, and James Stewart celebrate New Year's Eve at Romanoff's, 1957. (5/103) p. 184.
Photograph by Slim Aarons

Paul Robeson in *The Emperor Jones*, 1933. (5/34)
Photograph by Edward Steichen, lent by The Museum of Modern Art, Department of Photography

Gene Kelly, 1944. Strobe-lit time-exposure photograph. (5/104)
Photograph by Gjon Mili, courtesy Life Picture Service

Joan Crawford without conventional makeup, 1930. (5/105) p. 186
Photograph by George Hurrell, lent by John Kobal

Joan Crawford as Letty Lynton, 1932. (5/106) p. 187
Photograph by George Hurrell, courtesy Kobal Collection

Louise Brooks, 1928. (5/107) p. 192
Photograph by Eugene Robert Richee, lent by John Kobal

Carole Lombard, 1932. (5/108) p. 189
Photograph by Eugene Robert Richee, lent by John Kobal

Marlene Dietrich, 1935. (5/109) p. 188
Photograph by William Walling, Jr., lent by John Kobal

Jean Harlow on bearskin rug, 1934. (5/110)
Photograph by George Hurrell, lent by Allan Rich

The Departure of the Joads, 1940, lithograph by Thomas Hart Benton. One of a series commissioned from Benton by producer Darryl F. Zanuck to publicize *The Grapes of Wrath.*

Tyrone Power and Loretta Young, 1935. (5/111) p. 192
Photograph by George Hurrell, lent by Allan Rich

Greta Garbo in *The Kiss,* 1930. (5/114)
Photograph by Clarence Sinclair Bull, lent by John Kobal

Humphrey Bogart, 1941. (5/112)
Photograph by Scotty Welbourne, courtesy Kobal Collection

Katharine Hepburn in *Sylvia Scarlett,* 1936. (5/115)
Photograph by Ernest Bachrach, lent by John Kobal

NEW DEAL, 1933—41

Cel of seven dwarfs from Walt Disney's *Snow White and the Seven Dwarfs,* 1937. (5/2) p. 96
Lent by Maurice J. Noble Collection, courtesy Walt Disney Productions

Poster for *The Adventures of Robin Hood,* 1938. (5/4)
Lent by Steve Schapiro, courtesy Warner Bros.

A Night at the Opera by José Ramón Sánchez, 1981. Painting, acrylic on wood, 26″ × 34″. (5/5)
Lent by José Ramón Sánchez (Spain)

W. C. Fields in *David Copperfield,* 1935. (5/6)
Courtesy AMPAS and MGM/UA Entertainment

Poster for *Sons of the Desert,* 1933. (5/7)
Lent by Cincinnati Historical Society

German poster for *Tarzan the Ape Man,* 1932. (5/8)
Lent by Steve Schapiro

Poster for *The Phantom Empire,* 1935. (5/14)
Lent by Forrest J. Ackerman, Scientifilm Museum, Hollywood

Jean Harlow and George Cukor during production of *Dinner at Eight,* 1933. (5/15) p. 113
Courtesy AMPAS and MGM/UA Entertainment

Austrian poster for *The Painted Veil,* 1934. (5/16) p. 189
Lent by Harry Ransom Humanities Research Center, University of Texas at Austin, Theater Arts Collection

The Motion Picture Production Code, 1930. (5/17) p. 26
Courtesy AMPAS

Claudette Colbert and Clark Gable in *It Happened One Night,* 1934. (5/18)
Courtesy AMPAS and Columbia Pictures

Carole Lombard and John Barrymore in *Twentieth Century,* 1934. (5/19)
Courtesy AMPAS and Columbia Pictures

Rosalind Russell and Cary Grant in *His Girl Friday,* 1940. (5/20)
Courtesy AMPAS and Columbia Pictures

Spencer Tracy and Katharine Hepburn in *Woman of the Year,* 1942. (5/21)
Courtesy AMPAS and MGM/UA Entertainment

Production still from *Gold Diggers of 1933.* (5/22) p. 152
Courtesy Warner Bros. and MGM/UA Entertainment

Neon-edged violin used in *Gold Diggers of 1933.* (5/23) p. 152
Lent by Kenneth Anger Collection

Cartoon by Carl Rose, 1935. (5/24) p. 202
© 1935 The New Yorker Magazine, Inc.

Fred Astaire and Ginger Rogers in *Swing Time,* 1936. (5/26)
Courtesy AMPAS and RKO Pictures

Promotional cut-out for *Flying Down to Rio,* 1933. (5/25) p. 153
Lent by Cincinnati Historical Society

Ginger Rogers rehearsing with choreographer Hermes Pan for *Swing Time,* 1936. (5/27) p. 154
Courtesy AMPAS and RKO Pictures

Dance shoes worn by Fred Astaire in *Top Hat,* 1935. (5/28)
Lent by Los Angeles County Museum of Natural History

Shoes worn by Shirley Temple, 1937. (5/28.1)
Lent by Los Angeles County Museum of Natural History

Blacks-only movie house in Leland, Mississippi, 1939. (5/29) p. 42
Photograph by Marion Post Wolcott for the Farm Security Administration, courtesy Library of Congress

Stick 'Em Up Cinema, lithograph by Mabel Dwight, 1928.

Poster art for *Gone Harlem*, 1939. (5/30) p. 43
Courtesy Los Angeles County Museum of Art

Bill "Bojangles" Robinson and Shirley Temple in *The Little Colonel*, 1935. (5/31) p. 44
Courtesy Museum of Modern Art/Film Stills Archive and Twentieth Century Fox

Stepin Fetchit and Will Rogers in *Steamboat 'Round the Bend*, 1935. (5/33)
Courtesy AMPAS and Twentieth Century Fox

Adrian, chief costume designer at MGM, 1928–42, with Greta Garbo. (5/35) p. 112
Courtesy AMPAS and MGM/UA Entertainment

Re-creation of white ruffled chiffon evening dress designed by Adrian for Joan Crawford in *Letty Lynton*, 1932. (5/36)
Lent by the Giorgio Costume Collection

Joan Crawford in *Letty Lynton*, 1932. (5/37) p. 187
Courtesy AMPAS and MGM/UA Entertainment

Travis Banton, chief costume designer at Paramount, 1924–37, with Marlene Dietrich. (5/38) p. 113
Courtesy AMPAS and Paramount Pictures

Costume sketch by Orry-Kelly, leading designer at Warner Bros. in the 1930s and early 1940s, for *42nd Street*, 1933. (5/39)
Lent by Los Angeles County Museum of Art, Gift of Linda Descenna

Dorothy Lamour in *Beyond the Blue Horizon*, 1941 (Paramount). (5/40) p. 117
Courtesy Kobal Collection and Universal Pictures

Last page of MGM's 1935 contract with Greta Garbo. (5/41.1)
Courtesy MGM/UA Entertainment

Ball scene in *Marie Antoinette*, 1938. (5/42)
Photograph by George Hurrell, lent by Allan Rich, courtesy MGM/UA Entertainment

Costume sketch by Adrian for Norma Shearer in *Marie Antoinette*, 1938. (5/43)
Lent by Adrian Collection; Joseph Simms, Curator

Red velvet gown embroidered with pearls, designed by Adrian for Jeanette MacDonald in *Maytime*, 1937. (5/44) p. 111
Lent by Thomas S. Hartzog and Mrs. Joye B. Hartzog

Forest-green silk-velvet gown trimmed with gold, designed by Adrian for Norma Shearer in *Marie Antoinette*, 1938. (5/45) p. 111
Lent by Thomas S. Hartzog and Mrs. Joye B. Hartzog

Court dress, designed by Adrian for Greta Garbo in *Queen Christina*, 1933. (5/46)
Lent by Adrian Collection; Joseph Simms, Curator

Brown satin dress with lace underskirt, designed by Max Ree for Olivia de Havilland in *A Midsummer Night's Dream*, 1935. (5/47)
Lent by Jane Withers

Barbecue dress, designed by Walter Plunkett for Vivien Leigh in *Gone With the Wind*, 1939. (5/47.3)
Lent by Los Angeles County Museum of Art

Production sketch by Anton Grot for *A Midsummer Night's Dream*, 1935. (5/49) p. 92
Lent by Department of Special Collections, UCLA Research Library

Production sketch by Anton Grot for *The Sea Hawk*, 1940. (5/50) p. 93
Lent by Department of Special Collections, UCLA Research Library

Production sketch by Anton Grot for *The Private Lives of Elizabeth and Essex*, 1939. (5/51)
Lent by Department of Special Collections, UCLA Research Library

Production sketch by Ernst Fegté for *Design for Living*, 1933. (5/52)
Lent by La Cinémathèque Française, Paris

Production design by Roland Anderson for *Cleopatra*, 1934; sketch by Boris Leven. (5/53)
Lent by the De Mille estate

Production design by Lionel Banks for *Lost Horizon*, 1937; sketch by Cary Odell. (5/54)
Lent by the Frank Capra Collection at Wesleyan University

Production sketch by Boris Leven for *The Shanghai Gesture*, 1941. (5/56) p. 90
Lent by Boris Leven

Production design by Perry Ferguson for *Citizen Kane*, 1941; sketch by Claude Gillingwater. (5/57) p. 94
Lent by The Museum of Modern Art, Department of Film

Orson Welles and cinematographer Gregg Toland set up the final scene of *Citizen Kane*, 1941. (5/58) p. 132
Courtesy Museum of Modern Art/Film Stills Archive and RKO Pictures

"Rosebud," the sled that serves as a clue to the true character of Kane in *Citizen Kane*, 1941. (5/58.1)
Lent by Steven Spielberg

Production sketch by Robert Usher for *This Gun for Hire*, 1942. (5/59)
Lent by The Museum of Modern Art, Department of Film

Two sketches by Lyle Wheeler of a futuristic car in *The Young in Heart*, 1937. (5/62, 5/63)
Lent by David O. Selznick Archives, Harry Ransom Humanities Research Center, University of Texas at Austin

Matte painting of Oz used in *The Wizard of Oz*, 1939. (5/66) p. 97
Lent by Archives of Performing Arts, University of Southern California

Ruby slippers worn by Dorothy in *The Wizard of Oz*, 1939. (5/67)
Collection of National Museum of American History, Smithsonian Institution

Scarecrow costume worn by Ray Bolger in *The Wizard of Oz*. (5/69)
Lent by Ray Bolger

Costume sketch by Adrian for a Munchkin in *The Wizard of Oz*, 1939. (5/70)
Lent by the Adrian Collection; Joseph Simms, Curator

Production still from *The Grapes of Wrath*, 1940. (5/77)
Courtesy AMPAS and Twentieth Century Fox

Migrant woman who served as model for Ma Joad in *The Grapes of Wrath*, 1940. (5/78)
Photograph by Horace Bristol, courtesy Life Picture Service

Frank Capra and Gary Cooper during production of *Mr. Deeds Goes to Town*, 1936. (5/3) p. 81
Courtesy AMPAS and Columbia Pictures

Richard Day's set for *Dead End*, 1936. (5/71)
Courtesy the Samuel Goldwyn Company

Production still from *Fury*, 1936. (5/72)
Courtesy AMPAS and MGM/UA Entertainment

Joel McCrea and Veronica Lake in *Sullivan's Travels*, 1941 (Paramount). (5/76)
Courtesy AMPAS and Universal Pictures

Charlie Chaplin in *Modern Times*, 1936. (5/74)
Courtesy AMPAS

Overalls worn by Charlie Chaplin in *Modern Times*, 1936. (5/73)
Lent by Los Angeles County Museum of Natural History

Chaplin look-alike competition in Bellingham, Washington, ca. 1917. (5/113) p. 19
Photograph by J. W. Sandison, courtesy Whatcom Museum of History and Art, Bellingham, WA

Swedish poster for *The Great Dictator*, 1940. (5/75) p. 32
Lent by Swedish Film Institute, Stockholm

GONE WITH THE WIND, 1936–39

Unless otherwise indicated, the exhibits in this section have been lent by the David O. Selznick Archives, Theater Arts Collection, Harry Ransom Humanities Research Center, University of Texas at Austin. Courtesy MGM/UA Entertainment.

Teletype from Kay Brown to Producer David O. Selznick urging acquisition of motion-picture rights to *Gone With the Wind*, May 1936. (5/81)

Memo from Val Lewton to Selznick suggesting writers to revise the *Gone With the Wind* script, October 1938. (5/82) p. 65

Memo from Scott Fitzgerald to Selznick on the character of Melanie, January 1939. (5/83) p. 66

Opening titles by Ben Hecht for domestic and foreign versions of *Gone With the Wind*. (5/84) p. 67

Letter from Walter White, Secretary of the NAACP, to Selznick, June 1938. (5/101)

Selznick notation on competing offers for *Gone With the Wind* from MGM and Warner Bros. (5/85) p. 54

Letter from an Ohio fan suggesting Mae West for the role of Scarlett O'Hara. (5/86)

Publicity still of *Gone With the Wind* Production Designer William Cameron Menzies. (5/87)

Sketch by Dorothea Holt for the Butler House staircase. (5/88)

Sketch by Dorothea Holt of Rhett Butler on staircase. (5/88.1)

Sketch by Jack Martin Smith of Scarlett O'Hara on the road to Tara. (5/89)

Sketch by Jack Martin Smith of Scarlett O'Hara sheltering under a bridge. (5/89.1)

Publicity still of *Gone With the Wind* Art Director Lyle Wheeler with a model of the Atlanta set. (5/90)

Selznick on the Atlanta set. (5/91) p. 55
Photograph by Edmund Bert Gerard, courtesy Life Picture Service

Costume sketch by Walter Plunkett for Scarlett. (5/92) p. 120
Lent by Academy of Motion Picture Arts and Sciences

Cameo brooch worn by Scarlett. (5/93)
Lent by Academy of Motion Picture Arts and Sciences

Costume sketch by Walter Plunkett for Rhett Butler. (5/94)
Lent by Colin Higgins

Publicity still of cinematographers Ernest Haller and Ray Rennahan with Technicolor camera. (5/95)

Publicity still of Victor Fleming directing Vivien Leigh. (5/96)

Memo from Selznick to Jock Whitney announcing completion of *Gone With the Wind*. (5/97)

Two storyboards by William Cameron Menzies for Rhett and Scarlett's escape from Atlanta. (5/98, 5/98.1) p. 138

Best Picture Oscar, one of eight awarded to *Gone With the Wind*. (5/99)
Lent by Daniel Selznick

Hattie McDaniel with her Academy Award for Best Supporting Actress. (5/100)
Courtesy AMPAS

WORLD WAR, 1942–45

Production still from *This Is the Army*, 1943. (6/1)
Courtesy Warner Bros.

Production still from *Mrs. Miniver*, 1942. (6/2)
Courtesy AMPAS and MGM/UA Entertainment

Production still from *Air Force*, 1943 (Warner Bros.). (6/3)
Courtesy AMPAS and MGM/UA Entertainment

Production still from *Song of Russia*, 1944. (6/4) p. 10
Courtesy Museum of Modern Art/Film Stills Archive and MGM/UA Entertainment

Production still from *Sahara*, 1943. (6/4.1)
Courtesy Museum of Modern Art/Film Stills Archive and Columbia Pictures

Rita Hayworth and company in *Cover Girl*, 1944. (6/10)
Courtesy Kobal Collection and Columbia Pictures

Costume sketch by Irene Sharaff for Lucille Bremer in *Ziegfeld Follies*, 1945. (6/8) p. 114
Lent by Archives of Performing Arts, University of Southern California

Costume design by Helen Rose for Carmen Miranda in *Nancy Goes to Rio*, 1950; sketch by Elaine Owens. (6/6) p. 115
Lent by Donna J. Peterson

Sequined leotard with mink and sequined skirt designed by Mitchell Leisen and Edith Head for Ginger Rogers in *Lady in the Dark*, 1944. (6/9)
Lent by Paramount Pictures

Sketch for *The Three Caballeros*, 1945. (6/11)
Lent by the Walt Disney Archives, Burbank, CA

Cel and background for *Bambi*, 1942. (6/12)
Lent by the Walt Disney Archives, Burbank, CA

Roy Rogers with Trigger, 1943. (6/14)
Photograph by Walter Sanders, courtesy Life Picture Service

Fred MacMurray and Barbara Stanwyck in *Double Indemnity*, 1944 (Paramount). (6/15)
Courtesy AMPAS and Universal Pictures

Humphrey Bogart and Lauren Bacall in *To Have and Have Not*, 1944 (Warner Brothers). (6/16)
Courtesy AMPAS and MGM/UA Entertainment

Clifton Webb, Vincent Price, Judith Anderson, and Dana Andrews in *Laura*, 1944. (6/16.1)
Courtesy UCLA Theater Arts Library and Twentieth Century Fox

Humphrey Bogart and Dooley Wilson in *Casablanca*, 1943. (6/24)
Courtesy Warner Bros. and MGM/UA Entertainment

Piano and stool from Rick's Café in *Casablanca*. (6/17) p. 148
Lent by Dr. Gary Milan

Rattan chair from Rick's Café. (6/19)
Lent by Dr. Gary Milan

Table lamp from Rick's Café. (6/22)
Lent by The Burbank Studios

Moroccan style screen from Rick's Café. (6/23)
Lent by The Burbank Studios

Exchange of memos between Jack Warner and Hal Wallis on the casting of *Casablanca*. (6/27, 6/28)
Lent by Archives of Performing Arts, University of Southern California, courtesy Warner Bros.

Producer Hal Wallis's annotated copy of *Casablanca* script. (6/29)
Lent by Stanley Caidin, courtesy Warner Bros.

Ernst Lubitsch directing *To Be or Not to Be*, 1942. (6/30)
Courtesy AMPAS

Joel McCrea, Charles Coburn, and Jean Arthur in *The More the Merrier*, 1943. (6/31)
Courtesy AMPAS and Columbia Pictures

Bing Crosby and Bob Hope in *Road to Morocco*, 1942 (Paramount). (6/32)
Courtesy AMPAS and Universal Pictures

Poster designed by Vargas for *Moon Over Miami*, 1940. (6/33)
Lent by Steve Schapiro, courtesy Twentieth Century Fox

Publicity still for *The Outlaw*, 1943. (6/34)
Courtesy Life Picture Service

Starlet posing for 1943 calendar shot. (6/35)
Photograph by Ralph Crane, courtesy Black Star and Life Picture Service

Cartoon by Richard Decker on frontline screenings, 1943. (6/36) p. 116
© 1943, 1971 The New Yorker Magazine, Inc.

Postcard for the Hollywood Canteen. (6/37)
Lent by the Lester Glassner Collection

Marlene Dietrich entertaining the troops. (6/38)
Photograph by George Silk, courtesy Life Picture Service

Jennifer Jones, Claudette Colbert, and Shirley Temple in *Since You Went Away*, 1943. (6/39) p. 36
Courtesy Ron Haver

The Hilton family, models for the fictional characters in *Since You Went Away*, 1943. (6/40) p. 37
Courtesy Ron Haver

Paul Henreid and Bette Davis in *Now Voyager*, 1942. (6/40.1)
Courtesy Warner Bros. and MGM/UA Entertainment

Joan Crawford in *Mildred Pierce*, 1945. (6/41)
Courtesy Warner Bros. and MGM/UA Entertainment

Storyboard by Anton Grot for *Mildred Pierce*, 1945. (6/42)
Lent by Department of Special Collections, UCLA Research Library

Sketch of a production design by Salvador Dali for the dream sequence in *Spellbound*, 1945. (6/43) p. 98
Lent by David O. Selznick Archives, Harry Ransom Humanities Research Center, University of Texas at Austin

Production design by Salvador Dali for the dream sequence in *Spellbound*, 1945. (6/44) p. 98
Lent by Christopher Huss

END OF AN ERA, 1945–66

Violence on the picket line during the 1945 studio strike. (7/1) p. 11
Courtesy Bison Archives

J. Parnell Thomas, Chairman of the House Un-American Activities Committee (HUAC), conducting hearings, November 1947. (7/3) p. 30
Photograph by Francis Miller, courtesy Life Picture Service

Humphrey Bogart, Lauren Bacall, and Danny Kaye among the spectators at the HUAC hearings, 1947. (7/2)
Photograph by Martha Holmes, courtesy Life Picture Service

Gary Cooper testifying before HUAC. (7/4) p. 30
Photograph by Leonard McCombe, courtesy Life Picture Service

Dana Andrews in *The Best Years of Our Lives*, 1946. (7/5)
Courtesy the Samuel Goldwyn Company

Photograph from a *Time* Magazine article on returning veterans, 1944, which inspired *The Best Years of Our Lives*. (7/6)
Photograph by Gene Cook, courtesy Life Picture Service

Robert Ryan in *Crossfire*, 1947. (7/7)
Courtesy Museum of Modern Art/Film Stills Archive and RKO Pictures

Juan Fernandez and Claude Jarman, Jr., in *Intruder in the Dust*, 1949. (7/8)
Courtesy AMPAS and MGM/UA Entertainment

Gary Cooper in *High Noon*, 1952. (7/9)
Courtesy Museum of Modern Art/Film Stills Archive

Hat, boots, and gunbelt worn by Gary Cooper in *High Noon*, 1952. (7/10, 7/11, 7/12)
Lent by Archives of Performing Arts, University of Southern California

John Wayne and Montgomery Clift in *Red River*, 1948. (7/13)
Courtesy AMPAS and MGM/UA Entertainment

Alan Ladd and Brandon de Wilde in *Shane*, 1953. (7/14)
Courtesy AMPAS and Paramount Pictures

Polish poster for *Sunset Boulevard*, 1950. (7/16) p. 46
Lent by Gloria Swanson Archives, Harry Ransom Humanities Research Center, University of Texas at Austin

Orson Welles and Rita Hayworth in *The Lady from Shanghai*, 1948. (7/15)
Courtesy AMPAS and Columbia Pictures

Louis B. Mayer and his top stars at MGM's twentieth anniversary, 1943. (7/41) p. 57
Photograph by Walter Sanders, courtesy Life Picture Service

Front page of MGM's 1943 contract with Clark Gable. (7/42)
Courtesy MGM/UA Entertainment

Columbia Pictures chief Harry Cohn, 1958. (7/43)
Photograph by Allan Grant, courtesy Life Picture Service

Cartoon by Karl Hubenthal on death of Walt Disney, 1966. (7/44)
Courtesy Karl Hubenthal, *Los Angeles Herald-Examiner*

Pleated black silk dress designed by Milo Anderson for Patricia Neal in *The Fountainhead*, 1949 (Warner Bros.). (7/18)
Lent by The Burbank Studios

Patricia Neal in *The Fountainhead*, 1949 (Warner Bros.). (7/18.1)
Courtesy Museum of Modern Art/Film Stills Archive and MGM/UA Entertainment

Olivia de Havilland in *The Heiress*, 1949. (7/20) p. 103
Courtesy AMPAS and Paramount Pictures

Costume design by Edith Head for Olivia de Havilland in *The Heiress*, 1949. (7/19)
Lent by La Cinémathèque Française, Paris

Costume design by Edith Head for Elizabeth Taylor in *A Place in the Sun*, 1951. (7/21)
Lent by Leonard W. Stanley

Costume design by Edith Head for Grace Kelly in *To Catch a Thief*, 1955. (7/23) p. 121
Lent by La Cinémathèque Française, Paris

Arthur Freed, Vincente Minnelli, Leslie Caron, and Gene Kelly during the making of *An American in Paris*, 1951. (7/24)
Courtesy AMPAS and MGM/UA Entertainment

Costume sketch by Irene Sharaff for the ballet in *An American in Paris*, 1951. (7/25)
Lent by La Cinémathèque Française, Paris

Model of the fountain constructed at MGM for the ballet in *An American in Paris*, 1951. (7/26)
Lent by Vincente Minnelli

Climax of the ballet in *An American in Paris*, 1951. (7/27)
Courtesy AMPAS and MGM/UA Entertainment

Costume sketch by Mary Ann Nyberg for Cyd Charisse in *The Band Wagon*, 1953. (7/28)
Lent by Archives of Performing Arts, University of Southern California

Lobbying Congress: model designed by Ray Harryhausen for *Earth vs. the Flying Saucers* (1956), one of a spate of low-budget 1950s movies on alien invasion.

Costume sketch by Mary Ann Nyberg for male dancers in *The Band Wagon*, 1953. (7/29)
Lent by Archives of Performing Arts, University of Southern California

Production design by Oliver Smith for *The Band Wagon*, 1953. (7/31) Lent by Oliver Smith

Suburban sprawl in Levittown, Long Island, NY. (7/33)
Photograph by Joe Scherschel, courtesy Life Picture Service

Audience with polarized glasses at 1952 premiere of *Bwana Devil* in 3-D. (7/36)
Photograph by J. R. Eyerman, courtesy Life Picture Service

Cartoon by Anatole Kovarsky on problems of CinemaScope, 1954. (7/38)
© 1954, The New Yorker Magazine, Inc.

Screening of *The Ten Commandments*, 1956, in a drive-in. (7/39) p. 13
Photograph by J. R. Eyerman, courtesy Life Picture Service

Gloria Swanson mourns the destruction of New York's Roxy Theatre, 1960. (7/40) p. 193
Photograph by Eliot Elisofon, courtesy Life Picture Service

Golden calf from *The Ten Commandments*, 1956. (7/45) Lent by William Morris

Centurions' costumes for *Ben Hur*, 1959. (7/46)
Photograph by David Lees, courtesy Life Picture Service

Production sketch by John de Cuir for *Cleopatra*, 1963. (7/47)
Lent by Archives of Performing Arts, University of Southern California

Elizabeth Taylor and Loris Loddi in *Cleopatra* (1963). (7/47.1)
Courtesy 20th Century Fox

Production still from *The Ten Commandments*, 1956. (7/45.1)
Courtesy AMPAS and Paramount Pictures

Judy Garland in *A Star Is Born*, 1954. (7/49) p. 194
Photograph by Bob Willoughby, courtesy Warner Bros.

Soviet premier Nikita Khrushchev watching the filming of *Can Can*, 1959. (7/50) p. 220
Photograph by N. R. Farbman, courtesy Life Picture Service

Promotional sketch by Al Hirschfeld for *My Fair Lady*, 1964. (7/51)
Courtesy Warner Bros.

Dark green velvet dress and feathered hat, designed by Cecil Beaton for Audrey Hepburn in *My Fair Lady*, 1964. (7/52)
Costume lent by The Burbank Studios; hat recreated by Leah Barnes Kiernan

Costume sketch by Cecil Beaton for Audrey Hepburn in *My Fair Lady*, 1964. (7/53) p. 121
Lent by National Film Archive, London

Model designed by Ray Harryhausen for *Earth vs. Flying Saucers*, 1956. (7/56) p. 215
Lent by Forrest J. Ackerman, Scientifilm Museum, Hollywood

James Dean and Natalie Wood in *Rebel Without a Cause*, 1955. (7/58)
Courtesy Warner Bros.

James Dean and Elizabeth Taylor in *Giant*, 1956. (7/59)
Courtesy Warner Bros.

Burt Lancaster, Frank Sinatra, and Montgomery Clift in *From Here to Eternity*, 1953. (7/66)
Photograph by Bob Willoughby, courtesy Columbia Pictures

Production sketch by Ken Adam for the War Room in *Dr. Strangelove, Or: How I Learned to Stop Worrying and Love the Bomb*, 1964. (7/67) p. 38
Lent by Ken Adam

Sammy Davis, Jr., in *Porgy and Bess*, 1959. (7/68) p. 158
Courtesy the Samuel Goldwyn Company

Sidney Poitier and Rod Steiger in *In the Heat of the Night*, 1967. (7/71)
Courtesy AMPAS and MGM/UA Entertainment

French poster for *The Seven Year Itch*, 1955. (7/60)
Lent by Steve Schapiro

Costume sketch by William Travilla for Marilyn Monroe in *There's No Business Like Show Business*, 1954. (7/62) p. 115
Lent by Academy of Motion Picture Arts and Sciences

Groucho Marx as Shiva, the God of Business, 1935, pencil sketch by Salvador Dali. Dali sketched sets for an imaginary Marx Brothers movie, *Giraffes on Horseback Salad.*

Billy Wilder, cinematographer Charles Lang, Jr., Tony Curtis, and Marilyn Monroe during the filming of *Some Like It Hot,* 1958. (7/63) p. 133
Courtesy MGM/UA Entertainment

Nude marquisette dress embroidered with brilliants, designed by Jean Louis for Marilyn Monroe, who wore it to President Kennedy's birthday party, 1962. (7/61.1)
Dress lent by the estate of Lee Strasberg; fox stole lent by Edwards-Lowell Luxury Furs

Katharine Hepburn on location for *The African Queen,* 1951. (7/72) p. 195
Photograph by Eliot Elisofon, courtesy Life Picture Service

Henry Fonda and Lee J. Cobb in *Twelve Angry Men,* 1957. (7/73)
Courtesy Museum of Modern Art/Film Stills Archive and MGM/UA Entertainment

Rod Steiger and Marlon Brando in *On the Waterfront,* 1954. (7/74)
Courtesy AMPAS and Columbia Pictures

Gregory Peck and Mary Badham in *To Kill a Mockingbird,* 1962. (7/75)
Courtesy AMPAS and Universal Pictures

Paul Newman and Jackie Gleason in *The Hustler,* 1961. (7/76)
Courtesy Museum of Modern Art/Film Stills Archive and Paramount Pictures

Elizabeth Taylor and Richard Burton in *Who's Afraid of Virginia Woolf,* 1966. (7/77)
Photograph by Bob Willoughby, courtesy Warner Bros.

THE ARTIST'S VISION

Lillian in the Garden by Grover Cole, watercolor on paper, 21″ × 28″, 1982. (8/15)
From the collection of H. Lloyd and Judy Gay Burkley

A Paramount Picture by Reginald Marsh, tempera on board, 36″ × 28″, 1934. (8/16) p. 17
Marjorie and Charles Benton Collection

New York Movie by Edward Hopper, oil on canvas, 32¼″ × 40⅛″, 1939. (8/28) p. x
Collection, The Museum of Modern Art, New York, given anonymously, 1941

Stick 'Em Up Cinema by Mabel Dwight, lithograph, 10⅜″ × 10⁵⁄₁₆″, 1928. (8/29) p. 212
National Museum of American Art, Smithsonian Institution, Museum Purchase and Gift of Ben and Beatrice Goldstein Foundation, Inc.

Bob Hope by Marisol, painted wood sculpture for *Time* cover, 19″ h × 15″ w × 16″ d, 1967. (8/18)
Lent by National Portrait Gallery, Smithsonian Institution, gift of Time Inc.

The New Cinema, collage of images from *Bonnie and Clyde* by Robert Rauschenberg, for *Time* Magazine cover, 17″ × 13¼″, 1967. (8/13) p. 39
Lent by National Portrait Gallery, Smithsonian Institution, gift of Time Inc.

Painted bronze equestrian sculpture of John Wayne by Harry Jackson, for *Time* Magazine cover, 27½″ h × 33½″ l × 12½″ d, 1969. (8/21) p. 48
Lent by *Time* Magazine

The Departure of the Joads by Thomas Hart Benton, lithograph, 21″ × 26″, ca. 1939, inscribed by the artist to Darryl F. Zanuck. (8/14) p. 211
Lent by Richard D. Zanuck

Pencil sketch of Harpo Marx by Salvador Dali, 12½″ × 9½″, 1937. (8/23) p. 217
Lent by Mrs. Harpo Marx

Groucho Marx as Shiva, the God of Business, by Salvador Dali, pencil sketch, 1937. (8/24) p. 216
Lent by Jim Marx

Geometric Mouse — Scale C by Claes Oldenburg, black anodized aluminum construction, 24″ × 20″, 1971. (8/19)
Lent by Gemini G.E.L., © 1971, Los Angeles, and the artist

Miriam by Dan McCleary, oil on canvas, 56¼″ × 76¼″, 1983. (8/20) p. 198
Lent by William H. Bigelow III

Twentieth Century Fox by Robert Cottingham, oil on canvas, 52⅝″ × 72⅝″, 1969. (8/22) p. 50
Lent by Kent and Cara Wilson

Silver Marlon by Andy Warhol, acrylic and silkscreen on canvas, 70″ × 80″, 1964. (8/30) p. 208
Lent by A. Alfred Taubman

The General by José Ramón Sánchez, acrylic on wood, 26″ × 34″, 1982. (8/26)
Lent by José Ramón Sánchez (Spain)

Harpo Marx, 1935, pencil sketch by Salvador Dali. Dali became friends with Harpo when he first arrived in Hollywood, sending him a harp with barbed-wire strings as a present.

Marilyn by Mimmi Rotella, décollage, 52¼" × 37", 1962. (8/27) p. 196
Lent by Frits and Agnes Becht

The Empty Opera Set by Brian Shapiro, gouache, 32¼" × 44¼", 1983. (8/27) p. 99
Lent by Brian Shapiro

PRODUCTION DESIGN

Set design by Hilyard M. Brown for *Night of the Hunter*, 1955; watercolor rendering by David J. Negrone and David J. Negrone, Jr. (8/1)
Lent by Hilyard M. Brown

Storyboard by Mentor Huebner for *North by Northwest*, 1959; production designer, Robert Boyle. (8/2) p. 141
Lent by The Museum of Modern Art, Department of Film

Concept sketch by Boris Leven for *West Side Story*, 1961. (8/3)
Lent by Boris Leven

Storyboard by Maurice Zuberano for *West Side Story*; production designer, Boris Leven. (8/4)
Lent by Maurice Zuberano

Set sketch by Alexandre Trauner for *The Apartment*, 1960. (8/10)
Lent by Alexandre Trauner

Sketch for matte painting by Albert Whitlock for *The Birds*, 1963; production designer, Robert Boyle. (8/5) p. 169
Lent by Robert Boyle

Matte painting by Albert Whitlock for *Earthquake*, 1974. (8/6) p. 168
Lent by Universal Pictures

Sketch for matte painting by Joe Hurley for *The China Syndrome*, 1979; production designer, George Jenkins. (8/12) p. 38
Lent by George Jenkins

FOUNTAIN OF YOUTH, 1967–

Dustin Hoffman and Katharine Ross in *The Graduate*, 1967. (9/1)
Photograph by Bob Willoughby, courtesy the photographer and Embassy Pictures

Set sketch by Bill Magor for *The Graduate*, 1967; production designer, Richard Sylbert. (9/2)
Lent by George R. Nelson

Poster design for *Bonnie and Clyde*, 1967. (9/3.1)
Courtesy Warner Bros.

Costume sketch by Theodora Van Runkle for Faye Dunaway in *Bonnie and Clyde*, 1967. (9/4.1) p. 119
Lent by Theodora Van Runkle

Paul Newman and Robert Redford in *Butch Cassidy and the Sundance Kid*, 1969. (9/7)
Courtesy AMPAS and Twentieth Century Fox

Dennis Hopper and Peter Fonda in *Easy Rider*, 1969. (9/8)
Courtesy UCLA Theater Arts Library and Columbia Pictures

Production still from *American Graffiti*, 1973. (9/9.1)
Courtesy Universal Pictures

Al Martino and Marlon Brando in *The Godfather*, 1972. (9/10) p. 134
Courtesy Museum of Modern Art/Film Stills Archive and Paramount Pictures

Robert Shaw, Roy Scheider, and Richard Dreyfuss in *Jaws*, 1975. (9/11)
Courtesy Universal Pictures

Hollywood sign in ruins, ca. 1980. (9/19) cover
Photograph by David Strick

Poster for the Florida Motion Picture and TV Bureau, 1982. (9/20)
Lent by Florida Department of Commerce

Harrison Ford in *Witness*, 1985. (9/24)
Photograph by Nancy Ellison, courtesy Paramount Pictures

Milos Forman directing Jack Nicholson and cast in *One Flew Over the Cuckoo's Nest*, 1975. (9/21) p. 84
Photograph by Peter Sorel, courtesy Sygma and Fantasy Films

Robert Duvall and Tess Harper in *Tender Mercies*, 1983. (9/23)
Courtesy Universal Pictures

Susan Sarandon and Burt Lancaster in *Atlantic City*, 1981. (9/21.1)
Courtesy Paramount Pictures

Moving a billboard of Richard Pryor on Sunset Strip in Hollywood. Pryor's movies have built on his popularity as a stand-up comedian. Photo by David Strick.

Dustin Hoffman and Jon Voight in *Midnight Cowboy*, 1969. (9/25)
Photograph by Steve Schapiro, courtesy MGM/UA Entertainment

Robert de Niro with Martin Scorsese during the filming of *Taxi Driver*, 1976. (9/26) p. 84
Courtesy UCLA Theater Arts Library and Columbia Pictures

Peter Finch in *Network*, 1976. (9/27)
Photograph by Mary Ellen Mark, courtesy Visages and MGM/UA Entertainment

Diane Keaton and Woody Allen in *Annie Hall*, 1975. (9/28)
Courtesy MGM/UA Entertainment

Publicity still for *Prizzi's Honor*, 1985, with Jack Nicholson, Kathleen Turner, Anjelica Huston, and director John Huston. (9/29.1)
Photograph by Michael Childers, courtesy ABC Motion Pictures and Twentieth Century Fox

Costume sketch by Donfeld for Anjelica Huston in *Prizzi's Honor*, 1985. (9/29) p. 119
Lent by Mr. and Mrs. John Foreman

Roy Scheider in *All That Jazz*, 1979. (9/31)
Photograph by Alan Pappé, courtesy Lee Gross and Twentieth Century Fox

John Travolta and Karen Lynn Gorney in *Saturday Night Fever*, 1977. (9/71.1)
Courtesy Paramount Pictures

Hand-colored photograph by Dan Weaks of radical meeting in *Reds*, 1981. (9/57) p. 135
Lent by the photographer; courtesy Paramount Pictures

Production sketch by Joe Hurley for *Chinatown*, 1974; production designer, Richard Sylbert. (9/58) p. 101
Lent by Richard Sylbert

Production sketch by Stuart Wurtzel for *The Purple Rose of Cairo*, 1985. (9/59)
Lent by Stuart Wurtzel

Production sketch by George Jenkins for *Sophie's Choice*, 1983. (9/60)
Lent by George Jenkins

Peter MacNicol, Meryl Streep, and Kevin Kline in *Sophie's Choice*, 1983. (9/61) p. 136
Photograph by Douglas Kirkland, courtesy Sygma and Universal Pictures

Yellow silk chiffon dress and cape designed by Theoni Aldredge for Mia Farrow in *The Great Gatsby*, 1974. (9/62.1)
Lent by Paramount Pictures

Costume sketch by Ann Roth for Glenn Close in *Maxie*, 1985. (9/70)
Lent by Ann Roth

Costume sketch by Donfeld for Jane Fonda in *They Shoot Horses, Don't They?*, 1969. (9/50.2)
Lent by Donfeld Collection

Costume sketch by Anthea Sylbert for Vanessa Redgrave in *Julia*, 1977. (9/69) p. 118
Lent by Anthea Sylbert

Silver sequined evening dress, designed by Irene Sharaff for Faye Dunaway in *Mommie Dearest*, 1981. (9/66)
Lent by Bermans & Nathans, London

Costume sketch by Theadora Van Runkle for Liza Minnelli in *New York, New York*, 1977. (9/68.1) p. 118
Lent by Theadora Van Runkle

Production sketch by Arthur Lonergan for *M*A*S*H*, 1970. (9/33)
Lent by Arthur Lonergan

George C. Scott in *Patton*, 1970. (9/34)
Courtesy Twentieth Century Fox

Hal Ashby directs Jon Voight in *Coming Home*, 1978. (9/36) p. 84
Photograph by Nancy Ellison, courtesy MGM/UA Entertainment

Francis Coppola directing *Apocalypse Now*, 1979. (9/37) p. 82
Photograph by Nancy Moran, courtesy MGM/UA Entertainment

Continuity sketch by Tom Wright for *Apocalypse Now*, 1979; production designer, Dean Tavoularis. (9/38) p. 82
Lent by Dean Tavoularis

Production still from *Nashville*, 1975 (9/40)
Courtesy AMPAS and Paramount Pictures

Robert Redford and Dustin Hoffman in *All the President's Men*, 1976. (9/40.1)
Courtesy Warner Bros.

Sylvester Stallone in *Rocky*, 1976. (9/41)
Photograph by Neil Leifer/Camera 5

Sam Shepard in *The Right Stuff*, 1983. (9/43)
Photograph by John Bryson, courtesy Sygma and
Warner Bros.

Billboard for Clint Eastwood tribute in Paris,
1985. (9/85) p. 197
Photograph by Jacques Prayer, courtesy Gamma-
Liaison

Production still from *Sounder*, 1972. (9/44)
Courtesy Twentieth Century Fox

Richard Pryor billboard on Sunset Boulevard,
1981. (9/45) p. 218
Photograph by David Strick

Eddie Murphy in *Beverly Hills Cop*, 1984. (9/46)
Courtesy Paramount Pictures

Gregory Hines in *The Cotton Club*, 1984. (9/47)
p. 159
Photograph by Theo Westenberger, courtesy
Orion Pictures

Adolph Caesar and Robert Townsend in *A
Soldier's Story*, 1984. (9/48)
Courtesy Columbia Pictures

Sketch of space station in *2001: A Space Odyssey*,
1968. (9/80) p. 171
Lent by Stanley Caidin

Production sketch by Bill Magor for *Rosemary's
Baby*, 1968; production designer, Richard Sylbert.
(9/74)
Lent by Richard Sylbert

Life-size dummy of Linda Blair made up as the
"Regan" demon. Designed by makeup artist Dick
Smith, assisted by Rick Baker, for *The Exorcist*,
1973. (9/75) p. 164
Lent by Dick Smith, © Warner Bros. 1973

Miniature "Gozer Temple," created by Boss Films
under the supervision of Mark Stetson for
Ghostbusters, 1984. (9/76) p. 172
Lent by Columbia Pictures

Animated wolf created by Eoin Sprott Studio Ltd.
for *Wolfen*, 1981. (9/77)
Lent by the AMERICAN MUSEUM OF THE
MOVING IMAGE/Eoin Sprott Collection

Animated creature designed by Christopher
Walas for *Gremlins*, 1984. (9/79)
Lent by Christopher Walas

Steven Spielberg with set model for *Raiders of the
Lost Ark*, 1981. (9/12) p. 104
Photograph by Nancy Moran, courtesy Lucasfilm
Ltd., © 1981

Mother ship from *Close Encounters of the Third
Kind*. (9/13) p. 174
Lent by National Air and Space Museum,
Smithsonian Institution

Concept sketch by futurist Syd Mead for *Blade
Runner*, 1982. (9/81)
Lent by Syd Mead

Composite photograph of "Hades" zone in *Blade
Runner*, 1982. (9/82) p. 176
Photograph by Virgil Mirano, courtesy Boss Film
Corporation and Warner Bros.

Production painting by Anthony Masters for
Dune, 1984. (9/83) p. 175
Lent by Anthony Masters

Preparatory wax model of creature by Carlo
Rambaldi for *E.T.: The Extra-Terrestrial*, 1982.
(9/14)
Lent by Carlo Rambaldi, courtesy Amblin
Entertainment

Miniature of bicycle created by Industrial Light
and Magic for *E.T.: The Extra-Terrestrial*, 1982.
(9/14.1)
Lent by Steven Spielberg

Preparatory sketches of creature by Carlo
Rambaldi for *E.T.: The Extra-Terrestrial*, 1982.
(9/15.1) p. 175
Lent by Carlo Rambaldi, courtesy Amblin
Entertainment

Sketch of creature's points of movement by
Carlo Rambaldi for *E.T.: The Extra-Terrestrial*,
1982. (9/16)
Lent by Carlo Rambaldi, courtesy Amblin
Entertainment

STAR WARS 1975–82

*The exhibits in this section were created by Industrial
Light and Magic, which was established in 1975 as a
division of Lucasfilm Ltd. to create special effects for
the Star Wars trilogy. Unless otherwise indicated,
they have been lent by Lucasfilm.*

George Lucas with miniatures for *The Return of
the Jedi*, 1983. (9/86) p. 173
Photograph by Terry Chostner

Miniature of the *Millennium Falcon* from *Star
Wars*, 1977. (9/87) p. 174
Photograph by Terry Chostner

Preparing a set of the Death Star surface for *The
Empire Strikes Back*, 1980. (9/88)
Photograph by Terry Chostner

Matte painting by Chris Evans of the Death Star
and the planet Endor for *The Return of the Jedi*,
1983. (9/89)

Two-foot miniature of All Terrain-Armored
Transport (AT-AT) from *The Empire Strikes Back*,
1980. (9/90)

Two-inch miniature of All Terrain-Armored
Transport from *The Empire Strikes Back*, 1980.
(9/91)

Scale drawing by Joe Johnston of Imperial Walker.
(9/92)

First concept painting by Ralph McQuarrie for
Star Wars, 1977. (9/93)

Gilded suit worn by Anthony Daniels in the role
of C-3PO. (9/95)
Lent by National Museum of American History,
Smithsonian Institution

Sculpted figure of Yoda from *The Empire Strikes
Back*, 1980. (9/97)

Rancor puppet, designed by Phil Tippett for *The
Return of the Jedi*, 1983. (9/98)

Concept painting by Ralph McQuarrie of Luke
Skywalker in dungeon with Rancor for *The Return
of the Jedi*, 1983. (9/99)

Concept sketches by Ron Cobb for Cantina
creatures in Star Wars, 1977. (9/100, 9/101) p. 173

Concept painting by Ralph McQuarrie of Ewoks
attacking Imperial Walkers in *The Return of the
Jedi*, 1983. (9/102) p. 175

Ewok mask, paws, and feet worn by a little person in *The Return of the Jedi*, 1983. (9/103, 9/104,
9/105)

Neon-lit RKO sign from the facade of Radio City
Music Hall, 1932. (10/1) p. vii
Lent by Kenneth Anger Collection

Nikita Khrushchev watches the filming of *Can Can* (1959) at Twentieth Century Fox. The visiting Soviet premier pronounced the spectacle obscene. Photo by N. R. Farbman for *Life*.

INDEX

Italicized page numbers refer to the captions.